Teaching English to Speakers
of Other Languages

Teaching English to Speakers of Other Languages

Substance and Technique

BETTY WALLACE ROBINETT

Professor of Linguistics
and
Director, English as a Second Language Program
University of Minnesota

University of Minnesota Press · Minneapolis
and
McGraw-Hill International Book Company · New York

Printed at North Central Publishing Company, St. Paul
Published by the University of Minnesota Press,
2037 University Avenue Southeast, Minneapolis, Minnesota 55455,
and published in Canada by Burns & MacEachern
Limited, Don Mills, Ontario

The University of Minnesota is an equal-opportunity
educator and employer.

Library of Congress Cataloging in Publication Data

Robinett, Betty Wallace.
  Teaching English to speakers of other languages.

  Bibliography: p.
  Includes index.
  1. English language—Study and teaching—Foreign
students. I. Title.
PE1128.A2R55 428'.2'407 78-11448

ISBN 0-8166-0840-7 Univ. of Minn. Press, cloth
ISBN 0-8166-0868-7 Univ. of Minn. Press, paper
ISBN 07-053179-X McGraw-Hill, paper

To R. W. R.

Acknowledgments

It is impossible to single out the many persons who have contributed over the years to the development of the ideas in this book. My debt to the many authors listed in the bibliography and cited in the text is clear. I have, however, profited greatly from the careful reading of parts of the manuscript by Professors Bruce T. Downing of the University of Minnesota, David P. Harris of Georgetown University, and Christina Bratt Paulston of the University of Pittsburgh. My greatest debt of gratitude is owed to Virginia French Allen of Temple University, not only for her enlightening comments and her continued encouragement but also for initiating me into the world of teaching English to speakers of other languages. Sincere appreciation is also due the many students it has been my joy to teach, especially Eric Nelson for his insightful comments on the first three chapters. Finally, I would like to thank Beverly Kaemmer of the University of Minnesota Press for her skill and patience, and Marian Metcalf, who typed the manuscript, for making the routine aspects of this venture enjoyable.

Contents

Design
of the Book

BEING AN ENGLISH SPEAKER does not of itself qualify one to be a teacher of English to speakers of other languages. In order to teach a language, more than an intuitive knowledge of the subject is necessary. An effective teacher must have a solid grasp of the substance of the subject to be taught and, especially, the techniques for teaching it. This textbook provides both substance and techniques for teachers of English to speakers of other languages by describing the essential features of the English language by describing the essential features of the English language and by offering suggestions of ways in which the communication skills (listening, speaking, reading, and writing) can be taught. It is directed to both native and non-native speakers of English who are prospective teachers of English to speakers of other languages or who may already be teaching the language but would like to know more about it.

Format of the Text

The book is divided into two major sections. The first section (The English Language) includes a general description of the essential features of the grammatical system, the sound system, and the vocabulary system. A delineation of various kinds of grammatical drills and of specific techniques for teaching pronunciation is also included in this part of the book. The second part (Teaching English to Speakers of Other Languages) deals more generally with pedagogical matters. It provides a brief discussion of the relationship of language and culture, and its implications for language teaching; a delineation of current trends and issues in language teaching; a general discussion of what is involved in acquiring second language skills; detailed suggestions for teaching the various communication skills; and a brief discussion of testing and evaluation with particular reference to English as a second or foreign language.

ESOL— ESL — EFL

Since several different acronyms are used to identify this field, it seems appropriate to identify their use in this book. The phrase "English for speakers of other languages" (ESOL) is employed to describe the professional field to which this book is directed. Practitioners in this field often use the term "English as a second language" (ESL) to refer to English taught to non-English speakers in situations where it is the primary language of communication (as in the United States), and "English as a foreign language" (EFL) to refer to English taught to non-English speakers in situations where it is not the primary language (in Germany or Japan, for example). In this text, whenever a difference in pedagogical approach may be suggested because it is more appropriate in an ESL or an EFL situation, this is noted. In most cases, however, following a trend in the field, the term "second" language is used to convey the idea of "another" language and does not necessarily distinguish between an ESL and an EFL situation.

Bibliography and Exercises

One of the main objectives of this text is to develop in teachers a flexibility in their classroom teaching based on a broad background of sound information about the subject matter and of a variety of techniques. For this reason an extensive bibliography is provided with the hope that teachers will be encouraged to broaden and deepen their knowledge. The bibliography is placed at the end of the book and arranged by chapters, resulting more or less in an organization by subject categories. Although many of the items in the bibliography are referred to in the body of the text, others have been included, even when not specifically mentioned, if considered to be useful resources for further study. The bibliographic references for the first part of the book are separated into two categories — resource texts and teaching texts — within each of the three language areas: grammar, sounds, and vocabulary.

The exercises at the end of each chapter are meant to provide an opportunity for readers to check their comprehension of the information in the text or to apply this information to practical, pedagogically oriented tasks. Since this is a book for teachers, however, the exercises are not meant to be used in the language-learning classroom. The one exception to this may be that some of the exercises from the chapter on "Teaching the Communication Skills" might be adapted for classroom use.

The Sound System Chapter

The chapter on the sound system is quite detailed and includes specific pedagogical techniques for teaching pronunciation. The decision to discuss the sound system in such detail was made because relatively little attention is paid to this aspect of language teaching, and because it is of particular long-standing interest to the author. Furthermore, teaching techniques for pronunciation seemed to belong logically in this chapter since, like structural drills, they are closely related to the essential language background necessary for effective teaching of ESL/EFL.

The use of a modified International Phonetic Alphabet to symbolize English sounds may initially cause some concern to readers who are not familiar with this type of notation; but such symbolization is necessary because the regular spelling alphabet

does not contain sufficient letters to provide a one-to-one correspondence between sound and symbol in English. These special
symbols are carefully explained, and key words used to
exemplify them should make deciphering easy. (See page 70.)

This chapter should prove especially useful to readers who are
not native speakers of English.

Only a Beginning

No one textbook can be expected to do justice to all aspects of
the English language as well as to all matters pertaining to the
teaching of English to speakers of other languages. Certainly this
book does not claim to be all-inclusive. Nor is it meant to be
prescriptive. How the teacher makes use of the information con-
tained herein is an individual matter and will depend upon the
particular teacher and teaching situation.

This text can be only a beginning, whetting the appetite, it is
hoped, for a fuller range of study and experience, in which the
main course (to continue the metaphor) is the actual practice of
the art of teaching English to speakers of other languages. No
book can provide that experience; it can only hope to suggest the
variety of decisions ESOL teachers are called upon to make and
to give those teachers some means of making such decisions
intelligently. If this book serves as a useful resource for ESOL
teachers, it will have fulfilled its purpose.

The English Language

1

The Grammatical System

This section of the text contains a description of the major aspects of English grammar, an overview of the grammatical features of English that teachers of English to speakers of other languages must be familiar with. The information is presented in two parts: (1) a general description, in quite traditional terms, of the devices that signal grammatical relationships in English; and (2) a discussion of the grammatical arrangements characteristic of English sentences and the relationships that sentences have to each other. This second section draws more heavily on insights from modern linguistic study.

Grammatical Signals

In a sentence each word or phrase plays some special grammatical role or function in conveying the message of the sentence. In order to speak English one must be able to recognize the function of each sentence element. The English language signals some of these functions through the use of several syntactic devices. Below are listed seven major syntactic devices of English with examples of each type. Inflectional endings (-*s* plurals, for example), derivational affixes (prefixes and suffixes), and word stress belong to that part of the grammar which is often referred to as morphology, or the forms of words. The other signals operate over larger units of the language and are generally designated as belonging to syntax or, more simply, as syntactic features. We will refer to both kinds of items as grammatical features of English.

Examples of English Grammatical Signals

1. Inflection

   Plural of nouns: nuts, squirrels, branches
   Past tense of verbs: walked, lived, wanted

2. Structure or Function Words

   Articles: the, a/an
   Prepositions: of, to, by, for

3. Word Order

   Lexical item: chocolate milk; milk chocolate
   Functional item: He is. Is he?
   Where is he? I know where he is.

4. Derivation or Word Formation

   The wire acted as a magnet.
   They had magnetized the wire.
   The magnetic wire attracted pieces of metal.
   They had to demagnetize the wire.

5. Concord or Agreement

   The student reads a lot. The students read a lot.
   This man; these men.

6. Government

   I gave him the book.
   He gave me the book.

7. Stress and Intonation

   What will you do thén? (after that) I'll go downtown.
   What will you dó then? (instead of that) I'll go downtown.
   Her son is nineteen.

   Her son is nineteen?

Let us now look in some detail at the devices that signal various functions within English sentences.

1. Inflection

Modern English has relatively few inflectional endings, but they are used often. (The term *inflection* is used here in its grammatical sense and refers to a change in the form of a word to indicate different grammatical relationships; this should not be confused with its meaning of alteration in the pitch or the tone of the voice.) Grammarians classify these inflections in various ways; for our purposes we will specify eight inflections of English.

> Plural of nouns: nuts, squirrels, branches
> Possessive of nouns: cat's, man's, boss's
> Third-person singular (present tense) of verbs: eats,
>   runs, watches
> Past tense of verbs: walked, lived, wanted
> Past participle of verbs: asked, driven, meant
> Present participle of verbs: reading, studying
> Comparative of adjectives and adverbs: prettier, slower
> Superlative of adjectives and adverbs: prettiest, slowest

A peculiarity of English grammar is that what appears to be one -*s* suffix operates to signal plurality in nouns, possession in nouns, and third-person singular present tense in verbs. The potential confusion caused by such a similarity in signals, however, is balanced in the language learning process by the ease with which the pronunciation of these three inflections is taught because their pronunciation is determined by a phonological rule. This rule is discussed in the chapter on the sound system.
Below are examples of the three kinds of -*s* suffixes.

-S SUFFIXES

Plural of Nouns

book	book<u>s</u>
bird	bird<u>s</u>
church	churche<u>s</u>

Possessive of Nouns

singular	cat	cat<u>'s</u>
	writer	writer<u>'s</u>
	boss	boss<u>'s</u>
plural	cats	cats<u>'</u>
	writers	writers<u>'</u>
	bosses	bosses<u>'</u>

Third-Person Singular Present Tense of Verbs

stop	stop<u>s</u>
live	live<u>s</u>
wash	washe<u>s</u>

Irregular nouns such as *man*, *foot*, *tooth* do not form the plural in the same manner as regular nouns, although they follow the same rule for forming the possessive. The varying plurals of irregular nouns (*man*, *men*; *foot*, *feet*; *tooth*, *teeth*) often involve an inflectional change of another kind, an internal vowel change (technically called *umlaut*) which is characteristic of the Germanic family of languages. The plurals of these nouns must be learned as separate, irregular forms. Fortunately, they are few; but because they are used frequently, they should be learned as soon as possible.

Just as the *-s* suffix designates three functions (plurals of nouns, possessives of nouns, and third-person present tense of verbs), so the *-ed* suffix serves as a sign of the past tense (*added, cleaned, washed*) and the past participle of regular verbs (*has added, had cleaned, is washed*). A phonological rule for the pronunciation of the *-ed* suffix operates in a fashion similar to that of the *-s* suffix. (See the chapter on the sound system for a detailed description of this phonological rule.)

The past form of some irregular verbs in English, like the plurals of some irregular nouns, involves an internal inflectional change (technically referred to as *ablaut*): *eat, ate; drive, drove*. The past participle of many of these irregular verbs is formed by the addition of the suffix *-en* instead of *-ed*: *eaten, driven*. The past tense and past participle of others are formed by the addition of *-t*: *meant, left, brought*.

The present participle of verbs (*-ing* form) is used in several ways. Teamed with the auxiliary verb *be* it becomes the progressive verb phrase.

> The cat is watching the bird.
> The bird was eating a worm.

It may substitute for an adjective.

> Cats are fascinating creatures.
> Purring cats are happy cats.

Or it may replace a noun, in which case it is called a gerund.

> Flying is fun.
> Writing letters can sometimes be a chore.

Most adjectives and adverbs of one or two syllables form their comparative and superlative by adding the inflectional endings *-er* and *-est*.

slow   slower   slowest
pretty   prettier   prettiest

Adjectives and adverbs of more than two syllables generally employ the function words *more* and *most* instead of inflectional endings for the comparative and superlative.

important   more important   most important
beautiful   more beautiful   most beautiful

It should be noted that words like *simple* and *gentle* remain two-syllable words even after adding the inflectional endings: *simpler, simplest; gentler, gentlest.* Also, some two-syllable words do not generally employ the inflectional endings for comparison: *content, more content, most content.*

2. Structure Words

Words in English can be thought of as being of two types: content words or structure words. Structure words like *the, did, of, but,* and *because* form the framework on which we hang content words like *boy, leave, work, aspiration,* etc. Examples of the most frequently occurring types of structure words are the following:

articles (the, a/an)
prepositions (in, on, at, to, by)
auxiliary verbs (be, do, have; can, may, might)
coordinating conjunctions (and, or, but)
subordinating conjunctions (because, if, although)
interrogative pronouns (when, where, why, who, what)
relative pronouns (who, whom, which, that)
complementizer (that)

Structure words sometimes join smaller structures together into larger units.

They damaged the leg *of* the table.

Conjunctions like *but* join full sentences or parts of sentences.

They worked hard, *but* they enjoyed every minute of it.

The couple were young *but* mature.

Subordinating conjunctions like *because* connect a subordinate idea to the main idea, thereby producing a complex sentence.

They left *because* they couldn't wait any longer.

At other times, structure words act as markers of a particular grammatical class of words, e.g., *the* is a marker of nouns.

The dog barked.

In addition, the article *the* is often a sequence signal; that is, it refers to something which has been previously mentioned.

A young boy was at the door. *The* boy left before I got there.

Some structure words are used to signal specific grammatical constructions, as a form of *do* signals a question.

Did the onions make him cry?

Sometimes a certain structure word can be used instead of another syntactic device to express the same function.

Structure word:	the tail *of* the dog
Inflection:	the dog's tail
Structure word:	gave the book *to* them
Word order:	gave them the book

As can be deduced from these examples, structure words must be taught with the grammatical structure in which they appear, but content words can be rather freely substituted in many kinds of structures. This contrast between content and structure words is best exemplified in an exercise based on Lewis Carroll's 'Jabberwocky'.

'Twas brillig and the slithy toves
Did gyre and gimble in the wabe.

Because the content words consist of nonsensical lexical items, there is little semantic information offered by these lines. However, the structure is clear.

'Twas —— and the —— -y —— -s
Did —— and —— in the ——.

It is easy for an English speaker to select appropriate content words with which to fill the blanks because the structure words clearly indicate what grammatical constructions are present. One person's rendition of the lines might be this:

It was rainy and the slippery toads
Did hop and tumble in the pool.

In addition to this functional characteristic, there are other characteristics that distinguish structure words from content words:

1. Structure words tend to have little or no lexical meaning; their meaning is derived mainly from the function they serve.

2. There are few distinguishing forms that set them apart from other words. On the other hand, content words of the noun category, for example, have such formal characteristics as the *-ness* or *-ance* suffix (*kindness*, *compliance*); adjectives the *-ish* or *-ic* suffix (*childish*, *politic*); verbs the *-ize* suffix or the *en-* prefix (*magnetize*, *enlarge*).

3. They make up a relatively small class of words; most of the words in the dictionary are not structure words but nouns, verbs, adjectives, and adverbs.

4. They belong to a closed class; for example, we do not add to this class by borrowing from other languages or by invention, as we do with content words.

5. These words individually are used frequently; a page of English, for example, contains numerous repetitions of words like *the*, *in*, *that*, or the auxiliary verb *be*.

6. They are usually unstressed in spoken language; this makes them difficult for non-native speakers to identify.

We will discuss the content words, the principal vocabulary component of English, in a later section; but it should be remembered that the two kinds of words can never be divorced from each other; each plays an essential role in communication.

3. Word Order

Some languages have more flexibility than others in the order in which words can occur. English is a languge in which word order is relatively fixed; changes in the order of words often produce contrasts in meaning and in grammatical function.

The arm chair is damaged.
The chair arm is damaged.

He has finished the work.
Has he finished the work?

Paint that box.
Box that paint.

Only the child cried.
The only child cried.
The child only cried.

Sometimes a change in the order of content words is accompanied by other structural changes.

I gave a pencil to John.
I gave John a pencil.

I asked a question of Mary.
I asked Mary a question.

Placing the indirect objects (*John*, *Mary*) before the direct objects (*pencil, question*) in these sentences requires deleting the preposition (*to, of*).

If I had owned a yacht . . .
Had I owned a yacht . . .

I had owned a yacht.

The inversion of subject and verb (*I had* to *had I*) signals a conditional clause, semantically (although not stylistically) equivalent to an *if* clause. The third sentence, without inversion, contains no conditional meaning. It is, in fact, a simple statement.

4. Derivation or Word Formation

English, like many languages, forms new words by the addition of prefixes and suffixes: *like, likeable; kind, kindness; nation, national; critic, criticism; agree, disagree; rich, enrich.* Sometimes prefixes and suffixes are used in combination.

kind	kindness	unkindness
nation	national	international
light	lighten	enlighten

Acquaintance with the most frequently occurring, the most productive, derivational affixes (both prefixes and suffixes) is an effective means of increasing vocabulary. It is also an aid in identifying the functional use of a word. For example, the suffix *-ize* signals a verb: *realize, criticize, capitalize.* The suffix *-tion*, on the other hand, is characteristic of a noun: *action, condition, preparation.* The prefix *en-* often produces a verb: *enrage, enlarge, entitle.*

When more than one affix appears on a word, the order in which they are added should be pointed out so the constituent parts of words are identified.

" '*Hopefullywise*'! Did I understand you to say '*hopefullywise*'?"

enlighten = en + lighten (not enlight + en)
disgraceful = disgrace + ful (not dis + graceful)
ungraceful = un + graceful (not ungrace + ful)

Below is a chart that illustrates some of the most frequently used derivational affixes. Note that these can be added only to content words. Note also that the choice of affix is arbitrary, e.g., *realize* becomes *realization* (not *realizement*).

Examples of Derivational Forms

I. *Verb*	*Adjective*	*Noun*
act	active	activity
		action
despair	desperate	desperation
defy	defiant	defiance
depend	dependent	dependence
impeach	impeachable	impeachment

II. *Noun*	*Verb*	*Adjective*
horror	horrify	horrible
peace	pacify	peaceful
(pacifism)		pacific
alphabet	alphabetize	alphabetical
form	formalize	formal
(formality)		formalistic
courage	encourage	courageous

III. *Adjective*	*Noun*	*Verb*
clear	clearness	clarify
	clarity	
	clarification	
humid	humidity	humidify
civil	civility	civilize
	civilization	
dark	darkness	darken

IV. *Verb*	*Noun*	*Adjective*
avenge	vengeance	vengeful

5. Concord or Agreement

The grammatical device of concord, i.e., agreement of words that bear grammatical relationships, occurs very frequently in English. For example, there is agreement of subject and verb in the present tense.

$$\left.\begin{array}{l} \text{He} \\ \text{She} \\ \text{It} \end{array}\right\} \text{eats everything.} \qquad \left.\begin{array}{l} \text{I} \\ \text{We} \\ \text{You} \\ \text{They} \end{array}\right\} \text{eat everything.}$$

The most widely divergent forms that demonstrate agreement of subject and verb occur with the present and past tenses of the verb *be*.

$$\text{I am happy.} \qquad \left.\begin{array}{l} \text{He} \\ \text{She} \\ \text{It} \end{array}\right\} \text{is happy.} \qquad \left.\begin{array}{l} \text{We} \\ \text{You} \\ \text{They} \end{array}\right\} \text{are happy.}$$

$$\left.\begin{array}{l} \text{I} \\ \text{He} \\ \text{She} \\ \text{It} \end{array}\right\} \text{was happy.} \qquad \left.\begin{array}{l} \text{We} \\ \text{You} \\ \text{They} \end{array}\right\} \text{were happy.}$$

Concord or agreement is also indicated in the singular and plural forms of demonstrative adjectives.

Singular	*Plural*
this book	these books
that letter	those letters

The relative pronoun (except *that*) agrees with its antecedent, i.e., *who* is used with persons and *which* is used in other cases.

the woman who	the box which
the man who	the classes which
the editors who	

The relative pronoun *that* can, under certain circumstances, replace either *who* or *which*, thereby obviating the necessity for any agreement choice.

the box that arrived today
the man that arrived today

In many languages concord is required between adjectives and nouns, and articles and nouns. Thus students with such language backgrounds may be tempted to apply agreement rules where they do not belong, producing such ungrammatical phrases as *smalls classes* or *somes books*. (An asterisk before a word or sentence identifies an ungrammatical construction.) In other languages no concord or very limited concord is required, resulting in learning errors such as *they is* or *these book*.

6. Government

Another grammatical device in English is the use of different forms of pronouns to signal different functions in a clause. This device is traditionally called 'government' because certain functions are said to 'govern' the forms of words.

I bought *him* a book.	*She* has a book.	It's *her* book.
He bought *me* a book.	*We* have a book.	It's *our* book.
She bought *them* a book.	*He* has a book.	It's *his* book.
They bought *her* a book.	*I* have a book.	It's *my* book.

They bought *us* a book.
We bought *them* a book.

He and *she* argued.
The argument was between *him* and *her*.

He and *I* argued.
The argument was between *him* and *me*.

The pronoun forms shown above are the subject, object, and possessive adjective forms. The pronouns *you* and *it* do not change form when used as subject or object.

You told him a story.
He told *you* a story.
It destroyed the car.
The car destroyed *it*.

Some possessive adjectives and possessive pronouns have different forms for different functions, i.e., when they are used as modifiers and when they stand alone in the predicate.

$$\text{This is} \left\{ \begin{array}{l} \text{my} \\ \text{your} \\ \text{our} \\ \text{her} \end{array} \right\} \text{car.} \qquad \text{This car is} \left\{ \begin{array}{l} \text{mine.} \\ \text{yours.} \\ \text{ours.} \\ \text{hers.} \end{array} \right.$$

The reflexive pronouns sometimes match the possessive forms of pronouns and sometimes the objective forms.

$$\left. \begin{array}{l} \text{I} \\ \text{We} \\ \text{You (singular)} \\ \text{You (plural)} \\ \text{She} \end{array} \right\} \text{cut} \left\{ \begin{array}{l} \text{myself.} \\ \text{ourselves.} \\ \text{yourself.} \\ \text{yourselves.} \\ \text{herself.} \end{array} \right. \qquad \left. \begin{array}{l} \text{He} \\ \\ \text{They} \end{array} \right\} \text{cut} \left\{ \begin{array}{l} \text{himself.} \\ \\ \text{themselves.} \end{array} \right.$$

Although the use of government is not extensive in English, its occurrence with personal pronouns makes it an extremely important feature of English grammar since these words occur very frequently. Furthermore, since pronouns very often are not stressed in the stream of speech, they prove rather difficult for students to identify.

7. Stress and Intonation

Two features of the sound system also occur as grammatical signals. These are stress (intensity of sound) and intonation (pitch of voice). The three degrees of stress that occur on English words are symbolized thus: $/´/$ primary stress, $/ˋ/$ secondary stress, and weak stress, which is unmarked. Both stress and intonation will be dealt with more fully in the chapter on the sound system.

Word stress sometimes differentiates noun and verb

        récord (noun)   recórd (verb)

or verb and adjective.

        séparàte (verb)   séparate (adjective)

It can also distinguish a compound noun and a descriptive phrase (adjective + noun).

   bláckbìrd   bláck bírd

The difference between a present participle used as part of a verb phrase and one used as an adjectival modifier is signaled by stress.

  They're báking potátoes. (Oh, is that what they're doing!)
  They're báking potàtoes. (Oh, is that what they are!)

The use of a rising intonation on a statement can change it into a question.

     The baby is sleeping?

In fact, the mere use of rising intonation on a phrase indicates a question as opposed to a response.

    Okay? (as opposed to Okay.)
    Going? (as opposed to Going.)

Thus, not only are stress and intonation features of sound, but they are intimately tied to the grammar of the language, again illustrating the interaction of the various components of language.

Grammatical Arrangements

It would be impossible in a text of this kind to discuss in detail all the grammatical arrangements characteristic of English sentences, the relationships that sentences have to each other, and the meanings that these arrangements and relationships express. Nevertheless, sentences such as those in the language sample below, which incorporate many of the grammatical signals described above, illustrate what students need to be able to comprehend and to produce in order to use the language communicatively.

What's the matter with Johnny?
He must have seen something.
Do you see anything?
Yes, what I see is a huge kite way up in the sky.
That must have been what Johnny saw.

One bit of information in this verbal exchange can be expressed in a straightforward statement: *Johnny probably saw a kite*. However, very similar information, with a different focus, can be communicated by the following sentences which are quite different in structure.

A kite was probably seen by Johnny.
What Johnny probably saw was a kite.
It was a kite that Johnny probably saw.
It was Johnny that probably saw a kite.

Conversely, sentences that seem quite similar in structure can carry very different grammatical information. Even though the following three sentences look very much the same, the relationships within the third sentence are different from those in the other two.

The thought him a genius.
They proved him a fool.
They gave him a ticket.

The nouns *genius* and *fool* refer to *him* in each of the first two sentences; but *ticket* and *him* in the third sentence do not bear this same relationship.

Similarly, one of the three sentences below differs from the other two even though, superficially, they look very much the same.

They're easy to operate.
They're eager to work.
They're dangerous to own.

In the second sentence the subject *they* is also the subject of the infinitive *to work*; but in the other two sentences *they* is not the subject of the infinitives. Someone else will do the 'operating' or 'owning'. *They* refers to whatever someone 'owns' or 'operates', that is, it is used as the object of the infinitives.

The different relationships expressed in these two types of sentences can be shown by looking at the underlying ideas that make up such sentences and by considering the steps leading to the construction of their final form.

THEY ARE EASY TO OPERATE. IT is easy.

> IT = Someone operates them.
>
> For someone to operate them is easy.
>
> They are easy to operate.

Each step involves a process: nominalization by the use of an infinitive; deletion of *for someone*; placement of *them* in subject position with corresponding change in form; change in verb to agree with subject.

The second type of sentence is less complex.

THEY ARE EAGER TO WORK. They are eager.

> They will work.

The sentence to be embedded is nominalized into an infinitive with the subject deleted because the subject of the embedded sentence is the same as that of the matrix sentence. Notice that such a deletion would not take place in embedding a sentence whose subject was not the same as the subject of the main sentence: *They are eager for him to work*.

Before dealing with these more complex sentences, let us begin our discussion of grammatical arrangements in English with the well-known concept of a sentence as consisting of a subject and a predicate or, in more recent terms, a noun phrase (NP) and a verb phrase (VP). A sentence may be simple:

NP	VP
The teacher	laughed at the joke.

or complex:

The math teacher with red hair

laughed at the joke which was told by a young man in her class that she had always considered very shy.

The components of this complex sentence might be conceived of as several simple sentences added to the primary sentence, each of them having a subject and a predicate.

THE TEACHER LAUGHED AT THE JOKE.

The teacher teaches math.
The teacher has red hair.
The man told a joke.
The man is young.
The man is in her class.
She has always considered IT.
IT = The man is very shy.

Understanding that relatively long and complex utterances can be broken down into simple component sentences in this way will make the seeming complexity of sentences less formidable. Students will comprehend them more easily and will begin to create similar ones themselves.

Questions

Another way of illustrating the fact that complex sentences are made up of simple components is to pose several kinds of questions about a complex sentence, the answers to which are the simple sentences it conveys. First the content can be reconstructed by asking *yes/no* questions, so called because of the kind of response they elicit.

YES/NO QUESTIONS

Does the teacher teach math?
Yes, she does.
The teacher teaches math.

Does she have red hair?
Yes, she does.
She has red hair.
Is the man old?
No, he isn't.
The man is young.

A second type of question, the alternative question, allows for retrieving information through the use of one of the alternatives included in the question.

ALTERNATIVE QUESTIONS

Does she have red hair or black hair?
She has red hair.
Is the man young or old?
The man is young.
Did the teacher laugh or cry?
The teacher laughed.

A third question form may contain the information in exactly the order in which the answer should be stated. These are called 'tag' questions and are similar to *yes/no* questions in terms of the response they elicit.

TAG QUESTIONS

The man is in her class, isn't he?
Yes, he is.
He's in her class.
The man is shy, isn't he?
Yes, he is.
He's shy.
He told a joke, didn't he?
Yes, he did.
He told a joke.

Questions that cannot be answered by *yes* or *no* are often referred to as WH questions, since they are introduced by such words as *who, what, when*.

> Who laughed?
>> The teacher laughed.
>
> What does she teach?
>> She teaches math.
>
> What color is her hair?
>> Her hair is red.
>
> What did the young man do?
>> He told a joke.

The relationships illustrated by these questions and answers are an inherent part of the communicative process. We see that beginning with rather simple components, the end result can be a complex and intricately interwoven series of constructions. We need to take a closer look at the parts of these components and how they fit together so that we can better comprehend the end result. Let us look first at the verb phrase.

The Verb Phrase

Probably the most important feature of the English sentence is the verb phrase. As used here, the term *verb phrase* is equivalent to what is commonly thought of as the predicate of a sentence. It may be as simple as a single word.

> Birds *sing*.

Or it may be made up of auxiliary verbs and a main verb.

> She *is writing*.
> He *can write*.
> They *have been writing*.

Depending upon the choice of verb, the verb phrase (VP) may include an object or objects.

> She *writes long letters*.
> She *writes her mother long letters*.

Except when making a request or giving a command (*write the sentence; close the door; sit down*), it is necessary to make a choice in the verb phrase between one of two tense forms, present or past. In a single-word verb the tense is indicated by the verb itself.

Present:	eat(s)	like(s)	sing(s)	build(s)
Past:	ate	liked	sang	built

When the verb combines with auxiliaries to produce multiple word groups that signify mood (possibility, probability, etc.) or aspect (duration of action or completion of action), a certain order must be followed. Below is a formula that illustrates the restrictions on the arrangements of these auxiliaries within verb phrases in English.

tense + (MODAL) + (HAVE + -*en*) + (BE + -*ing*) + MV

In this formula MODAL represents any modal auxiliary (*can*, *may*, etc.); -*en* designates the past participle of a verb (*taken*, *written*, *liked*, *sung*, *sold*, etc.); -*ing* specifies the present participle (*sending*, *typing*, etc.); MV is the main verb; and the parentheses signify optional choices. That is, the sentence will dictate whether a progressive form (BE + -*ing*), a perfect form (HAVE + -*en*), or a modal form (*can*, *may*, *will*, etc.) is to be used or whether the main verb will appear alone. The formula is to be interpreted to mean that if a verb auxiliary (HAVE or BE) is used, the inflectional suffix that is selected with it (-*en* or -*ing*) must be added to the *following* word:

tense + HAVE +   -en   + MV (*go*)
     has
     have   gone
     had

tense + BE   +   -ing   +   MV
     is
     am
     are   going
     was
     were

tense + HAVE +   -en   +   BE   +   -ing   +   MV
    has
    have   been   going
    had

Tense must be indicated by the form of the first element in any verb phrase in a statement or question, whether the phrase is simple or complex. In addition to tense, the first element must also indicate subject-verb agreement, e.g. *has, have; is, am, are, was, were*.

	Present Tense	*Past Tense*
Simple	He *writes* well.	He *wrote* well.
Complex	He *can* write well.	He *could* write well.
	He *has* written well.	He *had* written well.
	He *is* writing well.	He *was* writing well.
	He *has* been writing well.	He *had* been writing well.
	He *may* have been writing well.	He *might* have been writing well.

The two final sentences above illustrate the use of all the optional portions of the rule.

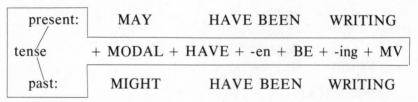

Learning the forms of verbs and the ways in which they are arranged in phrases, however, is only the first step toward being able to use verbs in a communicative situation. An essential part of the language learning process is to be able to use the form appropriately. For example, under what conditions would the following sentences occur?

He wrote letters yesterday.
He has been writing letters all afternoon.
He is writing letters now.

He writes letters every day.
He had written several letters before.
He might write several letters this afternoon.

Notice that although *might* is classified as a 'past' form in the last sentence, the time actually referred to is future. Thus, in English *tense* and *time* cannot be completely equated.

As an illustration of the importance of meaning as distinguished from form, let us turn to the use in the verb phrase of the infinitive (*to go*, *to ask*) and the gerund (*going*, *sleeping*). In many sentences these forms seem to be used almost interchangeably, with perhaps a distinction in aspect. (See Bolinger, 1968, for a discussion of the difference in meaning between the infinitive and the gerund.)

Infinitive	*Gerund*
He tried *to go*.	He tried *going*.
He hates *to sleep*.	He hates *sleeping*.
He started *to ask*.	He started *asking*.

However, with the verb *remember* the two forms indicate two very different meanings. They are not synonymous or nearly synonymous.

He remembered to go.
(The 'going' follows the 'remembering'.)
He remembered going.
(The 'going' precedes the 'remembering'.)

Examples such as these caution us to think always of the meaning of what we are teaching.

MODAL AUXILIARIES

The modal auxiliaries in English (*will*, *would*, *shall*, *should*, *can*, *could*, *may*, *might*, *must*) pose problems for non-native speakers of English because they differ in several ways from other auxiliaries. First, they differ in regard to formal characteristics. They do not employ the *-s* ending in the third person (*he cans; *it mays); they are regularly followed by the simple form of the verb (*can go*) rather than by the -*ing* form or the past participle; they cannot occur in infinitive phrases or as participles (**to may go* or **maying have gone*).

Another difference is that the relationship of the form of modals to tense is not clear. Traditional analyses (Francis, 1958; Quirk, et al., 1972) have attempted to pair the modals in a present-past relationship (*may-might*; *can-could*), as was done in the preceding section. However, both forms occur in sentences relating to the future: *he can (could) do it tomorrow*; *she may (might) leave next week*. Leech (1971) suggests that perhaps using the terms 'non-past' and 'past' instead of 'present' and 'past' might help avoid a too rigid classification of modals in terms of tense, especially since they are often used to refer to future time. Whitman (1975) suggests that in the analysis of the verb phrase (similar to that on page 23 of this chapter) a choice be made between modals and tense since modals cannot be related to tense in the same manner as other verbs. His verb phrase would then look like this:

$$
\left\{ \begin{array}{c} \text{Modal} \\ \text{Tense} \end{array} \right\} \quad + \quad \begin{array}{c} \text{(Perfect)} \\ \text{(have + -en)} \end{array} \quad + \quad \begin{array}{c} \text{(Progressive)} \\ \text{(be + -ing)} \end{array}
$$

However, it is not the formal characteristics or the lack of correlation with tense that cause the major problems in learning modals; it is the semantic content which poses real difficulty and which necessitates considerable attention. The exact meanings of modals are difficult to pin down. A distinction based on semantic considerations between 'epistemic' and 'root' meanings seems to be somewhat clarifying. Epistemic meanings carry a probabilistic or future connotation; Huddleston (1976:69) says that these meanings are epistemic "because they are concerned with the nature or limits of the speaker's knowledge of the proposition in question." Root meanings carry explicit information such as permission, ability, or necessity.

The accompanying table from Whitman (1975:82) assigns epistemic and root meanings to the modals.

Modal	Epistemic	Root
will	definite future	habit, obstinacy (in negatives)
shall	definite future	opinion (in questions)
would	conditional future	past habit; obstinacy
should	probably future	advisability
can	[a] . . .	ability, capacity, permission
could	[a] . . .	past or conditional ability
may	possible future	permission
might	possible future	. . .
must	logical conclusion	necessity

[a]According to Traugott (1972), epistemic meanings never developed for *can* and *could*.

The following examples of epistemic and root meanings of modals are also from Whitman.

Epistemic	Root
John will be here in five minutes.	Boys will be boys.
I shall not ask again.	Shall we go?
John should be here by now.	You really should read that book.
He may be there by five.	Yes, you may go.

An additional problem with modals is caused by the fact that some of them have a different meaning when used in negatives and questions from their meaning in affirmative statements. (Note the comment in Whitman's table concerning *will* and *shall*.) The negative of *I must go* is not *I must not go* but *I don't have to go*. The meaning of *I must not go* is, in effect, "I am obliged not to go." The main verb is negated, not the modal auxiliary.

Since modals involve complicated semantic problems, students must learn them as lexical items, relating meaning to context as with other lexical items. Because they are so commonly used considerable attention must be paid to them.

Negative and Interrogative Sentences

Negative and interrogative sentences are closely related in English. Table 1 shows the characteristic forms of affirmative, negative, and interrogative verb phrases in sample sentences. Notice that verb phrases which begin with forms of *be*, *have*, or any modal auxiliary are negated by the addition of *not* (contracted form *n't*) to *be*, *have*, or the modal (*isn't*, *hasn't*, *can't*). Interrogative sentences are formed by inverting the order of the subject and *be*, *have*, or the modal. In verb phrases that contain no auxiliary verb the appropriate form of the verb *do* must be introduced to form the negative and interrogative. This form of *do* carries the appropriate tense and person, receives the negative particle *not*, and is inverted with the subject to form questions. When a form of *do* is used, the main verb is reduced to its simple form since the form of *do* indicates tense and person.

Another illustration of the close relationship between negative and interrogative sentences is in the use of what Quirk (1972) calls 'non-assertive' forms. Examples of the use of assertive and non-assertive forms appear in Table 2.

A very clear illustration of the formal characteristics of affirmative, negative, and interrogative forms occurs in English tag questions, illustrated in Table 3. However, it must be remembered that intonation plays an important role in the use of tag questions. The rising intonation on the tag indicates uncertainty about the answer, a real request for information.

   They're early, aren't they? (I'm not really sure.)

On the other hand, a falling intonation on the tag indicates not so much a question as a request for confirmation of what the speaker already is quite convinced of.

   They're early, aren't they? (Tell me that I'm right.)

Table 1. Affirmative, Negative, and Interrogative Verb Phrases

Verb	Affirmative	Affirmative Interrogative	Negative	Negative Interrogative
Be	He is early.	Is he early?	He isn't early.	Isn't he early?
Modal Verbs	He can be early.	Can he be early?	He can't be early.	Can't he be early?
Have	He has arrived.	Has he arrived?	He hasn't arrived.	Hasn't he arrived?
Other Verbs	He eats at six.	Does he eat at six?	He doesn't eat at six.	Doesn't he eat at six?
	He arrived late.	Did he arrive late?	He didn't arrive late.	Didn't he arrive late?

Table 2. Assertive and Non-Assertive Forms

Assertive	He wants *some* money.	He *sometimes* complains.
Non-Assertive	He doesn't want *any* money.	He doesn't *ever* complain.
	Does he want *any* money?[a]	Does he *ever* complain?
	Doesn't he want *any* money?	Doesn't he *ever* complain?

[a]The use of *some* instead of *any* in a question (*Does he want some money?*) signifies the expectation of an affirmative answer.

Table 3. Tag Questions

Affirmative Statement + Negative Tag	Negative Statement + Affirmative Tag
He is early, isn't he?	He isn't early, is he?
He can be early, can't he?	He can't be early, can he?
He has arrived, hasn't he?	He hasn't arrived, has he?
He eats at six, doesn't he?	He doesn't eat at six, does he?
He arrived late, didn't he?	He didn't arrive late, did he?

Phrasal Verbs

One very frequently occurring type of verb in English, which speakers of other languages have difficulty with, is called a phrasal verb. Phrasal verbs consist of a verb plus one or more adverbial elements such as *out*, *off*, or *up*. Notice the way in which they function.

She *put on* her coat.	She *put* it *on*.
She *tore up* the paper.	She *tore* it *up*.
She *called up* her adviser.	She *called* her *up*.
She *put up with* the situation.	She *put up with* it.
She *looked into* the matter.	She *looked into* it.
She *came across* the reference.	She *came across* it.

These phrasal verbs are idioms, that is, the meaning of the complete phrase is something different from a sum of the meanings of the individual parts.

As seen above, when pronouns appear as objects in the first group of sentences, the phrasal verbs must be separated and the pronoun inserted between the verb and the particle. These are called *separable* phrasal verbs. That same order may also be used when the object is a short noun phrase: *She tore the paper up*. However, if the object is a lengthy phrase, the verb and the particle are not separated: *She tore up the paper that she had written earlier. Inseparable* phrasal verbs are those that are never separated in this way (as in the second group of sentences above).

These phrasal verbs must be differentiated from sequences that appear to be similar but that contain a verb followed by a preposition. As with all prepositional phrases, the noun or pronoun object must follow the preposition.

Wait for the girl.	Wait for her.
Look at the puppy.	Look at it.
Ask for an extension.	Ask for it.
Go over your work.	Go over it.
Keep up with the others.	Keep up with them.

The Noun Phrase

Noun phrases (i.e., NPs), the second important element in English sentences, may be simple

Novels
Some people
Few interviews   } can be interesting.
Two pets
Many paintings

or complex (containing notions that can be expressed as sentences).

Novels written by
   young authors
Weirdly dressed people
Fast moving interviews
   of newsworthy figures   } can be interesting.
Affectionate pets from
   exotic places
Surrealistic paintings
   of melting clocks

All the above sentences contain noun phrases (NPs) in subject position. All words or phrases that function as subjects and objects (including objects of prepositions) are NPs, and they always have the same form (except for the case form of pronouns) whether used as subjects or objects of various kinds.

The company consulted *a lawyer*.
The lawyer gave *advice* to *the company*.
Some members of *the organization* disagreed with *the decision*.
The decision displeased *some members*.

Because nouns often appear with articles (*a/an*, *the*, *some*, etc.), it is necessary to consider a count/mass distinction that is relevant in English when selecting the appropriate article. Certain nouns are countable (*table*, *cat*, *glove*, *aspect*), i.e., they can be pluralized and used with *a/an* and numbers. Others are noncountable or mass nouns and have only one form (*coffee*, *music*, *gold*). However, some noncount nouns appear as count nouns in phrases like *three coffees* or *three milks* where the noun of measurement has been deleted (*three cups of coffee*; *three glasses of milk*). When the noun has or designates a definite, nongeneric referent, all forms of the noun (singular count, plural count, and mass) appear with the definite article *the*.

$$\left.\begin{array}{l}\text{the table}\\ \text{the tables}\\ \text{the coffee}\end{array}\right\} \qquad \text{that they sold}$$

When the noun designates an indefinite, generic referent, singular count nouns appear with *a/an* and plural count nouns and mass nouns with *some* or without any article.

$$\text{I need} \left\{\begin{array}{ll}\text{a} & \text{table.}\\ \text{(some)} & \text{tables.}\\ \text{(some)} & \text{coffee.}\end{array}\right.$$

However, when the noun is generic (referring not to a specific member of a class but to the class as a whole) count nouns use either *a/an* or *the* in the singular and no article in the plural. Mass nouns with generic reference appear without articles.

A cat	is a fascinating creature.
The cat	is a fascinating creature.
Cats	are fascinating creatures.
Gold	is a precious metal.

Notice the use of the articles in the sentences below.

I want a new *dress*.
   (singular count noun; indefinite, nongeneric reference)
The *dress* I like most is the blue one.
   (singular count noun; definite, nongeneric reference)
I'd like some *coffee*.
   (mass noun; indefinite, nongeneric reference)
I don't like the *coffee* in this restaurant.
   (mass noun; definite, nongeneric reference)

Truth is beauty.
  (mass noun; generic reference)
The *truths* expressed by the author are well known.
  (plural count noun; definite, nongeneric reference)

Order of Noun Modifiers

Just as the order of auxiliaries in the verb phrase is restricted, so is the order of modifiers before the head word in a noun phrase.

> an old red wool shirt
> that child's three large plastic blocks
> the first two rectangular boxes

There is no reason for English to use this particular order rather than another. Some languages have quite different rules of word order in this regard. But students must learn this particular sequence in noun phrases and the proper sequence in verb phrases if they are to produce comprehensible sentences in English.

Articles (*the*, *a/an*), pre-articles (*some of*, *all of*, *both*), demonstratives (*this, that*), and possessive nouns appear first in the phrase. Adjectives denoting age generally precede those of color (*old red*). Ordinal numerals generally precede cardinal numerals (*first two*). Nouns modifying other nouns quite generally immediately precede the noun modified (*wool shirt, plastic blocks*).

> Jennifer's ⎫
> that child's ⎬ three large plastic blocks
> Jimmy's ⎭

Modifiers that precede nouns are usually single words, although an adjective can be modified by an intensifier (a *very* large cat). Phrasal and clausal modifiers follow the noun.

> Millicent is the girl *with blonde hair*.
> The girls *who own the blue car* are sisters.

One of the ways to develop the ability to produce complex noun phrases is to conceive of the premodifiers above as derived from simple statements about the noun: e.g., *the shirt is old*, *the shirt is red, the shirt is made of wool*. These simple statements can then be combined to make the complete phrase: *an old red wool shirt*.

In similar fashion, a sentence like *The girl has blonde hair* can be embedded in a simple sentence such as *Millicent is the girl*, by making certain syntactic changes (the concept of *have* being related to the preposition *with*), to produce *Millicent is the girl with blonde hair*. Or the statement *The girls own the blue car* can be embedded into the simple sentence *The girls are sisters* by the use of a relative clause to produce a more complex utterance: *The girls who own the blue car are sisters*.

One of the best ways to teach the distinction between *who* and *whom* in relative clauses (a difficulty encountered by native speakers of English as well as those for whom it is not a native language) is through this concept of embedding one sentence into another, the main sentence.

> The person is extraordinarily tall.
> (main sentence)
> The person is standing near the door.
> (sentence to be embedded)

The noun subjects of the two sentences are the same; therefore the subject relative pronoun *who* is used in the embedded clause to avoid repetition of the subject and to introduce the embedded clause.

> The person   is extraordinarily tall.
> who is standing near the door

However, in the following two sentences, the noun phrases that have the same referent and for which a relative pronoun will be used in one instance do *not* fulfill the same function. One is a subject and the other, the noun phrase in the clause to be embedded, is an object of a preposition.

> The person is extraordinarily tall.
> (main sentence)
> You spoke to the person.
> (sentence to be embedded)

In this case (at least in formal usage) the relative pronoun *whom* is used in the embedded clause; *who* is colloquially acceptable in the first sentence below.

The person *whom* you spoke to is extraordinarily tall.

The person to *whom* you spoke is extraordinarily tall. (very formal)

Adverbial Modifiers

We have seen that auxiliaries in verb phrases, and articles and adjectives in noun phrases, follow rather strictly prescribed rules of order in their respective constructions. Adverbs, on the other hand, tend to be more flexible, occurring in a number of sentence positions.

> He will do the work *today*.
> *Today* he will do the work.
> He *often* goes to the movies.
> He goes to the movies *often*.
> He is *usually* early.
> He *usually* is early.
> *Usually* he is early.
> He left *quickly*.
> He *quickly* left.

Although the first sentence in each group above probably represents the most frequent position of the adverb illustrated, the others are perfectly acceptable. Moving the adverb to initial position in the sentence tends to place special emphasis on it. It should be noted that there are still restrictions on the placement of adverbs: e.g., *He will do today the work* and *He goes often to the movies*.

There are in fact a number of different kinds of adverbs, and each adverb class tends to be restricted to use in certain positions only. For example, *always* is a 'pre-verbal adverb' and is placed before all verbs except *be*.

> The teacher *always* asks us to repeat.

Always answer the telephone.
The teacher is *always* on time.

Teachers should be familiar with the traditional classification of adverbs or adverbial phrases into those of frequency (*often*, *sometimes*, *every day*); place (*there*, *home*, *to the store*); time (*tonight*, *yesterday*, *at ten o'clock*); and manner (*quickly*, *easily*, *in a loud voice*). A useful rule of thumb to follow if more than one of these adverbs occurs in a sentence is the sequence of PLACE + MANNER + TIME: *He rode his bicycle to school carefully yesterday*. Sometimes adverbs of manner precede adverbs of place: *He walked quickly to the door*, but the PLACE + TIME sequence is regularly followed: *They drove to Chicago last weekend, but will leave for Europe on Sunday*.

A separate category of adverbial modifiers that is not mobile in this same way is the adverb of degree (*very*, *rather*, *somewhat*). These adverbs in general immediately precede the words they modify.

The lecture was *very* long.
The *rather* large room was filled to capacity.
She spoke *extremely* well and *quite* interestingly.
John is *much* taller than Jim.
Why did they stay *so* long?
That tie is *too* loud.

Combining Sentences

There are several ways in which sentences can be combined in English. One way is to conjoin them so that they are still easily discernible as separate sentences.

Phyllis is a lawyer and *Laura is a psychiatrist*.

A second way of combining sentences is by making one subordinate to another. The two sentences are still quite clearly identifiable, but one is *embedded* in another. The subordinate element generally modifies the other in some way, rather than making a separate statement.

Bill left early *because he was busy*.
The man *who was busy* left early.

A third means of joining sentences, also by the process of embedding, results in sentences like the following, where the subordinate element is an integral functional unit of the sentence (usually functioning as a noun phrase) that may or may not be easily recognizable as a sentence.

What he said meant everything to me.
His saying that meant everything to me.
He gave *whatever he wanted to give* to *whoever asked him*.
I wish *that he had answered the question*.
The problem is difficult *for him to solve*.

CONJOINED SENTENCES

Sentences such as *Phyllis is a lawyer* and *Laura is a psychiatrist* are most commonly connected by the conjunctions *and*, *or*, and *but*, the choice depending upon the relationship between the sentences that the speaker wishes to express. *And* signifies an additive relationship, *or* an alternative relationship, and *but* designates a contrast.

Sentences that are joined in this way are often interchangeable: that is, there is no priority in the order of sentences.

He has long hair and he wears blue jeans.
He wears blue jeans and he has long hair.

He's going to the movies or he's going to see a friend.
He's going to see a friend or he's going to the movies.

Fiats are very maneuverable but Buicks are safer.
Buicks are safer but Fiats are very maneuverable.

In many cases, however, the order of statements in conjoined sentences is significant, revealing more than just a stringing together of additional thoughts, alternatives, or contrasts. In these cases conjunctions carry additional meaning which can be inferred from the context of the situation. Following are examples of conjoined sentences that cannot be reversed. Notice the additional interpretation inherent in the conjunction.

He has long hair and (so) he keeps it tied with a leather thong. (result)

They are going to the movies or (else) Bill's girl friend will be unhappy. (inference)

Fiats are very maneuverable but (can you believe it?) Jim can't even park one. (denial of expectation)

The above sentences can just as well be joined together in a subordinate relationship and maintain comparable meanings. Notice, however, that the subordinating conjunction introduces the clause that precedes the coordinating conjunction in the sentences above.

Because he has long hair, he wears it tied with a leather thong. (causal)

If they don't go to the movies, Bill's girl friend will be unhappy. (conditional)

Although Fiats are very maneuverable, Jim can't even park one. (concessive)

Elements within sentences can also be joined together. Following are examples of sentences in which various constituents are made up of combined elements.

SUBJECT
Bill and Mary are revising a series of books.

DIRECT OBJECT
Bill is rewriting lessons one and two of the first book.

VERB
Mary is rearranging and editing the last five lessons.

OBJECT OF PREPOSITION
Bill added material to the beginning and the end of the first book.

INDIRECT OBJECT
The publishers will send Mary and Bill more work soon.

EMBEDDED SENTENCES

There are two major types of embedded sentences that are easily discernible in English. One is the relative clause, which was mentioned above.

The child *who is sick* left early.

The man *whom you met* is a German professor.

The woman *whose book was just published* is from Maine.

In relative clauses the introductory word, a relative pronoun, refers to a noun phrase in the main clause (or main sentence into which the relative clause is being embedded). For example, in the sentences above, *who* refers to *the child*, *whom* refers to *the man*, and *whose* refers to *the woman*. In addition to its function as a word that introduces a subordinate clause, the relative pronoun serves a particular function in the clause in which it appears: *who*, above, is subject; *whom* is direct object; and *whose* is a modifier. Furthermore, relative clauses usually follow closely after the noun to which they refer.

The second kind of transparently visible embedded sentence is the adverbial clause, introduced by such words as *because*, *if*, *although*, *when*.

He didn't finish the work *because he ran out of material.*

Carol will be unable to buy the car *if she doesn't work this summer.*

Janet went with the group *although she was uneasy about the trip.*

They returned to the house *when the heat became unbearable.*

These differ from relative clauses in two ways: (1) they are introduced by words that function as introductory words while at the same time revealing a semantic relationship to the main clause (condition, cause, concession, time); and (2) they may be placed either before or after the main clause.

He didn't finish the work because he ran out of material.
Because he ran out of material, he didn't finish the work.

We have already mentioned in the preceding section the relationship of these adverbial clauses to conjoined sentences. Thus, the above sentence might be conjoined and result in *He ran out of material so he didn't finish the work.*

The decision of when to use conjoining or embedding when combining two or more sentences is not always an easy one to make. It is best to remember that embedded sentences of the type shown above, sometimes called subordinate clauses, are usually those that have a dependency relationship to the main sentence. If two sentences seem to be of equal importance, it is best to join them together with coordinating conjunctions.

Embedded sentences sometimes function as noun phrases and take the place of subjects, direct and indirect objects, and objects of prepositions. These, too, are quite easily recognized as sentences within sentences.

SUBJECT
What he said produced a favorable reaction.

DIRECT OBJECT
He said whatever he pleased.

INDIRECT OBJECT
She presented whoever won with an award.

OBJECT OF PREPOSITION
They packed the books in whatever boxes were available.

DIRECT OBJECT
I wish that he had answered the question.

A type of embedding in English that is not quite so transparent occurs in what appear to be simple sentences but in reality are complex embedded ones. A knowledge of the simple sentences from which the sentence is constructed can help students understand the meaning of the sentence. Notice the structural changes that occur during the process of embedding.

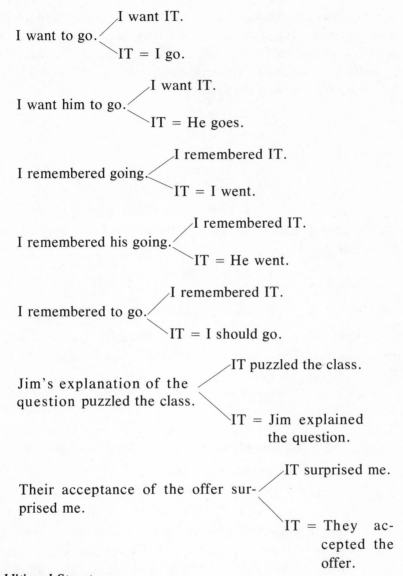

I want to go.
  I want IT.
  IT = I go.

I want him to go.
  I want IT.
  IT = He goes.

I remembered going.
  I remembered IT.
  IT = I went.

I remembered his going.
  I remembered IT.
  IT = He went.

I remembered to go.
  I remembered IT.
  IT = I should go.

Jim's explanation of the question puzzled the class.
  IT puzzled the class.
  IT = Jim explained the question.

Their acceptance of the offer surprised me.
  IT surprised me.
  IT = They accepted the offer.

Additional Structures

REQUEST SENTENCES

Simple sentences (statements and questions) and conjoined and embedded sentences produced by combining simple sentences have been discussed in a general way. However, there are other types of frequently occurring sentences that have so far not been mentioned. For example, classroom activities necessitate the use of request (imperative) sentences which take the following form in English.

> Open your books.
> Use a pencil.
> Repeat after me.
> Read the first sentence.
> Answer the questions.
> Ask John . . .

These requests may be made in a more polite fashion by adding the word *please*.

> Please open your books.
> Please use a pencil.
> Please repeat after me.

The phrase *would you please* may also be added to make a polite request which then results in a typical question structure: *Would you please open your books?*

Request sentences can be described as having the same structure as simple sentences (NP + VP) except that the NP is usually deleted. Traditionally, this subject has been referred to as '*you* understood' since this subject is always the second person.

> (You) open your books.
> (You) use a pencil.
> (You) repeat after me.

It is clear that the deleted NP must be second person because the grammar of English prescribes that when the direct object refers to the same person as the subject, that object must be reflexive in form; that is, it 'reflects' the subject. Notice the following sentences, which are not requests, in which the subjects are expressed.

> John washed himself. (*John washed John.)

Ruth asked herself a question. (*Ruth asked Ruth a question.)

Because of this rule we know that the underlying or unexpressed subject of the following request sentences is second person because the pronoun objects 'reflect' the subject.

Wash yourself.
Help yourselves.
Don't cut yourself.

SENTENCES WITH IT AND THERE

Two other common sentence types are those beginning with the expletives *it* and *there*. Sentences with *it* are frequently used in talking about the weather or in telling time.

It's cold today.
It was rainy yesterday.
It's seven o'clock.
It's after ten.

Sentences with *there*, which contain indefinite subjects and some form of the verb *be*, are used to avoid what seem to English speakers to be awkward statements, such as *Several men are in the room* or *A book is on the table*. In these sentences unstressed *there* is substituted in the normal position for the subject, which still determines concord with the verb although it is now placed after the verb.

There are several men in the room.
There is a book on the table.

Unstressed *there* (sometimes referred to as 'existential' *there*) differs from the adverb *there*, which is normally stressed. The contrast between these two words is clear in a sentence like *There were several men there* in which the first *there* is an expletive and the second an adverb.

In like manner, *it* can be used to substitute for a subject that is moved to the end of a sentence; this is especially true if the subject is a clause.

What you say makes no difference.

It makes no difference what you say.

To do that is foolish.

It is foolish to do that.

EXCLAMATIONS

A sentence type that does not appear too often in EFL/ESL textbooks, but that is fairly common in speech, is the exclamation with *what* and *how*.

What a horrible day it is!

What a magnificent concert that was!

How thoughtful she is!

How silly they are!

Even though these contain WH words, they do not contain the word order characteristic of questions. Notice that the last two sentences become questions when the word order is shifted.

How thoughtful is she?

How silly are they?

Exclamations, like any other structure, should be practiced in context. Perhaps examples from reading assignments can be used to introduce them, and the weather can generally be used as an excuse for practicing them.

ELLIPSIS

The preceding exclamations illustrate a very common phenomenon in English, the use of ellipsis, a process whereby portions of a sentence are deleted. The exclamations above can be expressed elliptically without subject and verb.

What a horrible day!

What a magnificent concert!

How thoughtful!

How silly!

Other types of elliptical expressions are provided below; the ellipted portion of each sentence is enclosed in parentheses.

John can play the violin, and Mary can (play the violin), too.
John didn't understand it, and neither did I (understand it).
John is going to Paris today and (John is going) to London
   next week.
John likes to travel, but his friends don't (like to travel).
John will drive to (Chicago) but fly back from Chicago.
John's car is newer than Jim's (car).

It will be noted that ellipsis often occurs when sentences are combined.

PASSIVE SENTENCES

Of the two sentences below one is active, the other passive; that is, in the first sentence the subject is the agent or doer, but in the second sentence the subject is that which is acted upon (actually, the object in the first sentence).

The teacher announced the results of the contest.
The results of the contest were announced by the teacher.

Passive sentences contain a form of the auxiliary verb *be* followed by the past participle; *were announced* in the second sentence above is a passive verb. The agent in the active sentence is expressed in the passive sentence in a prepositional phrase beginning with *by*. The agent is often omitted when this information seems unimportant or is not known, as in the following examples.

The bridge was constructed in 1950.
The work was inspected every week.
The problem was investigated immediately.
The window was broken last night.
The candidate was notified of his selection.

Whitman (1975:124) says that in addition to the reasons given above we avoid mentioning the agent in passive sentences because we prefer to withhold information about the agent for reasons of security, fear, or vindictiveness, or because there is a scholarly dictum that says writers should avoid using "I," which can be done by using the passive.

The agentless passive appears frequently in scientific and technical writing (Huddleston, 1971) where attention is focused on something other than the agent, as in the following examples.

> The experiment was completed in record time.
> Samples were prepared . . .
> The solution was added . . .
> The correct amounts were measured . . .

Thus, to treat the passive as a transformation of active sentences is bound to be misleading, since many passive sentences do not contain the agent that is explicitly required in its active counterpart.

Sequencing of Grammatical Items

The selection and sequencing of grammatical items for instruction will depend upon the specific needs of students, but there are certain elements of grammar that are undoubtedly essential to all speakers in the early stages of learning English. Below is a suggested list of such structural items; the next step would be the addition of conjoined and embedded structures.

statements
yes/no questions (with *be* and *do*)
requests
questions with WH words (interrogative pronouns)
number in nouns
tense in verbs (present, present progressive, past, present
    perfect)
modal auxiliaries
modifiers of nouns

The above list is not complete nor is the order fixed; the communicative needs and interests of the students should determine priorities within the list and the addition of other structures.

Finocchiaro (1969:66–82) and the less recent Fries (1945:35–36) contain suggested sequences of structures. Leech and Svartvik (1975) is a useful resource for selecting grammatical items according to their communicative use: e.g., denial and affirmation; comparison; place, direction, and distance; describing emotions. Structural items are arranged according to communicative meaning, and a grammatical compendium explains them in detail.

Knowledge of the syntactic features outlined briefly in this section of the book should provide an elementary grasp of English grammar. Fluency in the use of the language will depend upon many factors, foremost of which is probably a great deal of practice. The next section of this chapter will suggest ways in which these structures may be practiced.

Teaching the Grammatical Patterns

Practice in using the structural patterns described in the first section can be provided in a variety of ways. Here we will describe drills that are especially useful in the early stages of learning English grammar. Although drills are used in teaching all the communicative skills, structural drills are those that have been most often described and categorized (Cook, 1968; Dacanay, 1963; Hok, 1964; Kaszmarski, 1965; Ney, 1967; Paulston, 1970, 1971). Dacanay's classification lists four major types of drills: substitution, transformation, response, and translation. In our discussion of grammatical pattern drills we will follow Dacanay's terminology, but we will add one more type: the imitation or repetition drill. It should be remembered that all of these are mechanical or manipulative drills, especially useful in the early stages of learning a particular grammatical item.

Structural Drills

IMITATION

This type of drill — repetition of a model provided by the teacher — is employed primarily at the very beginning stages of language learning. It is often used in teaching grammar but is also effective for practicing pronunciation, including the prosodic features of language (stress, intonation, and rhythm). The first exercise that follows could also be used for teaching vocabulary, especially if accompanied by suitable visual aids. In this and subsequent exercises T indicates *Teacher* and S indicates *Students*.

Practice on the simple sentence with contracted form of *is*.

T: She's a nurse.   S: She's a nurse.
 She's a teacher.   She's a teacher.
 She's a doctor.   etc.
 She's a lawyer.
 She's an engineer.

Practice on verb forms, and on stress and rhythm.

T: The bóys eárn móney. S: The bóys eárn móney.
 The bóys are eárning   The bóys are eárning
  móney.   móney.
 The bóys are going to   etc.
  eárn móney.
 The bóys are going to
  be eárning móney.

SUBSTITUTION.

This kind of exercise can be of various types, from simple one-word substitutions to the more complicated moving-slot substitutions requiring other changes for purposes of agreement. Substitution drills are very useful for establishing the word order of sentences or parts of sentences, or for emphasizing correlative changes within sentences.

Simple Substitution

Practice on word order of statements with *be*.

T: The book is on   S: (repeats to start drill)
 the table.   The book is on the table.

 pen   The pen is on the table.
 box   The box is on the table.
 eraser   etc.
 pencil

Correlative Substitution

Practice on the present progressive verb form; subject/verb agreement.

T: Mary is studying.	S: (repeats)
	Mary is studying.
Mary and John	Mary and John are studying.
My brother	My brother is studying.
His friend	etc.
My friends	

Moving-Slot Substitution

Practice on the word order of direct object and time adverb.

T: She bought a car yesterday.	S: (repeats) She bought a car yesterday.
He	He bought a car yesterday.
house	He bought a house yesterday.
last week	He bought a house last week.
sold	etc.

Combined Moving-Slot and Correlative Substitution

Practice on word order and agreement of verb and time adverb.

T: She is buying a car today.	S: (repeats) She is buying a car today.
yesterday	She bought a car yesterday.
sold	She sold a car yesterday.
drove	She drove a car yesterday.
every day	She drives a car every day.
they	etc.

TRANSFORMATION

These drills are perhaps better referred to as *conversion* drills, to differentiate the use of the term 'transformation' in this sense from its use in transformational-generative grammar. Although these drills sometimes resemble the manipulative operations in certain rules of transformational grammar, they are not meant to be equated with such rules.

Transposition

Practice on statements and questions.

T: She can swim. S_1: Can she swim? S_2: Yes, she can.

  play tennis S_3: Can she play S_4: Yes, she can.
  drive a car   tennis?   etc.
  ride a bicycle   etc.
  play the piano

At this point the teacher should consciously make an effort to reduce the amount of 'teacher talk' in the classroom by organizing the practice in such a way as to force students to produce most of the language. Thus, in the above drill, the teacher will merely provide the cue for the structural practice; the students will formulate the questions and make the responses.

Integration

Practice on indirect questions.

T: Who is she? S_1: Do you know S_2: No, I don't.
   Do you know?   who she is?   (Yes, she's
                                            ———.)

   How far is it to S_3: Do you know S_4: No, I don't.
   Chicago? Do   how far it is   (Yes, it's
   you know?   to Chicago?   ———.)
   How much is   etc.   etc.
   the plane
   fare? Can you
   tell me?

What time is it?
  Do you
  know?
When is her
  birthday? Do
  you remem-
  ber?

In an exercise like the preceding one, students should be encouraged to answer affirmatively if they can provide the appropriate information. If not, they should reply negatively. Thus, while drilling a particular structural item, students concentrate on the meaning and attempt to *use* the language communicatively.

In the following exercises, the teacher establishes the pattern to be practiced (shown by the materials enclosed in the small boxes) and then merely cues the students, who carry on the practice.

Reduction

Practice on paraphrase construction.

> She's going to have someone paint the garage.
> She's going to have the garage painted.

T: mow the lawn	S_1: She's going to have someone mow the lawn.
	S_2: She's going to have the lawn mowed.
fix the sidewalk	S_3: She's going to have someone fix the sidewalk.
	S_4: She's going to have the sidewalk fixed.
wash the windows	etc.
repair the screens	

It should be noted that integration and reduction drills sometimes necessitate other changes: for example, a change in word order in the integration exercise (*who is she . . . who she is*) or a change in form in the reduction exercise (*paint* becomes *painted*). These are similar to the changes that occur in the correlative substitution drills described above. Every change, of course, increases the difficulty of the exercise and should be taken into account when sequencing drills according to relative ease or difficulty.

RESPONSE

Response drills probably come closer to the communicative use of language than do other types of manipulative drills because they depend upon imitation of a communicative situation for their operation; and even though they may be quite mechanical, they can provide practice on idiomatic uses of language and on such important devices as conversational rejoinders.

Practice on response involving count and noncount nouns.

Do you need any envelopes? Yes, just a few, please.
Do you need any paper? Yes, Just a little, please.

T: chairs	S₁: Do you need any chairs?
	S₂: Yes, just a few, please.
help	S₃: Do you need any help?
	S₄: Yes, just a little, please.
stamps	etc.
pens	
ink	

Practice on emphatic rejoinder.

Did you finish your homework? As a matter of fact, I did.

T: go to the movie	S₁: Did you go to the movie?
	S₂: As a matter of fact, I did.
call your mother	S₃: Did you call your mother?

buy a car	S₄: As a matter of fact, I did.
write your brother	etc.
wash the dishes	

Practice on short rejoinders (affirmative and negative).

(1) She likes hamburgers.	I do, too. (So do I.)
T: French fries	S₁: She likes French fries.
	S₂: I do, too. (So do I.)
potato chips	S₃: She likes potato chips.
	S₄: So do I. (I do, too.)
ice cream	etc.
pie	
cake	

(2) She doesn't like liver.	I don't either. (Neither do I.)
T: pork	S₁: She doesn't like pork.
	S₂: I don't either. (Neither do I.)
radishes	S₃: She doesn't like radishes.
	S₄: Neither do I. (I don't either.)
cucumbers	etc.
lamb	

(3) She likes hamburger.	I don't.
T: French fries	S₁: She likes French fries.
	S₂: I don't.
	S₃: I don't either. (Neither do I.)
potato chips	S₄: She likes potato chips.
	S₅: I don't.
	S₆: Neither do I. (I don't either.)

(4) She doesn't like liver. I do.	
T: pork	S_1: She doesn't like pork.
	S_2: I do.
	S_3: I do, too. (So do I.)
radishes	S_4: She doesn't like radishes.
	S_5: I do.
	S_6: So do I. (I do, too.)

Notice the way in which this last exercise must be operated to produce natural responses. The affirmative statement (1) allows either form of the affirmative response (*I do, too* or *So do I*). Similarly, the negative statement (2) allows either form of the negative response (*I don't either* or *Neither do I*). However, when an affirmative statement is followed by a negative response (3), or a negative statement by an affirmative response (4), the straightforward contradictory statement (*I do* or *I don't*) must be used by the first person responding; then a second person, who is agreeing with this first person, may use one of the alternative response forms (of the type *So do I* or *I don't either*), depending upon whether the first response was affirmative or negative.

Drills that are poorly written sometimes do not take into account these kinds of structural rules; and if great care is not taken in writing them, they can easily falsify actual language use. Materials writers sometimes become so enthralled with the structures being drilled that they forget to test the products of the drills to see if they are more than just manipulative exercises without any real base in language use. It is particularly important for teachers who are not native speakers of English to check with a native speaker, if possible, when they suspect that exercises have become nothing but manipulation of language to the point of distorting actual usage.

TRANSLATION

Translation exercises can be used by teachers in classes where all students speak the same first language, but probably not otherwise; in a class of students of heterogeneous language background, the teacher's ability to use the native language of some of the students and not of others may cause some to feel slighted. However, a limited use of translation exercises, particularly by bilingual teachers in a homogeneous class, can be advantageous and timesaving. Its use is particularly effective in checking the comprehension of difficult items of structure, vocabulary, and idiomatic usage, or in developing varieties of style in the expressive use of language at the advanced level. (See Dacanay, 1963:147–50 for examples of translation exercises.) Under no circumstances, however, should this be the only or the dominant kind of classroom activity.

The structural drills described above can be implemented in the classroom in a variety of ways: (1) they can be practiced orally or used as written exercises; (2) they can be drilled individually or in chorus; or (3) the teacher may select a student with particularly good pronunciation to act as a model for imitation (this is especially useful for teachers who are not native speakers of English).

Although choral drills have disadvantages, they are sometimes an absolute necessity in classes that are so large as to prohibit much individual recitation. If properly conducted (and that word is chosen purposely), they can be helpful in developing correct rhythm. They also provide a cover for very timid language learners until they can gain enough confidence to attempt individual responses. On the negative side, they do not allow the teacher the close observation of individual performance which is most desirable; and the lazy student can sometimes avoid practice altogether. However, a cautious use of choral drills can be effective as a change of pace, a setter of sentence rhythm, and an aid to the shy student.

In large classes where individual drills are impossible and more than choral drills are desired, practice in smaller groups can be effected by indicating that responses be made by rows, or by dividing the class in half (either vertically or horizontally), or by all the men (boys) and women (girls) to respond in turn.

The structural drills described here exemplify the kinds of practice that may be necessary to introduce specific grammatical constructions to students at various levels of learning English. Ways in which such grammatical structures can be practiced in more meaningful, more nearly communicative situations will be discussed in Chapter 7, Teaching the Communication Skills.

Exercises

A. Read the following 'Jabberwocky'-type sentences; then replace the unfamiliar italicized words with typical English words so that the sentences have 'meaning'. What kinds of syntactic devices enable you to replace these words?

1. *Bosk*, are you *tedding* or *hoppling*?
2. The *hoplite fugitated*, but the *fugleman* was *premiated* in *crispated mufti*.
3. Some *glibbery tallages* may have been *swashed*.
4. The *refection* cannot be *saponified* in *stoups*.
5. The *suttee* was *shriven* and is now *sanable*.
6. An *intendant silicified* the *kishy dehisence*.

B. Fill in the blanks below by adding derivational affixes or deleting them from the words supplied. More than one word can sometimes be supplied for some categories.

Noun	Verb	Adjective
1. analysis		
2. beauty		
3.	compare	
4.		creative
5.	destroy	
6.	determine	
7.		excitable
8.		identical
9.	judge	
10. magnet		
11. optimum		

12.	participate	
13.	rebel	
14. renunciation		
15.		resistant
16.		simple
17.		social
18.	supply	
19. sympathy		
20.	transfer	

C. Read the following sentences aloud paying attention to the stress on words that look alike.

1. The police have a suspect in mind.
   Is there anyone you suspect?

2. My freshman English instructor left her imprint on me. I shall never forget how to use a semicolon because she imprinted its correct usage so strongly on my mind.

3. He has a watch pocket but no pocket watch.

4. There's the picture frame I've been looking for! There are others in the attic but none this size.

5. I like milk chocolate but not chocolate milk.

6. What are they? They're cooking apples.

7. What are they doing? They're cooking apples.

8. They're racing cars, that's what they're doing.

9. What did you say they were? They're racing cars.

10. Let's have a clam bake. We can bake clams on the beach.

D. Change the phrases and sentences below to questions simply by using a different intonation pattern as you read them aloud.

1. Here.

2. In the drawer.

3. The mail box at the corner.

4. They scored.

5. Put it in the box.

   6. Matt said he would leave at six.

   7. Dinner isn't ready yet.

   8. Her parents met her at the airport.

   9. Millions of people use it.

  10. He told you who it was.

E. Arrange the words in each of the items below into grammatical sentences. Use only the words given. Sometimes you will be able to make more than one sentence out of the groups of words. What generalizations can you make about the order of words in English sentences after completing this exercise?

  1. table
    typewriter
    the
    radio
    he
    set
    the
    on

  2. eat
    the
    daisies
    don't

  3. philanthropist
    the
    is
    hallmark
    humanitarianism
    true
    a
    of

  4. John
    anymore
    sister
    scarcely
    his
    sees

5. cramming
   systematic
   better
   than
   results
   review
   test
   a
   produces
   for

6. personal
   more
   conversations
   are
   interviews
   telephone
   effective
   sometimes
   than

F. Identify the nouns in the following sentences as singular or plual count nouns, or mass nouns. Then tell whether they are used in a nongeneric (either definite or indefinite) or generic sense.

   1. Water can be taken from the pumps in the village.
   2. Fuel can be purchased from vendors who deliver it directly to the homes.
   3. The women of the village, sometimes accompanied by their daughters, walk as far as five miles several times a week to cut wattle trees and to carry the loads of wood to their homes.
   4. A few families keep chickens so that they can sell eggs.
   5. Others sell surplus milk from the cows they raise.
   6. An increase in the size of farms was announced last year.
   7. There has been an advance in farm cultivation by owners.
   8. Lumber played an important role in the economic development of the Upper Midwest.

9. Men in Minnesota showed great ingenuity in getting logs to mills.

10. Lumberjacks, who often came from Michigan, helped make it the 'Golden Age'.

G. What are the simple sentences out of which the following sentences are made?

1. Three large high-rise apartments with the same design have already been built or are nearing completion.

2. She looked at him as if she had not understood a word he had said.

3. John has an identical twin, a lawyer who lives in the same city, and this sometimes causes confusion.

4. His constant laughing was an irritating nuisance.

5. Your first assignment is to reorganize the files in the cabinet behind my desk.

6. Families with some economic resources are able to obtain tin rain barrels in which to collect water from their roofs, thereby saving the cost of water from pumps.

H. Construct tag questions for the following sentences. Note any sentences for which a tag is not easily decided upon.

1. Sally is intelligent.

2. The air conditioner isn't working.

3. He has lots of money.

4. The instructor didn't announce a quiz.

5. My father seldom watched TV.

6. Either Tom or Mary will do it.

7. Neither Sue nor Mary can do it.

8. Everyone should help.

9. Not everyone likes everyone else.

10. Cuba supports communism.

I. Change the following affirmative sentences to negative sentences, making any other structural changes that are necessary.

1. I think someone is coming.

2. Consider some of the consequences.

3. Do you sometimes wish you were a politician?
4. Is he already here?
5. They are still listening to the music.
6. Her parents are visiting her, too.
7. She is going to ask one or the other to help her.
8. We've left the keys to the car somewhere.
9. They were somehow disappointed in the results.
10. I must finish this assignment.

J. Which of the following sentences contain separable phrasal verbs? Can you paraphrase their meanings with one word?

1. They turned down the offer.
2. They looked after the child.
3. They turned in the manuscript.
4. They fell off the wagon.
5. They thought up an excuse.
6. They looked up the word.
7. They woke up the baby.
8. They talked about the movie.
9. They talked over the assignment.
10. They thought of the answer.

K. Join the two sentences in each item by using the conjunctions *and*, *or*, or *but*. Identify them as being interchangeable or non-interchangeable conjoined sentences.

1. We ran out of bread for the sandwiches.
   Mother sent my brother to the store to get some.
2. Algernon is intelligent.
   He is irresponsible.
3. The applicant may be a woman.
   The applicant may be a man.
4. They must clip the grass around the trees and shrubbery.
   They can't mow the grass at all.
5. She was a famous architect herself.
   Her father was a famous architect.

L. Combine the two sentences in each item by making the second sentence a relative clause to be embedded in the first sentence.

1. The woman is a judge.
    The woman is signing the papers.

2. They finally discovered the address of the woman.
    Mrs. Clark had given the letter to the woman.

3. His sister is a baseball player.
    He is very fond of his sister.

4. The car is full of gadgets.
    The gadgets can do everything imaginable.

5. The events are described in his memoirs.
    The events led to his resignation.

6. We are restricting the writing to specific material.
    The students should be able to understand and to produce the material.

7. The total price does not include additional fees.
    Additional fees must be paid by the customer.

8. Testing items should be arranged in contexts.
    Students should be familiar with the contexts.

9. The publisher is very much interested in the biography.
    A former English professor wrote the biography.

10. I would like to get in touch with Mary.
    Mary's aunt is a friend of mine.

M. Express the underlined portions of the complex sentences below as simple sentences.

Example: I didn't approve of her being fired.
              She was fired.

1. The boat whose picture I took belongs to my uncle.

2. I was hoping to leave by six.

3. The person to whom you pay the rent is the manager.

4. We enjoyed seeing his slides of Africa.

5. He had <u>his hair cut</u>.
6. I asked <u>him to go</u>.
7. <u>Sam's flunking the exam</u> didn't surprise us.
8. We wish <u>that the Vikings would win the title</u>.
9. I hope <u>that you will both be very happy</u>.
10. I recall <u>his saying exactly what you said he said</u>.

2

The Sound System

One of the most important aspects of learning a second language is the effort to master the sound system, to pronounce the language. But what exactly *is* pronunciation? One of the most detailed dictionary definitions states that it is "the act or the result of producing the sounds of speech, including articulation, vowel formation, accent, inflection, and intonation, often with reference to the correctness or acceptability of the speech sounds." [1]

The sounds of speech that are generally assumed to be the basis of pronunciation are the consonants and vowels; but what the above definition refers to as "accent, inflection, and intonation" proves to be an equally important part of the sound system. These are sometimes called the covering patterns of language: stress, pitch, juncture, and rhythm. If students concentrate only on the individual sound segments of the language (the *th* sound, for example), they may produce accurate renditions of the individual sounds but be grossly misunderstood if the 'tune' of the language is missing. The teacher must, therefore, emphasize all the elements of the sound system in teaching pronunciation: the individual vowels, consonants, and semivowels; word and sentence stress; intonation or patterns of voice pitch; juncture or pause; and the characteristic combinations of stressed and unstressed syllables in discourse which produce the rhythm of American English.

The above definition also refers to "acceptability" and "correctness." Another dictionary definition of pronunciation emphasizes this same idea: "the way or ways in which a unit of language is usually spoken or on the basis of analogy would probably be spoken by persons qualified by education or otherwise to be speakers worthy of imitation." [2]

Thus an acceptable pronunciation of a linguistic item is one that is not condemned by native speakers as being overly different from their own speech or the speech of those whom they would be willing to imitate. Another way of saying this is to describe as acceptable any pronunciation that does not draw attention away from *what* a person is saying to *how* he or she is saying it. Variant pronunciations of a word, e.g., *wash* pronounced as /waš/ or /wɔš/ (but perhaps not /wɔrš/) would be accepted by speakers who are familiar with such alternatives. It is essential to keep an open mind toward variation in the pronunciation of English words because we are not always familiar with dialects that may be far removed from our own. Fries's admonition in this respect is clear.

> It must be evident that in dealing with matters of pronunciation, especially in attempting to determine what is acceptable English speech, it is well to cultivate the virtue of tolerance. There is comparatively little difficulty in settling upon some one pronunciation for any word that must be acknowledged acceptable. Justly to render a negative judgment, however, to condemn any pronunciation one hears generally used, demands much greater caution as well as knowledge. [3]

More recent statements of this attitude can be found in H. B. Allen (1973) and Dickerson (1976).

Teachers need to be acquainted with dialect variation for another reason. Textbooks in English for speakers of other languages are written by people from many different geographical areas of the United States and from countries in which different dialects of English are used; and the pronunciation in these texts will necessarily reflect, to some degree, the dialect of the authors. Thus, although one author, a native of the northern part of the United States, may transcribe *on* as /an/, an author from the midland or southern area may transcribe it as /ɔn/. Since textbooks are not generally chosen because of their applicability to certain geographical areas, teachers must be aware of the fact that their own pronunciation may differ from that of the text and still be acceptable. Conversely, they must not believe that any pronunciation in the text, which may not agree with their own, is therefore unacceptable. (A useful reference for pronunciation is Lewis [1972].) They should, however, adhere to their own pronunciation and not try to simulate another dialect.

When dialect differences are discussed with students, care must be taken that the student does not receive an incorrect impression. Often the statement is made that persons in certain sections of New England pronounce such words as *glass*, *dance*, *bath* with an /a/ sound rather than with the /æ/ sound which is typical of much of the rest of the country. Because some students have particular difficulty producing the /æ/ sound, they often express enthusiastic interest in learning such a dialect. They say, "It would be easier to learn that dialect because we wouldn't have to pronounce 'that other vowel sound'." They must be shown that New England speakers, along with all other speakers of English, have to pronounce 'that other vowel sound' — the /æ/ sound — in such words as *man*, *sat*, *alphabet*.

Similarly, when certain dialects are referred to as '*r*-less', students conceive the notion that they would not have to pronounce the /r/ (another difficult sound for many students) if they were taught such a dialect. Again, they have to be shown that this '*r*-less-ness' occurs only under certain restrictions and that no dialect of English is completely without the /r/ sound. All speakers produce /r/ in syllable initial position: *read*, *ring*, *arrest*. And even those who omit it in word or syllable final position as in *fa(r)*, *ove(r)*, *teache(r)* usually insert it when the following word or syllable begins with a vowel: *far away*, *over and out*, *teacher evaluation*.

Wise teachers refuse to become too concerned about dialect differences but are alert to those that may confuse their students; and wise students, insofar as possible, pattern their pronunciation after one particular regional type of speech that represents a large number of speakers and has broad acceptance.

Describing the Sound System

Returning to our definition of pronunciation we come to the term 'articulation', the way in which sounds are produced. It is through an understanding of the articulatory process that teachers are best able to help students pronounce sounds with which they have difficulty.

The Need for a Special Alphabet

In order to discuss the articulatory process involved in producing the vowels, consonants, and semivowels of English (the three kinds of segments that make up syllables and words) we need to have a systematic means of referring to these sounds. English is phonetically spelled, that is, the letters that we use to spell English represent sounds in the language. However, these letters do not always stand in a one-to-one relationship with the sounds they are supposed to represent. We grapple with many spellings of the same sound: we, need, read, key, believe, receive, people, machine. Conversely, the same sequence of letters may be pronounced in a variety of ways: through, although, thorough, bough, cough, hiccough.

The history of the English language has involved borrowing words from many languages, often with the spelling approximating the sound of the word when it was borrowed and sometimes with a spelling change later; e.g., *dette, debt*. Furthermore, between the time of Chaucer and that of Shakespeare, our language underwent the impressive 'great vowel shift', which has put our language out of step with the pronunciation of vowels in other Indo-European languages. Compare, for example, the pronunciation of the vowels *a*, *e*, *i*, *o*, *u* in Spanish, French, or German with their pronunciation in English. Nor has there been a spelling reform in English as there has in languages like Spanish, Turkish, and Finnish.

Otto Jespersen made the following statement concerning the difficulties presented by English spelling:

> Max Müller once said that English orthography is a national misfortune, and Viëtor has improved upon this observation by declaring that it is an international misfortune, since it is not only Englishmen but also all educated persons in other lands who have to be bothered with it.[4]

Although it is true that there are many regularities in English spelling patterns that help us in pronouncing words, there are indeed many irregularities. In addition, there are simply not enough letters in our alphabet to make all the distinctions necessary to represent the sounds of English. We need a one-to-one correspondence between each significant sound and the symbol used to represent it. Such a representation facilitates talk about sounds and, especially for adult students, serves as an aid in learning pronunciation.

Phonetics and Phonemics

Persons dealing with language have for many years used some kind of symbolization to represent speech sounds. Phoneticians often recorded all the minute differences that they could hear when a person spoke. In such a narrow transcription the English *k* sounds in *kill, cool, call* would be differentiated, since there is a phonetic difference between them that can be acoustically perceived and described in articulatory terms. The *k* in *kill* is pronounced with the back of the tongue upon the hard palate; the *k* of *cool* is pronounced with the back of the tongue upon the velum or soft palate; the *k* of *call* is produced with the tongue farther back than for either of the other two. These *k* sounds would be represented by different symbols in a purely phonetic alphabet, since the purpose of such an alphabet is to symbolize acoustically perceptible differences.

More recently, linguists have emphasized language as a system of contrasts. From this idea of contrasts within the system has come the concept of a phonemic alphabet that symbolizes only those sounds that contrast meaningfully with one another. In such an alphabet the three *k* sounds in *kill*, *cool*, and *call* would be represented by one symbol /k/, since the slight phonetic difference between them is never a contrastive feature; that is, if we should pronounce *kill* with the *k* of *call*, the meaning of the word would not change.

The sound symbolized by /k/ does contrast with /g/ (thereby necessitating a distinctive symbol) since the substitution of /g/ for /k/ results in a word with a different meaning: *gill*. The use of a phonemic alphabet, providing a systematic representation of these contrasting sounds, is extremely valuable in teaching these contrasts.

From time to time, however, there is a need to refer to certain nonphonemic characteristics of English such as aspiration or vowel length. These phonetic characteristics are often as important in the communicative process as are phonemic distinctions. Pedagogically they are sometimes crucial in helping students both in distinguishing and in producing contrasts. For example, the difference between *hiss* and *his* can be explained on the phonemic level as a contrast between the two sounds /s/ and /z/ (voiceless and voiced counterparts of a sound produced at the same point of articulation and in the same manner). However, the pronunciation of the final voiced sound in *his* is accompanied by a lengthening of the preceding vowel sound (a phonetic feature that occurs regularly in English). By emphasizing the length of the vowel, students produce a better 'phonemic' contrast than when they concentrate only on the voicing distinction between the two sounds.

Traditionally, linguists have agreed upon a stylized notation to distinguish phonetic and phonemic symbolization. Phonetic transcription is enclosed in brackets: [pʰ] represents the phonetic transcription of the first sound in the word *pen*, showing the heavily aspirated initial consonant. A phonemic representation of the same sound would not include this phonetic feature of aspiration and would be enclosed in slashes: /p/.

A Phonemic Representation of English Sounds

A phonemic representation of English sounds is provided in Table 4. Since English uses more sound contrasts than the Latin alphabet can accommodate, some special symbols have had to be added. Seven special consonant symbols are needed: /ŋ/ si*ng*, /θ/ *th*ink, /ð/ *th*ey, /š/ *sh*e, /ž/ vi*si*on, /tš/ *ch*ild, /dž/ *j*et. Three are needed for the vowel sounds: /æ/ m*a*t, /ə/ c*u*t, /ɔ/ c*augh*t (also used in the diphthong /ɔy/ t*oy*). All other symbols are those of the regular alphabet, each symbol (letter of the alphabet) always representing one sound and only one sound. For example, /g/ will always represent the 'hard' *g* sound as in *get*, and /s/ will always represent the sound in *see* but not the sound in *as*.

Through the use of this augmented alphabet the student will be able to relate sound to symbol.[5] However, the alphabet should not be used as an end in itself, only as a means to an end. It is a device to aid the student's memory, but it cannot be expected to

Table 4. The Sounds of English

CONSONANTS

/b/	/bæd/	bad	/m/	/mæn/	man	/ŋ/	/siŋ/	sing
/d/	/duw/	do	/n/	/now/	no	/θ/	/θiŋk/	think
/f/	/fæt/	fat	/p/	/pen/	pen	/ð/	/ðey/	they
/g/	/get/	get	/s/	/siy/	see	/š/	/šiy/	she
/h/	/hat/	hot	/t/	/tuw/	two	/ž/	/vižən/	vision
/k/	/kowm/	comb	/v/	/véri/	very	/tš/	/tšayld/	child
/l/	/leyt/	late	/z/	/zuw/	zoo	/dž/	/džet/	jet
/r/	/reyt/	rate						

SEMIVOWELS OR GLIDES

| /y/ | /yet/ | yet | /w/ | /wet/ | wet |

VOWELS AND DIPHTHONGS

/iy/	/miyt/	meet				/uw/	/kuwl/	cool
/i/	/mit/	mit				/u/	/kud/	could
/ey/	/meyt/	mate				/ow/	/kowt/	coat
/e/	/met/	met	/ə/	/kət/	cut	/ɔ/	/kɔt/	caught
/æ/	/mæt/	mat	/a/	/kat/	cot			
/ay/	/taym/	time	/aw/	/tawn/	town	/ɔy/	/tɔy/	toy

STRESS

| /´/ | /téybəl/ | table | /`/ | /béysbɔ̀l/ | baseball |

work miracles. If, for example, students are shown that the vowel sounds in *leave* and *live* are represented by two different symbols, /iy/ and /i/, they will be more aware of the need to make this distinction in sound. But this does not guarantee that when they see the symbol /i/ they will immediately pronounce the sound accurately. The symbol should be thought of as a mnemonic device, useful in teaching the pronunciation of the sound it represents.

It should also be remembered that the same symbol can represent one sound in a particular language and another sound in a second language. It is impossible to predict the phonetic actualization of a sound simply by looking at a symbol. For example, the symbol /t/ does not represent the same sound in English and in Spanish. It is the responsibility of the teacher to show students the phonetic quality of each sound in the language being learned, utilizing the symbolization to fix these contrasts in sound firmly in their minds.

Stress Markings

In defining a phonemic alphabet we have said that it is a symbolization of the significant sound contrasts, those that produce changes in meaning. Since word and sentence stress are meaningful, they must also be symbolized. We need to distinguish between such pairs of words as *recórd* (verb) and *récord* (noun) or *insért* (verb) and *ínsert* (noun) which carry different stress patterns depending upon their function in a sentence.

I need to insért something in the envelope.
The ínsert doesn't add much to the weight.

In order to illustrate the essential characteristics of word stress, three degrees of stress must be symbolized: /´/ primary stress, /`/ secondary stress, and weak stress, which is left unmarked.[6] The three levels can be distinguished in the word *récognìze*. Secondary stress on *ize* is signaled by the fact that a full vowel sound /ay/ is present in the final syllable. Most weak syllables contain either /ə/ or /i/, and the final syllable of *recognize* cannot be reduced to those sounds. Clearly contrasting with this word is *reckoning* in which no secondary stress appears and in which the syllables without primary stress can be reduced to /ə/ and /i/. This phenomenon of reducing vowels in unstressed syllables is an important characteristic of the English sound system, and words in isolation often have a vowel quality different from the vowel quality of these same words when they appear in the stream of speech. For example, *to* /tuw/ can become /tə/ in the phrase *go to the bank*. Care should be taken not to implant the pronunciation of isolated forms so strongly in the minds of students that they cannot later reduce them.

English sentence stress must also be symbolized. Contrasts that are intuitively apparent to native speakers of English are not automatic to others, particularly those whose own language does not use stress in this way. Notice the contrastive stress in the following sentences.

> How áre you?
> I'm fine. How are yóu?
>
> Where are the paper plátes?
> Oh, don't use the páper plates. Use the
> chína plates.
>
> Where's the apple píe?
> How did you get the idea that it was an ápple
> pie? It's a chérry pie.

Rhythm

Developing from sentence stress is the rhythm typical of English which is produced by the relatively even spacing of stress in English sentences. In other words, major stresses in an English phrase or sentence tend to produce a kind of rhythmic beat in the language that speakers try to maintain no matter how many syllables happen to fall between these stresses. An illustration of this phenomenon in English is seen in the stress patterns in the following 'reverse pyramid' exercise.

Énglish is ínteresting.
The Énglish book is ínteresting.
The Énglish book is very ínteresting.
The Énglish book isn't very ínteresting.

Notice that the greater the number of syllables between stresses, the faster the syllables are pronounced and the greater the tendency to use contracted forms. Because of this tendency we say that English is a 'stress-timed' language. Many other languages, on the other hand, are 'syllable-timed' because they seem to require almost equal amounts of time to produce each syllable. This feature of English necessitates a great deal of practice by students whose native language happens to give almost equal stress to each syllable.

A simple illustration of the way in which English speakers try to maintain a certain timing in stress within a phrase is the change that occurs in the stress pattern of the words *afternoon* and *comprehend* when in isolation and in a phrase.

àfternóon   but   áfternoòn téa
còmprehénd   but   cómpreheǹd Jóhn, not Bíll

In English primary and secondary stresses are sometimes reversed in order to maintain a certain number of syllables between primary stresses rather than to have primary stresses close together in sequence.

Intonation

Just as the contrasts in sounds and stress need to be symbolized, so do the pitch levels of the voice. These pitch patterns, or intonation, express meanings in the same manner as contrasts in sounds and stress. The statement

He is go|ing.

can be distinguished from the question

He is go|ing?

simply by the use of a different intonation.

Similarly a contrast in intonation on the one word *where* can signal two different kinds of questions.

Where? (I'm asking for some information.)

Where? (I didn't hear your answer; I'm repeating the question.)

English intonation uses four distinct pitch levels in various combinations. These levels can be graphically symbolized in a linear fashion. This type of intonation marking has proved useful because it provides a visual reinforcement of what students are asked to imitate with their voices, pitch 4 being very high, pitch 3 high, pitch 2 mid, and pitch 1 low.

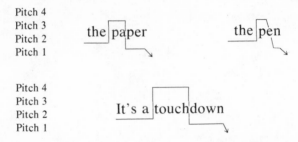

Pitch 4
Pitch 3
Pitch 2   the |paper   the |pen
Pitch 1

Pitch 4
Pitch 3
Pitch 2   It's a |touchdown
Pitch 1

It should be noted that pitch 2 is drawn immediately below the line of writing and pitch 3 immediately above. Pitch 4 is quite a distance above the line and pitch 1 considerably below. Care should be taken to distinguish pitch 3 from pitch 4, which should appear very far above the line of writing. Pitch 2 is usually the level on which one starts an utterance if there is no special stress:

The book is on the |table.
                2

Pitch 3 is used to express stress or prominence in the sentence or phrase:
                                3
                    That's |the one!

Pitch 1 is sometimes referred to as 'final' because it often occurs at the end of utterances:

She isn't here. Tell me about it.
1
1

Pitch 4 expresses some special emotion and is not used as frequently as the other three pitches:

4 4 4
Help! He's drowning! Look out!

The perpendicular and diagonal lines illustrate the difference between a change of pitch that occurs between syllables (perpendicular line)

the paper

and a change that necessitates a glide on the vowel sound of a single syllable (diagonal line)

the pen.

This gliding change within the syllable requires special practice because it necessitates a lengthening of the vowel sound which students may find difficult.

Intonation patterns are referred to by the use of the numbered pitch levels described above, starting with the stressed syllable on which a change occurs. For example, the 3-1 intonation indicates a pattern that begins on level 3 and ends on level 1. The following sentence illustrates the use of 3-1 intonation.

He left the house in a hurry.

The most common intonation patterns are 3-1, 2-3, and 3-2. The 3-1 intonation occurs on many different grammatical structures and often has the meaning of finality.

He left. I don't know anything about him.

Notice that the 3-1 intonation regularly occurs on WH questions.

Who is he? Where did he go? How much is it?

The 2-3 intonation, on the other hand, denotes incompleteness. It often occurs in a series or with a *yes/no* question.

Is she early? She needs a pen, some paper, and a ruler.

Notice that at the end of the series in the preceding sentence the 3-1 intonation occurs.

The 3-2 intonation (instead of the 3-1) is found quite often in the middle of sentences, indicating nonfinality, where a fall to level 1 would indicate finality. This fall only to level 2 indicates that the speaker is going to continue.

He has already finished . . . (but he'll wait for you.)

It must be clearly understood that intonation is not tied directly to grammatical structure. It possesses a meaning of its own, revealing the speaker's attitude or feeling toward what he or she is saying. For example, the same sequence of words in an utterance can be spoken with different intonations depending upon what the speaker wishes to convey.

She's a lawyer.   (statement of fact)

She's a lawyer!   (disbelief or surprise)

She's a lawyer . . .   (nonfinal signal, "and
                               she's extremely busy.")

The use of two different intonations (rising or falling) on *yes/no* questions reveals a difference in attitude on the part of the speaker. The use of 3-1 instead of the more frequent 2-3 may be an attempt to provide variation in intonation or it may be a desire to emphasize an idea.

Is he young? Is he a good student? Is he well prepared?

Can he swim? Is he prepared to take a life-saving test?

In the section of this book on the grammatical system we

have mentioned the implications inherent in the use of rising and falling intonation on tag questions (see page 28). Below is the typical intonation found on alternative questions.

Would you like coffee or tea?   (These are the two beverages available; the response would probably be either one or the other of the alternatives.)

Since an alternative question involves a limited kind of series, the first of the alternatives offered has the rising intonation (2-3) and the second or final alternative the falling intonation (3-1). This intonational combination distinguishes it from a *yes/no* question which may look very much like an alternative question but which entails a different presupposition in the mind of the speaker.

Would you like coffee or tea?   (Or would you like something else? The response would probably be, "Yes," or "No, thank you.")

Classification of Sounds

Having examined the various aspects of the English sound system in a general fashion, let us now turn to a detailed discussion of the individual sound segments of English: the vowels, consonants, and semivowels or glides. We will discuss first a phonetic classification of the sounds of English as a basis for a thorough understanding of the differences in the articulation of these various sound segments. Table 5 should be referred to in connection with the following discussion.

All English sounds can be divided into two categories: *stops* and *continuants*. In stop sounds, the air stream is completely impeded before it is released. The simple stop sounds in English are six in number: /p/, /t/, /k/, /b/, /d/, /g/. These six sounds have

Table 5. Phonetic Classification of English Sounds

SOUNDS

CONTINUANTS   STOPS /p, t, k/ /tš/
/b, d, g/ /dž/

ORAL   *NASAL* /m, n, ŋ/

RESONANT   FRICATIVE /f, θ, s, š, h/
/y, w, l, r/   /v, ð, z, ž/
and all vowels

Adapted from Kenneth L. Pike, *Phonetics* (University of Michigan Press, 1944).

special phonetic features that separate them into two groups of three sounds each. The sounds /p/, /t/, /k/ are pronounced without voice, that is, without vibration of the vocal cords. (A more detailed explanation of voicing and voicelessness is forthcoming. See pages 85–86.) Furthermore, they also require aspiration or a puff of air when they appear at the beginning of a word or a stressed syllable. Notice the difference in the /t/ sounds in *top* and *stop*, for example. The sounds /b/, /d/, /g/, on the other hand, are voiced and are never aspirated.

The second category of sounds, continuants, can be subdivided into two groups: *oral continuants* and *nasal continuants*. Nasals are produced with air emitted from the nose and are three in number: /m/, /n/, /ŋ/.

Oral continuants can be further classified into *resonant* or *fricative* sounds. Fricatives are sounds in which there is audible friction of the articulators. In English these are the voiceless sounds /f/, /θ/, /s/, /š/, /h/ and the voiced sounds /v/, /ð/, /z/, /ž/.

A special group of complex sounds, composed of a stop plus a fricative, are the two English *affricates*: /tš/ (voiceless) and /dž/ (voiced).

Resonant sounds, those in which there is no audible friction, can be of two types: *central* and *lateral*. In English there is only one lateral, the /l/ sound, produced by the air stream being released around the sides of the tongue.

The remaining sounds in English are the central resonant sounds produced without audible friction and with the air passing over the center of the tongue in a continuing stream. These central resonants include all the vowel sounds, the /r/ sound, and, in addition, the so-called semivowels or glides (/y/ and /w/). In manner of production it can be seen that the semivowels and /r/ are much more similar to vowels than to consonants, and they can be taught much more effectively if this phonetic characteristic is emphasized. The /r/ sound particularly should be introduced as a nonfricative continuant sound because in so many languages it tends to be just the opposite. The same holds true, in many respects, for the /y/ and /w/ sounds. More will be said later about specific techniques for teaching these individual sounds.

Visual Aids to Pronunciation

In teaching the sounds of the language, it is seldom sufficient (except with very young children) for students simply to imitate the teacher. The majority of students need specific help; and visual aids, such as diagrams and charts that clarify the articulatory processes involved in making sounds, can help students gain greater accuracy in pronunciation. They seem to provide a better grasp of the manner of production and the points of articulation than do simple descriptive paragraphs.

For example, in teaching the pronunciation of the English /t/ we can ask students to imitate our pronunciation. If their native language happens to be Spanish, they will probably put their tongues against the back of their upper teeth to pronounce the sound because this is what they do in pronouncing the comparable sound in Spanish. We can tell them that the /t/ sound is pronounced with the tongue placed against the alveolar ridge, higher and farther back in the mouth than they are accustomed to, but a diagram illustrating such a tongue position is more effective because of its visual impact.

One type of diagram found useful in teaching articulatory positions is the simple face diagram in which the positions of the various 'organs of speech' are shown. Figure 1 is a diagram of the speech mechanism which can be used as a model for describing the various articulatory processes involved in producing sounds.

The face diagram is more effective in illustrating some sounds than others: /θ, ð/ with the tongue between the teeth; /p, b, m/ with the lips completely closed; /t, d/ with the tongue on the tooth ridge; /n, ŋ/ with the tongue on the tooth ridge for one and against the velum for the other, and the nasal passage open; and the contrast between the 'clear' /l/ of *leave*, in which the front of the tongue is relatively high, and the 'dark' /l/ of *veal*, in which the back of the tongue is relatively high. Even other modifications such as the thrusting outward of the lips in the pronunciation of /š/ in *shoe* or the jaw movement in the /w/ of *wall* can be shown on these so-called static diagrams by the use of dotted lines or arrows.

Vowel Sounds

The points of articulation for the vowel sounds are less easily discerned than those for consonant sounds because in producing vowels the tongue moves freely without contact within a small area inside the mouth. If, however, we superimpose a chart of the vowel sounds on a face diagram, the relationship of the tongue position to the sound produced becomes much clearer. Figure 2 illustrates the position of English vowel sounds within the mouth.

If we are teaching the contrasting vowel sounds in *leave* and *live*, for example, we can show through the use of the vowel chart that the /iy/ sound of *leave* is produced with the front of the tongue in a higher and more forward position than for the /i/ sound of *live*. Likewise, when we turn to the back vowels, it can be pointed out that all of them are produced with some degree of lip rounding.

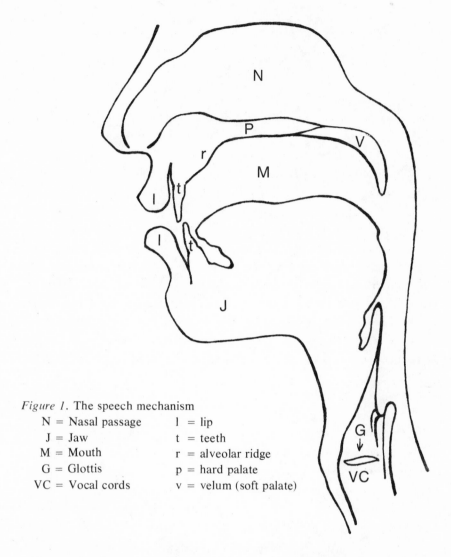

Figure 1. The speech mechanism

N = Nasal passage	l = lip
J = Jaw	t = teeth
M = Mouth	r = alveolar ridge
G = Glottis	p = hard palate
VC = Vocal cords	v = velum (soft palate)

To attain the most effective results when using these charts students must have some feel for the movement of the tongue within the mouth. Flexibility exercises, which help students become adept at changing tongue position, are desirable. General exercises for attaining this flexibility can begin with the repetition in sequence several times of the sounds /iy/ — /a/ — /uw/ which require extremes in tongue movement, thereby making students aware of the movement of the tongue in their mouth.

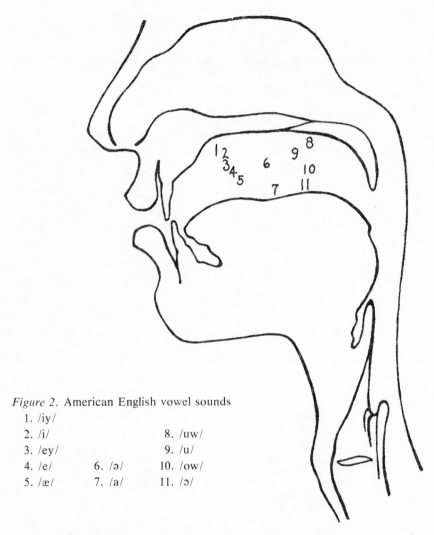

Figure 2. American English vowel sounds

1. /iy/
2. /i/
3. /ey/
4. /e/   6. /ə/   8. /uw/
5. /æ/   7. /a/   9. /u/
                       10. /ow/
                       11. /ɔ/

Then when they attempt to pronounce such contrasts as /iy/ and /i/, in which the tongue movement is less noticeable, they will be better able to discern this movement.

Some students have greater trouble than others controlling tongue movement. It is often very difficult for them to produce the /i/ sound. In these cases the 'bracketing' exercise may help.[7] In this exercise the two sounds closest in position to the sound under consideration are pronounced in contrast several times: /iy/ — /ey/; /iy/ — /ey/; /iy/ — /ey/. Then students are asked to

move the tongue to a position midway between these two bracketing sounds, approximating the difficult sound: /iy/ — /i/ — /ey/;
/iy/ — /i/ — /ey/. This can be done with words as well as with
sounds in isolation: b*eat* — *bait*; *beat* — *bait*; *beat* — *bit* — *bait*.

Another aid for students in pronouncing English vowels is the
use of muscular control. In differentiating /uw/ and /u/, for
example, students can be told that /uw/ is produced with considerable muscular tension and with the lips quite rounded. Then
when they are told that /u/ is pronounced with the muscles more
relaxed and with less lip rounding, this seems to bring forth a
more accurate production of the sound because the tongue low-
ers a bit through relaxation. Attention should be called to the
fact that /i/, /e/, /ə/, /u/ are lax vowels, that is, they are produced
without muscular tension.

Often the statement is made that the vowel sound in *beat* is
longer than the vowel in *bit*. This is true, but it should be pointed
out that the quantitative distinction is not the essential difference
between them. A qualitative distinction, due to the difference in
tongue position, causes the essential difference. Tenseness of
muscles for the higher glided /iy/ accounts for the slight difference
in length; tense muscles will hold a sound for a longer time than
muscles that are more relaxed.

After the approximate positions of the various vowel sounds
have been pointed out by the use of a vowel chart within the face
diagram (as in Figure 2), the chart can be used alone each time a
new vowel is introduced without the necessity of including a
careful drawing of the face. (See the vowel chart that appears as
part of Table 6.) When students see the chart, they will associate
the various vowels with the actual tongue position in the mouth.
The use of the vowel chart in teaching seems to produce better
results than the introduction of vowel sounds from a purely arbitrary list which has not been arranged in relation to articul-
tory production. Relating vowel quality to method of articulation
is equally important in teaching the recognition or perception of
vowel sounds.

Table 6. English Phonemes

General Type		Point of Articulation						
		Bi-labial	Labio-dental	Inter-dental	Alveolar	Alveo-palatal	Velar	Glottal
Stops	Voiceless	p			t	tš	k	
	Voiced	b			d	dž	g	
Fricatives	Voiceless		f	θ	s	š		h
	Voiced		v	ð	z	ž		
Nasals	Voiced	m			n		ŋ	
Liquids	Voiced				l			
	Voiced				r			

		Front	Central	Back
Semivowels		y		w
Vowels	High	iy		uw
		i		u
	Mid	ey	ə	ow
		e		
	Low	æ	a	ɔ

Consonant Sounds

The consonant sounds are more satisfactorily described than the vowels from the point of view of articulation because students can see more clearly either from a spoken model or from charts and diagrams exactly how to arrange the vocal apparatus to produce the sound. A master consonant chart similar to that in Table 6 can be used in the same manner as the vowel chart to illustrate point and manner of articulation. Students and teachers can refer to this chart each time a new sound is introduced in order to keep more clearly in mind the contrasts within the consonant groupings.

Voiceless and Voiced Sounds

When learning to produce the consonant sounds in English students must learn the distinction between voiceless and voiced sounds. They see, for example, that when they pronounce /p/ and /b/, the mouth is closed for both sounds. What then causes the difference between them? If they hold their hands over their ears or place their finger on their throat, they will be able to hear or feel the difference between the two sounds. When they produce /b/ they hear a buzzing sound in their head or feel a vibration in their throat. No such buzzing or vibration occurs when they pronounce /p/. This buzzing sound is caused by the vibration of the vocal cords, and sounds produced with such vibration are called voiced sounds. It is helpful for students to practice a contrasting series of voiceless and voiced continuant sounds until they can gain control over them:

/sssssssss zzzzzzzzz sssssssss zzzzzzzzz/.

Often words in English are contrasted solely by voiceless and voiced sounds: *sue*, *zoo*; *pet*, *bet*. And voiced-voiceless contrasts in syllable or word initial position are extremely important. However, although it may seem that voicing is the major distinction between such words as *ice* /ays/ and *eyes* /ayz/, the length of the vowel preceding the voiced consonant is actually more important than the voicing. Thus, students should be taught to lengthen the vowels preceding voiced consonants in producing such words as *eyes* [ay::z]; *bad* [bæ::d]; *stand* [stæ::nd]. In so doing the effect will be much closer to the pronunciation of a native speaker. Students should be taught to listen for this feature, too.

Practice on minimally distinctive pairs of words that contrast in this way can prove a helpful exercise, but emphasis should be placed on the length of the vowel and not on an exaggeration of the final voiced consonant.

write /rayt/	ride [ray::d]
cease /siys/	seize [siy::z]
cents /sents/	sends [se::ndz]

The phonetic feature of voicing plays an important part in the morphological structure of English words, specifically in the pronunciation of the *-s* and the *-ed* suffixes. Here students need to distinguish differences in voicing in order to select the correct pronunciation of the suffixes. The spelling of these suffixes does not give students the necessary clues to pronunciation; they must understand the phonological rule that enables them to pronounce them accurately.

Let us look first at the phonological rule for the pronunciation of the *-s* suffix (used to signal plural of nouns, possessive of nouns, and third-person singular present tense of verbs). This same rule can also be applied to the pronunciation of the contracted form of *is*: The teacher*'s* here.

Pronunciation of the -S Suffixes

When a noun or verb ends in a sibilant sound /s, z, š, ž, tš, dž/, the *-s* suffix is pronounced /əz/. (A sibilant sound is one that is heard as a relatively loud hissing or buzzing sound.)

glass	/glæs/	glasses	/glǽsəz/
rise	/rayz/	rises	/ráyzəz/
Charles	/tšarlz/	Charles's	/tšárlzəz/

When a noun or verb ends in a voiced sound that is not a sibilant, the *-s* suffix is pronounced /z/:

bird	/bərd/	birds	/bərdz/
see	/siy/	sees	/siyz/
David	/déyvid/	David's	/déyvidz/

When a noun or verb ends in a voiceless sound that is not a sibilant, the *-s* suffix is pronounced /s/:

book	/buk/	books	/buks/
stop	/stap/	stops	/staps/
Patrick	/pǽtrik/	Patrick's	/pǽtriks/

The *-ed* suffixes, inflections that indicate the past tense and the past participle of verbs, also follow a phonological rule which necessitates distinguishing voiceless and voiced sounds.

Pronunciation of the *-ED* Suffixes

When a verb ends in the sound /d/ or /t/, the *-ed* suffix is pronounced /əd/:

| add | /æd/ | added | /ǽdəd/ |
| test | /test/ | tested | /téstəd/ |

When a verb ends in a voiced sound other than /d/, the *-ed* suffix is pronounced /d/:

| clean | /kliyn/ | cleaned | /kliynd/ |
| play | /pley/ | played | /pleyd/ |

When a verb ends in a voiceless sound other than /t/, the *-ed* suffix is pronounced /t/:

| practice | /prǽktis/ | practiced | /prǽktist/ |

Notice that the *-ed* suffix of regular verbs is pronounced the same whether it is the past tense or the past participial form.[8]

Teaching the Sound System

The techniques illustrated in the following section of this chapter are suggested as a means of helping students attain intelligible pronunciation. They can be utilized at any stage of the learning process, whenever students manifest difficulty with particular aspects of pronunciation. Detailed techniques for developing listening comprehension and speaking ability (which depend in great part upon control of the sound system) will be found in Chapter 7, Teaching the Communication Skills.

Use of Minimal Contrasts

Communication in a second language necessitates not only the production of sounds but the recognition of them in the stream of speech. This demands practice in discriminating distinctive sound contrasts. Because sound contrasts are more easily perceived in minimally distinctive utterances, the use of minimal pairs has been found to be quite successful in teaching sound discrimination (both at the receptive and productive levels). These minimal pairs may be single-word contrasts, phrasal contrasts, or even contrasts within complete sentences.

Suppose, for example, students are having difficulty hearing and producing the /s/ — /θ/ contrast. Lists of minimally distinctive words can be arranged on the blackboard and a variety of exercises developed using these lists.

/s/	/θ/
sick	thick
some	thumb
sing	thing
sought	thought
sink	think

Instead of using only minimal pairs of words, groups of contrasting words can also be useful, particularly to students whose native language has few final consonants of any kind. Then lists of words such as *mass*, *match*, *math*, *mat*, *map*, etc. could be used.

If a vowel distinction is to be introduced, even a three-way contrast can be shown through such minimally distinctive sets of words. Here the use of phonemic transcription is more useful than regular orthography because it emphasizes the fact that the sole distinction in the sets of words is in the vowel sound. The regular spelling (*psalm*, *calm*) may obscure the problem under consideration.

/ə/	/a/	/æ/
səm	sam	sæm
kəm	kam	kæm
lək	lak	læk
kət	kat	kæt

When contrasting vowel sounds in exercises such as this it is best to contrast them first in final position: /biy — bey — bow — buw — baw/; then before a voiced consonant: /fiyd — feyd/; /fuwl — ful/; and finally before a voiceless consonant: /siyt — sit/; /mes — mæs/. This sequence is suggested since in the first two positions the vowel tends to be longer and more easily recognizable.

Although the temptation will be to pronounce these pairs with the intonation used on alternative sequences

(sick-thick),

the same intonation should be used on both items in order to maintain the minimal distinction:

sick-thick.

The following procedures are suggested for the use of minimal pairs in the beginning stages of recognizing and producing contrasts:

1. The teacher pronounces the items in each list and students repeat them.
2. Individual students are asked to pronounce all the items in a given list. Articulatory descriptions of the sounds, face diagrams, flexibility or bracketing exercises may be used at this point for students having great difficulty in producing the sounds.
3. The teacher pronounces pairs of items in contrast (*sick*, *thick*) being certain to use the same intonation on both items. Students repeat the pairs in unison.
4. The teacher pronounces an item from either list and individual

students signal which list it is from. This can be done by numbering the columns and having students call out the number, or hold up the appropriate number of fingers (especially with younger students who sometimes tend to want to shout). This can also be carried out as a dictation exercise with students writing their answers on paper.

5. Individual students are asked to pronounce pairs of items in contrast.
6. Individual students are asked to pronounce an item from one of the lists with the teacher signaling which he or she hears.
7. Individual students are asked to pronounce an item and another student signals which list it is from. This student in turn pronounces an item, and the exercise continues.

Using lists of words such as those described here is recommended only to ensure the student's ability to recognize and produce troublesome sounds. Practice on sounds in context should be implemented into classroom activities from the earliest stages (see Bowen, 1973, 1976).

Techniques for Teaching Specific Sounds

A teacher often develops specific techniques for helping students learn to produce sounds that are not in their own language or that are slightly different from those in their own language. These devices are sometimes directly related to articulatory description but are couched in terms that the students can readily understand. The following are some tricks of the trade that the author has used and that are not often found in textbooks.[9]

We will begin with the vowel sounds. In teaching /æ/, emphasis should be placed on the spread position of the lips. This can be achieved most easily by asking students to smile while they pronounce this sound, forcing them to spread their lips.

The /ə/, /a/, /ɔ/ sounds need contrastive practice since many speakers of other languages confuse them. The /ə/ sound can be described as the sound one makes when one is suddenly hit in the stomach. Furthermore, it must be made without rounding the lips. This sound can be contrasted with /a/ by having students notice the difference in jaw position; /ə/ is made with the jaw almost closed, but /a/ requires a very open mouth with the jaw quite low. Students can also be reminded that this is the sound doctors ask patients to make when they want them to open their mouths wide for throat examinations. Distinguishing /ɔ/ from /ə/ requires attention to jaw position, /ɔ/ being produced with a lower jaw position than /ə/, and to the presence or absence of lip rounding (/ɔ/ with slight lip rounding and /ə/ entirely without).

The English vowels /ey/ and /ow/ are clearly diphthongal in quality, that is, they consist of two sounds, the first of which is the most prominent. The upward movement of the jaw and tongue for the second part of the diphthong should be pointed out. Although the vowels /iy/ and /uw/ are also diphthongs, they are not quite so easily discernible as such because the distance that the tongue has to travel in going from the first element of the diphthong to the second element is very slight. The three remaining diphthongs in English, /ay/, /aw/, /ɔy/, are also clearly seen as diphthongs because the jaw moves perceptibly in producing these sounds.

The contrasts between /iy/ and /i/ and between /uw/ and /u/ can be clarified through the use of muscular tension, as has been mentioned previously. One way to call attention to this is to have students clench their fists when they are practicing tense vowel sounds, and to open and relax them when they are producing lax sounds.

Flexibility exercises and bracketing drills as means of producing particular vowel sounds accurately have also been discussed previously. They can be extremely effective in the early stages of learning vowel distinctions.

As stated previously, the articulation of consonant sounds is more clearly visible to the speaker; thus imitation of them seems to be easier than imitation of vowel sounds. However, the following techniques for individual consonant sounds have been found helpful.

The tongue position for the initial sound of *thing*, the /θ/

sound, can be illustrated in such a way that the symbol itself becomes a memory clue. The symbol is enlarged on the blackboard to represent an open mouth, and the crossbar is drawn as if it were a tongue protruding between the teeth.

In teaching the glides /y/ and /w/, two things should be emphasized. First, these are vowel-like sounds, that is, they should be pronounced with no contact of the tongue within the mouth. Second, the tongue glides rapidly into the position of the following vowel sound. The beginning position for the /y/ glide is close to that of the vowel /iy/. In producing the word *yes* /yes/, the tongue begins in the position for /iy/, then moves rapidly into the position for the following vowel /e/:/iy — e/. The first sound glides smoothly into the position of the vowel that follows, hence the source of the name for this type of sound.

The /w/ sound needs additional attention because it is a rounded sound. The lips are tightly rounded at the beginning of the sound, which starts in a position similar to the vowel /uw/. As the tongue glides into the position of the vowel that follows, the lips are rapidly unrounded. Thus in the word *wet* /wet/ the students begin with the rounded vowel /uw/, glide into the sound /e/, simultaneously unrounding their lips: /uw — e/. If /w/ is followed by /uw/ or /ow/ as in *woo* or *woke*, the lips are rounded at the beginning of the /w/, rapidly unrounded for the glide to the vowel, then rounded again for these vowels. When /w/ is followed by slightly rounded vowels as in *woman* or *wall*, the extreme rounding for /w/ is followed by slight unrounding for the vowels /u/ and /ɔ/. Since these are relatively difficult articulatory processes, it is best to begin the practice of /w/ with words in which it is followed by unrounded front and central vowels. Words such as *we*, *way*, *won* should be practiced first; then the student can progress to the more difficult sequences in words like *wool*, *would*, *walk*, and *woe*.

Similarly the /r/ sound should be taught as belonging to a group of sounds in English that is closely allied to vowels in manner of articulation. /r/ is produced without any contact or vibration of the tongue within the oral cavity usually by retroflection, or curling back of the tip of the tongue. Since most languages make use of an *r* sound that is more consonantlike in its production (often a trill, a flap, or a fricative), a great amount of practice is required to avoid contact within the mouth. A particular sequence in teaching the pronunciation of this sound is suggested.

Teaching /r/ first in postvocalic position seems to produce better results. Students should be asked to pronounce /a/ and then to raise and curl back the tip of the tongue while continuing to produce the vowel sound. This should produce the word *are* /ar/. If this can be done satisfactorily, students may then practice other words and phrases in which /r/ follows a vowel: *car, farm, near the door*.

Incorrect pronunciation of the /r/ sound, perhaps more than any other in English, is a deterrent to good pronunciation. First, in normal speech the /r/ sound tends to 'color' the vowel sounds that precede it; that is, the vowel sounds are somewhat blurred when the tongue glides into the position for /r/. Second, this vowel-like articulation reinforces the smooth rhythm of English. The substitution of a consonantlike /r/ sound on the part of speakers of other languages tends to create a staccato kind of rhythm that is strange to the ears of an English speaker.

Following the successful articulation of the postvocalic /r/ comes the next step: production of /r/ in prevocalic position, as in *road* and *read*. In addition to the possibility of contact within the mouth, this poses the problem of the lip rounding required when /r/ is in syllable initial position. Building upon what has already been learned, students should be asked to produce /a/ + /r/ again, lengthening the /r/ and following it with the vowel /ow/ which will force a rounding of the lips: /a-rrr-ow/. This sequence should be practiced several times to be sure students are not touching the roof of the mouth or using velar contact. Then they can omit the vowel before the /r/: /row/.

In teaching the lip rounding that accompanies /r/, obvious reinforcement is gained by beginning the practice with words in which the /r/ is followed by rounded back vowels: *road, wrote, room*. After this, students are ready to attempt words in which the vowel sounds themselves are not rounded but the /r/ must be: *red*, *ran*, *write*.

The confusion between /r/ and /l/ which plagues speakers of certain East Asian languages can best be handled by concentrating on the distinction between tongue contact and no tongue contact, and lip rounding and no lip rounding in such pairs as *load*, *road*; *lice*, *rice*; *play*, *pray*.

Similar emphasis upon manner of articulation will help remedy the problem of substituting one consonant for another, e.g., /v/ for /w/ or /dž/ for /y/.

When the voiceless stop sounds, /p, t, k/, appear in initial position in a word or in initial position in a stressed syllable within a word, they are produced with aspiration, that is, a slight puff of air, an *h* sound. The 'match trick' is a device that can be used to enable students to observe whether or not they are producing aspiration when they pronounce these sounds. Students hold a lighted match in front of their mouths and attempt to blow it out as they pronounce such words as *pie*, *time*, *cat*. As an alternative to the match, a piece of paper (not too heavy in weight) can be held in front of the mouth while pronouncing *pen*, *piece*, *apartment*, *appearance*. This device is not quite so successful with the /t/ and /k/ sounds since fairly strong aspiration is required to move the paper, and this is more readily done with /p/.

Students very often substitute the kind of /l/ that generally occurs before front vowels in English (*let*, *lead*, *last*) when they pronounce words in which /l/ follows the vowel (*call*, *will*, *feel*). In English these are two phonetically distinct sounds. When pronouncing the 'clear' /l/, the variant occurring before front vowels, not only the tongue tip but the entire front of the tongue is pressed against the alveolar ridge with a great deal of muscular force. On the other hand, postvocalic /l/ ('dark' /l/) requires that the tongue touch the tooth ridge very gently and that there be a slow transition between the vowel and the /l/, allowing the middle of the tongue to assume a low or mid-low position. To help students make this slow transition and lower the middle of the tongue, an extra vowel should be inserted between the vowel and /l/, thus producing two syllables: /kɔ-əl/, /wi-əl/, /fiy-əl/.

The six sibilant sounds /s, z, š, ž, tš, dž/ are often confused. They can be arranged in such a way that students are made aware of the oppositions in the series both in terms of voicing and point of articulation.

$$
\begin{array}{cc}
s & š \\
z & ž \\
 & tš \\
 & dž
\end{array}
$$

As a matter of fact, the symbols /tš/ and dž/ were selected for the English affricates, instead of other symbols that are commonly used, for purely pedagogical reasons. They more clearly illustrate the articulation of these sounds which combine a stop and a continuant sound.

Imitation of various hissing and buzzing sounds sometimes helps students understand the difference between /s/ and /z/. The /s/ sound can be compared to the sound a snake makes, the sound of steam escaping from a teakettle, or air from a tire. A flying mosquito or a buzz saw work quite well as illustrations of the /z/ sound.

An additional characteristic of the sibilants (except /s/ and /z/) is protrusion of the lips. Although the acoustic effect is not altered completely by omitting this protrusion, as with other facial movements in uttering sounds, the lack of such protrusion tends to alter the general effect of speech.

The 'pencil trick' is helpful in distinguishing the points of articulation for /n/ and /ŋ/ since these are difficult to see and to hear. A pencil is placed sideways across the mouth and students are asked to pronounce the two sounds. If the /n/ is pronounced correctly, the tip of the tongue will touch the pencil; if the /ŋ/ is produced accurately, the tip of the tongue will be down behind the front teeth and will not touch the pencil.

It is hoped that with the use of the simple devices and techniques described here the difficulty of learning new sounds will be eased. It should be emphasized that teachers who have had some training in phonetics will be better able to guide students to the proper articulation of sounds. (See, for example, a book like that of Ladefoged [1975].) They can more readily detect improper articulation and provide the means for correcting the fault.

Techniques for Teaching Consonant Clusters

The sound system is more than a mere inventory of individual sounds. These sounds are arranged according to certain restrictions just as there are particular grammatical arrangements in the language. This is especially true of the consonant sounds that combine to make clusters. The clusters are of two kinds, those found in initial position in the syllable and those in final position.[10] Examples of both types are found in the following words:

/st-/	stop	takes	/-ks/
/kl-/	clean	cold	/-ld/
/pr-/	price	heart	/-rt/

Students who have learned to master the final sound in *brush* may find difficulty in producing the related word *brushed* because it involves a cluster of two consonants /-št/. It will be remembered from our discussion of the pronunciation of the *-s* and *-ed* suffixes that the addition of these inflections often produces consonant clusters and that these are very active inflections within the language.

Troublesome sequences of consonants in clusters like these require special attention. Many of these seemingly difficult sequences can be made easier to pronounce by changing the juncture between syllables through the use of phonetic syllabication. For example, if students are having difficulty pronouncing such clusters as /-zd/ in *raised it* or /-ks/ in *speaks a lot*, they can be shown that the final /d/ or final /s/ can be moved to the following syllable (which begins with a vowel sound):

/reyz-dit/   /spiyk-sə-lat/

Or if we are teaching the /-št/ sequence in *washed*, we can first ask students to pronounce the phrase *wash two cups* in which this consonant sequence occurs between two syllables /-š t-/. Then we can change the phrase to *washed a cup* in which the two sounds are more closely combined, at the same time pointing out that they can be separated into two syllables because of the following vowel sound.

/wɔš-tə kəp/

This type of exercise can be devised for almost all the consonant clusters. Naturally these clusters will not always occur in positions preceding vowel sounds where they may be divided by this use of phonetic syllabication; but once students have learned the sequence involved in the articulation of such phrases as *washed it*, *looked at it*, *changed it*, it will be easier to produce these sounds before a consonant as in *cashed them*, *looked for them*, *changed them*.

The pronunciation of initial consonant clusters with /r/ (/pr-, tr-, gr-, etc./) can be facilitated by first introducing a vowel sound between the two consonants: /pərə/, /tərə/. Students may need to be reminded again that they are not to touch the tongue to the interior of the mouth when pronouncing the /r/. Then the pronunciation should be speeded up until the intrusive vowel is omitted. A reminder should also be given that lip rounding for the /r/ should begin on the preceding consonant.

Spanish speakers and Iranians, among others, often insert a vowel sound before the initial clusters beginning with /s/. They tend to say *es-peak*, *es-kate*, *es-top*. Concentrating on lengthening the /s/ seems to alleviate this problem.

/sssspiyk/   /sssskeyt/   /sssstap/

The same technique helps students who have trouble devoicing the /s/ before voiced consonants in such initial clusters as /sm-/, /sn-/, /sl-/, which they tend to pronounce as /zm-/, /zn-/, /zl-/. They, too, should be asked to lengthen the initial /s/.

/ssssmayl/   /ssssnow/   /ssssliyp/

Final consonant clusters are difficult for students to hear as well as to produce. An exercise that is helpful in beginning systematic practice on final consonant clusters is illustrated by the series *were*, *word*, *world*. Beginning with a single final consonant students must either recognize or produce one or more consonants in order to distinguish the other words: /wər — wərd — wərld/.

Often students fail to differentiate the present and past forms of regular verbs because they do not hear the final consonant in the cluster. In many verbs the sole distinguishing feature of the past form is the addition of /t/ or /d/.

like	/layk/	liked	/laykt/
pull	/pul/	pulled	/puld/

Exercises using minimal differences in sound can provide practice in discriminating the present and past forms of verbs. Sentences are especially effective and can be used just as in any other minimal pair exercise.

They talk about it.	They talked about it.
They learn about it.	They learned about it.
They discuss it.	They discussed it.
They wash it.	They washed it.

Another difficulty involving consonant clusters occurs in the use of the highly frequent -*s* suffixes, either plurals of nouns or third-person singular present tense of verbs. Thus in a pair of sentences such as the following, students have to pinpoint both for production and recognition the placement of the /s/ or /z/ of the -*s* suffixes.

> The girl takes piano lessons.
> The girls take piano lessons.

For a more varied response than those of the typical minimal pair drill, students can be asked to supply a correlative sentence indicating that they recognize what they hear. Thus, depending upon which statement the teacher makes, students would respond, *She takes piano lessons* or *They take piano lessons*.

Consonant sequences that occur contiguously in separate words such as /z-θ/ in *he's thinking* may be termed consonant combinations in order to differentiate them from clusters, which are close-knit sequences within the same syllable. These consonant combinations, which are many in number, demand a manipulation of the tongue which is difficult for many students.[11] Flexibility exercises can be helpful in achieving fluent production of such combinations. The continuous repetition of /zzzθθθzzzθθθzzzθθθ/ may be necessary before students can pronounce this sentence easily.

The description of sounds as they occur in these combinations may differ somewhat from the description of the sound in an isolated word. Teachers should be aware that phonetic environments tend to modify sounds. For example, students are taught that the English /t/ is pronounced with the tongue on the alveolar ridge (not touching the teeth). But in pronouncing the phrase *get things*, the /t/ becomes dental, that is, it is partially assimilated to the position of the /θ/ which follows. The /θ/ sound, which is classified as an interdental sound (produced with the tongue between the teeth), in this case is produced with the tongue against the teeth, being partially assimilated to the sound that precedes it. This assimilation process will become easier for students the more practice they have and the more fluent they become.

Many consonant clusters in final position are reduced in normal conversation. Thus in *The lists are on the table* the /-sts/ of *lists* is often reduced to a single lengthened consonant: [lis::]. Reductions like this are helpful for those who have great difficulty pronouncing these clusters. (Even native speakers of English find them difficult.)

When a final three-segment cluster contains a medial /t/ or /k/, this medial sound is sometimes omitted, resulting in pronunciations like the following:

asks	[æs::]
guests	[ges::]
masked	[mæst]

In dealing with these consonant clusters, it is well for the teacher to examine his or her own speech, and the speech of others, and to give the student the benefit of whatever reduction is normally used.

When preparing English-teaching materials, it is useful to remember a statement made by Otto Jespersen, an unusually talented phonetician and an experienced teacher of English to non-English speakers: "The difficult sounds ought not to occur too many in succession and in too difficult combinations."[12] These difficult combinations can sometimes be avoided in classroom exercises if the teacher watches for them.

Techniques for Teaching Stress, Rhythm, and Intonation

Word stress can be practiced by the simple repetition of various groups of words arranged according to stress patterns. Students can be asked to place additional words in the appropriate group once the model has been practiced. The following patterns, or others like them, can be written on the board and students given additional words to add to the lists.

táble	pronóunce	álphabèt	ùnderstánd
pencil	direct	yesterday	afternoon
study	explain	criticize	engineer

Students should be alerted to the relationship between the quality of the vowel and the amount of stress given. Syllables that are, or potentially can be, uttered with weak stress (the third degree of stress discussed earlier in this chapter) are pronounced with reduced vowels (usually /ə/ or /i/); syllables with primary or secondary stress must have what is termed 'full' vowel quality: /iy, ey, a, ow, uw, etc./. This is important for two reasons. First, if students know the vowel sounds in a word, they can make a good guess at stress placement since any reduced vowel will not receive primary or secondary stress. On the other hand, if they know which syllable is stressed, they know that the unstressed syllables should not be produced with full vowels. Thus if they know that only the first syllable of *vegetable* is strongly stressed, they know the other syllables must be pronounced with reduced vowels: /védžtəbəl/. If they know that the vowel sounds' in *cashier* are /æ/ and /iy/, they realize that neither syllable can be reduced; both must have more than weak stress. This may not tell them which of the two receives the stronger stress, but it does tell them that neither can be reduced.

After practice has been provided on stress patterns in single words, these words should be used in context so that students learn to control stress in complete utterances, not merely in isolated words.

Contrastive stress within sentences is another aspect of the English phonological system which students must learn to control. They need practice in varying the placement of sentence stress as the situation demands it. Sentence stress can be shifted in a sentence such as the following to give students practice in acquiring the ability to fix stress appropriately.

Mary went to the movies last night.

The teacher can ask, "Who went to the movies?" A student answers, "Mary," and then pronounces the entire sentence with stress only on *Mary*.

Máry went to the movies last night.

Next the teacher asks, "Where did Mary go?" Another student answers, "To the movies" and follows this with the complete sentence.

Mary went to the móvies last night.

This sequence can be followed with the question "When did Mary go to the movies?" eliciting

last níght

as opposed to "Which night did Mary go to the movies?" which should elicit

last níght.

Dialogues prove to be a useful means of setting situations that elicit special stress. The following telephone conversation might be used for practice on stress.

A. May I speak to Mr. Ánderson, please?

B. There are twó Mr. Andersons in this department. They're brothers. Which one did you want?

A. I'm not sure, but I think I want the older brother.

B. That's Jím Anderson. Just a minute and I'll get him.

A. Thank you.

There are two types of exercises that are especially useful in teaching English sentence rhythm. One, described earlier in the chapter, is the reverse pyramid exercise in which students start with a relatively short sentence with two major stresses and build up to a relatively long sentence while adding words to consecutive sentences in the pyramid. Notice that contractions make it easier to maintain the rhythm.

The mán is eating a sándwich.
The old mán is eating a sándwich.
The old mán's eating a chicken sándwich.
The old mán's eating a delicious chicken sándwich.

Another means of practicing the more or less evenly spaced sentence stresses which seem to be characteristic of English rhythm is by adding phrases to an utterance, each phrase containing a primary stress.

The proféssor
The proféssor in the óffice
The proféssor in the óffice is a línguist.
The proféssor in the óffice is a línguist from Rússia.

The rhythm of English, as we have said, tends to pressure speakers into reducing or weakening unstressed syllables in order to maintain an evenness of beat throughout the utterance. This reduction especially affects words of one syllable that are unstressed. The ability to use these reduced or weakened forms will enable students to maintain better sentence rhythm, and their speech will sound much more natural. Some of the most frequent one-syllable words that occur with reduced forms are given below. Notice that these are structure words, which were discussed in Chapter 1, The Grammatical System.

a	/ə/	in *a* minute
an	/ən/	in *an* hour
the	/ðə/	in *the* house
and	/ən/	black *and* white
to	/tə/	ten *to* six
or	/ər/	this *or* that

These reduced forms are very difficult for students to hear in the stream of speech, and practice in the comprehension of such forms will be discussed in the section on teaching listening comprehension.

The most successful technique for teaching intonation is imitation or mimicry. However, the use of gestures can reinforce this mimicry; that is, when the utterance requires a falling intonation, better results are sometimes achieved if the teacher raises a hand and lets it fall in imitation of the change in voice pitch.

Linear intonation marking, such as that advocated in this text, is a mnemonic device in itself, since it shows visually when a rise or fall of the voice is required.

When falling intonation is difficult for students to imitate, especially on a question or a long statement, it is helpful to begin at the end of the utterance and work backward. Thus in

Where did he go?

students can be asked to produce only the word *go* in imitation of the teacher. As an isolated word, they usually have little difficulty producing it with a falling intonation. Then they can be asked to pronounce

he go, did he go, and finally When did he go.

This cumulative 'backward buildup' usually results in the use of the proper falling intonation.

The importance of the linear markings cannot be overemphasized. Students receive tremendous support from this visual aid; and as they continually practice utterances that are marked for them, they begin to develop a sense of the pattern of English intonation which will carry over into more communicative situations.

One of the intonational problems arising in the classroom is that students produce utterances in a questioning manner — using a rising intonation because they are asking by means of the intonation, "Is this right? Am I doing this correctly? Is this what you want?" — often when the rising intonation is not suitable. The teacher needs to call their attention to exactly what they are doing, assure them that they are performing well, and attempt to get across the idea of finality at the end of an utterance. This usually remedies the problem.

A question often raised by teachers is "How much should we correct students' pronunciation?" The answer to this varies with the students involved. First, some students take criticism well; others do not. This factor must be taken into consideration. Second, overcorrection can interfere with students' attempts to communicate. The teacher should never interrupt students to correct them; they should always be allowed to finish what they are saying.

One procedure for avoiding this problem (both in pronunciation and in grammar) is to select one or two items to be emphasized in a particular classroom activity and correct only those items.

A rather successful activity in terms of motivation in pronunciation activities is the practice of taping a short segment of students' speech at the beginning of a course of study, practicing it with them several times and pointing out their errors, and then retaping it at the end of a four- to eight-week period, allowing them to compare their 'before and after' efforts. Usually the greatest improvement is in the overall covering patterns of intonation, stress, and rhythm. However, very often decided improvement is discerned in vowel contrasts and the /r/ sound.[13]

In summary, a word of caution is in order. Many of the activities described in this chapter involve exaggerations of actual speech. Students should never be dismissed from the classroom until that which has been practiced is produced in normal conversational style. It is wise for the teacher to repeat an utterance in a natural fashion both before and after using exaggerated styles. But above all, students should always be given the opportunity to produce the material in a normal fashion as the last step.

Exercises

A. Read the following paragraph at normal speed. Mark the stress and intonation that you use. Ask someone else to read it, and compare that reading with yours. Ask a speaker of another language who is just beginning to learn English to read the paragraph and compare the sounds, as well as the stress and intonation, with those of a native speaker.

This paragraph can also be used as a 'before and after' exercise for those trying to improve their English pronunciation. It can be recorded before any instruction is begun and after specific help on pronunciation has been provided. (The sentences are numbered for easy identification.)

(1) Watching television is a popular pastime. (2) Both children and adults can participate. (3) Some programs are intellectually stimulating; others are disappointing. (4) Many housewives watch 'soap operas' during the day. (5) Sports lovers especially enjoy football, basketball, baseball, and soccer games on TV. (6) Monday night football appeals to armchair quarterbacks. (7) Educational TV provides an alternative to commercial programming. (8) It also offers courses of study for college credit. (9) However, most people watch TV purely for recreation. (10) What kind of programs do you like?

B. To illustrate the relationship between punctuation and intonation, mark the following nonsense syllables with what might be an appropriate intonation. Pay attention to the stress markings.

1. le lá.
2. le le lá, le lá le.
3. le le lá le le?
4. le lá!
5. le le lá le . . .

C. Match the sentences below with the nonsense utterances in the preceding exercise and check to see whether the intonation you have marked may be appropriate. When you finish, the sentences should be arranged in the form of a short dialogue by following the sequence in the preceding exercise.

1. of course
2. I just wondered
3. John left
4. did you answer it
5. after he left, the phone rang

D. Pronounce the plural of the following words. Write the pronunciation of the -*s* suffix (/s/, /z/, or /əz/) in the space provided.

1. shoe	_____	6. country	_____
2. dish	_____	7. arm	_____
3. question	_____	8. song	_____
4. map	_____	9. glass	_____
5. lunch	_____	10. paragraph	_____

E. Pronounce the third-person present tense form of the following verbs. Write the pronunciation of the -*s* suffix in the space provided.

1. make	_____	6. provide	_____
2. change	_____	7. hear	_____
3. see	_____	8. finish	_____
4. confuse	_____	9. laugh	_____
5. write	_____	10. stand	_____

F. Pronounce the following words. In the space provided write the pronunciation of the -*s* suffix which may be that of noun plural, noun possessive, third-person singular of a verb, or the contracted form of *is*.

1. cat's   _____   6. colleges _____
2. bushes   _____   7. days'   _____
3. Alice's   _____   8. lights   _____
4. lamps   _____   9. day's   _____
5. Paul's   _____   10. singers _____

G. Pronounce the past or past participial form of the following verbs. Write the pronunciation of the -*ed* suffix (/t/, /d/, or /əd/) in the space provided.

1. plan   _____   6. breathe _____
2. permit   _____   7. live   _____
3. hope   _____   8. collect _____
4. admire   _____   9. wash   _____
5. cause   _____   10. taste   _____

H. Form as many words as possible by inserting vowel or diphthong sounds in the items below. Compare the spelling of these words with their phonemic representation. What regular spelling patterns do you find?

1. /s_____k/   6. /g_____d/
2. /r_____d/   7. /p_____l/
3. /br_____k/   8. /p_____nt/
4. /l_____v/   9. /k_____st/
5. /w_____l/   10. /sm_____l/

I. Form as many words as possible by inserting consonant sounds in the items below. Compare the spelling of these words with their phonemic representation. What regular spelling patterns do you find?

1. /_____ru/   4. /mi_____/
2. /_____ik/   5. /_____awnd/
3. /_____owz/   6. /briy_____/

   7. /_____ay/   9. /_____en/

   8. /_____ip/   10. /le_____/

J. Mark the stresses on the words below. Use three degrees (primary, secondary, and weak). Arrange the words in columns so that all the words in one column have the same number of syllables and the same stress pattern.

1. advertise	6. basement
2. include	7. patient
3. animal	8. contain
4. maintain	9. teacher
5. excellent	10. celebrate

K. Identify the items in the following paragraph that are probably reduced in normal conversation. One way to discover which items are reduced is to record the paragraph at normal conversational speed and listen to it.

The robbery took place in the early afternoon. Two men entered the bank and went directly to the manager's office. While they held him hostage, two of their companions, who had previously stationed themselves in strategic positions in the bank, ordered everyone to lie on the floor. This included the manager. The robbers quickly collected the money from the open vault, filling two large laundry bags. Finally, after warning everyone to remain on the floor for five minutes, they rushed out the door and into a waiting car which was driven by a young boy. They were all apprehended later because, ironically, the police stopped the car for a traffic violation and found that the boy was driving without a license. In checking further, of course, they discovered the laundry bags full of money and arrested them all.

Notes

1. *The American College Dictionary* (New York: Random House, 1963).

2. *Webster's Third New International Dictionary* (Springfield, Mass.: G. and C. Merriam Company, 1961).

3. Charles C. Fries, *The Teaching of English* (Ann Arbor, Michigan: George Wahr Publishing Company, 1949), p. 72.

4. Otto Jespersen, *How to Teach a Foreign Language* (London: Allen and Unwin, 1947), p. 166.

5. Numbers and combinations of numbers, instead of letters, have been very successfully used by Allen, Allen, and Shute (1966) to symbolize English vowel sounds.

6. Although acknowledging the validity of the Trager-Smith (1957) system of four degrees of stress, it has been found pedagogically more satisfactory to mark only three degrees. Thus the Trager-Smith primary and secondary stresses are both marked as primary in this text, the difference being that primary stress always coincides with the intonation contour in the utterance. What is termed secondary stress in this text /ˋ/ corresponds to the Trager-Smith tertiary level. Weak stress is used here in the same sense as in the Trager-Smith analysis except that it is sometimes referred to as 'unstressed' and is not marked.

7. This exercise was first described in Kenneth L. Pike, *Phonemics* (Ann Arbor: University of Michigan Press, 1947), p. 16.

8. A few past participles used as adjectives are sometimes pronounced with /əd/ instead of /d/ or /t/: a *learned* /lə́rnəd/ man; a *beloved* /bilə́vəd/ relative; a *blessed* /blésəd/ event.

9. Some of the information included here is also found in Betty Wallace Robinett, "Simple Classroom Techniques for Teaching Pronunciation," in *On Teaching English to Speakers of Other Languages,* ed. V. F. Allen (Champaign, Illinois: NCTE, 1965), pp. 135–38.

10. For a detailed list of English consonant clusters see Clifford H. Prator and Betty W. Robinett, *Manual of American English Pronunciation*, 3rd ed. (New York: Holt, Rinehart and Winston, 1972), pp. 151–53. Some of the information on teaching techniques is found in Betty Wallace Robinett, "Teaching English Consonant Clusters," in *Studies in Language and Linguistics in Honor of Charles C. Fries*, ed. Albert H. Marckwardt (Ann Arbor: University of Michigan, English Language Institute, 1964), pp. 335–42.

11. For a list of these consonant combinations see Betty J. Wallace, "A Quantitative Analysis of Consonant Clusters in Present-Day English," unpublished Ph.D. dissertation, University of Michigan, 1951.

12. Jespersen, *How to Teach a Foreign Language*, p. 29.

13. An example of this type of exercise is the "Accent Inventory" that accompanies the *Manual of American English Pronunciation* by Prator and Robinett (1972).

3

The Vocabulary System

In the two preceding chapters we have discussed the grammatical system of English — the structural arrangements and relationships of words — and the sound system — the structural arrangements and relationships of sounds. A third system, separate yet interrelated, is the vocabulary or the lexical system, without which there would be no way of dealing with the meaning of our experience. A major difference exists between the lexical system and the other two: whereas the sound system and the grammatical system are mastered quite early in the language learning experience, speakers continually add to their lexical store. Lenneberg describes this situation aptly when he says, "A lexicon is like a photograph that freezes motion."[1] When changes take place in our experience, additional "photographs" (different lexical items) are added.

Semantics, or the study of meaning in language, is complex; but it is clear that there are at least three kinds of meaning which can be differentiated in describing the semantic content of a language. Although these have been given various names, we shall refer to them as *lexical*, *grammatical*, and *experiential* meaning.

Meaning

Lexical Meaning

Lexical meaning is that found in the dictionary when we want to know what a word means. The meaning is given in terms of the relationship of the symbol (the word) to our cognitive experience in the real world. For example, the question ''What does *porch* mean?'' conjures up in the mind of a speaker of English a picture of a structurally attached appendage to a house. The meaning can be further specified by the addition of other lexical items: *screened, enclosed, side, front, upstairs*. The lexical meaning is learned by connecting *porch* (either in its spoken or written form) with the category of things to which it belongs in the world of experience, either directly or vicariously (perhaps through pictures).

In the discussion of the grammatical system of English two types of lexical items were mentioned: structure words and content words. The lexical system generally concerns itself with content words, those symbols that are more directly correlated with experience in the outside world. Concrete nouns such as *typewriter* and *bookcase*, and abstract nouns such as *truth*, *idea*, and *interpretation* are content words, as are verbs like *propose*, *investigate*, *sleep*, *drive* and adjectives like *clear*, *intelligent*, *pink*, *solitary*. The description of the vocabulary system in this chapter will concern itself primarily with the lexical meaning of content words.

Grammatical Meaning

Grammatical meaning is derived from syntactic or grammatical relationships within the language. For example, the lexical item *man* in the utterance *the man hit the dog* brings with it, in addition to the lexical meaning 'an adult male human being', the meaning of 'agent' or 'doer' because of its relationship in that particular utterance to the verb *hit*. However, in the sentence *the car hit the man* the word *man*, while retaining the same lexical meaning as in the sentence above, now has the grammatical meaning of 'receiver' because it bears a different relationship to the verb *hit*. On the other hand, the lexical item *man* in the sentence *the man saw the dog* has the grammatical meaning of 'experiencer' or 'receiver' (rather than 'doer') because of the peculiar properties of the verb *saw* which are different from those of the verb *hit* in the previous example. Thus, whenever a lexical item occurs in a grammatical construction, it carries with it grammatical as well as lexical meaning.

The relationship between syntax and semantics or grammar and meaning can be further illustrated by the structure word *have* in the following sentences.

(1) She has been to Moscow several times.
(2) I have got nothing to do.
(3) She has to write a letter.
(4) They had her wash their car.
(5) They had their car washed.
(6) They had their car stolen.

The meaning of each of these sentences is determined in great part by the grammatical relationship between *have* and the verb that follows it. In (1) it is followed immediately by the past participle, thereby producing the perfect aspect (*has been*). *Have got* in (2) is an idiomatic phrase consisting of a form of *have* and the past participle of *get*, and is an alternative form of the simple verb *have* meaning 'possess'. The phrase *has to* in (3), followed directly by the simple form of the verb (*write*), signifies necessity. In (4) *have* is followed, this time with an intervening pronoun, by the simple form of the verb (*wash*); *have* in this sentence expresses a causative meaning, and the subject of the following verb is expressly stated (they had *her* wash the car, that is, *she* washed the car). In (5) *have* is also used in a causative sense, but it is followed, again not immediately, by the past participle (*washed*); in this use of *have* the object of the following verb is expressed, but the subject is not: (someone) washed their *car*. This use is comparable to a passive expression, and the last part of the sentence may be paraphrased as *the car was washed by someone*. Sentence (6) is ambiguous since it has a meaning similar to that of (5), that is, 'they arranged it so that their car was stolen' or 'they arranged it so that someone stole their car'; it may also have the meaning 'what happened to them was that someone stole their car'.

Grammatical meanings such as those mentioned here are essential to a total understanding of the language.

Experiential Meaning

In addition to lexical and grammatical meaning, there is the very special interpretation that is brought to each word by both speaker and hearer because of each person's own particular, personal experiences and those experiences that are common to the culture of which he or she is a part. It is not always enough to know the lexical meaning of a word in order to understand and be understood completely. The lexical meaning of the word *dog* is quite easy to comprehend: 'a four-footed animal, domesticated, often kept as a pet'; but there are special connotations to the individual speaker and hearer which are part of the meaning of that word. Thus, what may connote a lovable, happy, affectionate family friend to one person may be thought of as a mischievous, dirty, dangerous enemy to another. This difference will certainly result in different total understandings of the simple sentence *someone killed the dog yesterday*. These differing interpretations result from experiential meaning, which is part of the total semantic system.

Words, then, are more than just symbols of something in the real world. They carry with them special connotations evolving from the individual, personal experience of each speaker as well as from the society of which he or she is a part, and these connotations are inextricably bound up in the meaning of words. This indicates, then, that matters of culture and experience must be taught when teaching vocabulary, for it is essential that words be understood in the sense that they are intended if accurate communication is to be achieved.

Lexical Characteristics of English

A knowledge of the specific characteristics of the English lexical system will be of great value to students learning English as a second language. These lexical characteristics are of two types:

those related to the forms of words and those related to meaning categories.

Form

English lexical categories that involve forms can be described in this way: (1) sets of lexical items that exhibit internal change in form (*man, men; sing, sang*); (2) sets of lexical items that exhibit external change in form (*kind, kindness, unkindly*); (3) lexical items that exhibit both internal and external changes in form (*serene, serenity; maintain, maintenance; inflame, inflammatory*); and (4) lexical items that exhibit no change in form but differ in function (*cut* as present or past tense; *sheep* as singular or plural; *chair* as noun or verb).

IRREGULAR NOUNS AND VERBS

Lexical items that manifest internal change comprise words that occur very frequently in English. These include the irregular nouns, verbs, and adjectives which are part of the basic lexicon of the language: *woman, tooth, foot; get, eat, ride; better, worst*. Since they occur so frequently, they must be acquired early in the language learning process. The constant necessity to use them aids the learning process because it provides motivation for their acquisition.

DERIVATIONAL FORMS

Many of the lexical items in the second category, those manifesting external change in form, are of Latin origin, although by no means all of them; for example, *kind, kindness, kindly* are Germanic in both root and affixes. But whatever their origin, a knowledge of the process of word derivation can be an effective aid to vocabulary building. This process, involving the addition of affixes (prefixes and suffixes) to base words, provides a flexibility within the English lexical system which is not common to all languages. Thus, by learning the meaning of the word *define*, students will also understand the basic meaning of other related words such as *definition*, *definable*, and *redefine*. They can also be made aware of the correlation between various affixes and their functions and meanings: e.g., *-tion* signaling a noun, *-able* an adjective; *in-* meaning negation and *re-* repetition. Such generalizations will increase the students' ability to utilize the vocabulary system. This relates especially to the students' *recognition* rather than to their *production* of vocabulary items.

However, a word of caution must be injected here since it is not possible to predict in every case which suffixes will be used with a given word. Furthermore, not all words ending in *-al*, which is commonly designated as an adjectival suffix, are adjectives: e.g., nouns such as *revival* or *denial*. There are, of course, certain obvious relationships which are usually predictable, such as that between the noun suffix *-ence* and the adjective suffix *-ent*. If students see the word *evidence*, they might expect the existence of a word like *evident*.

Another word of caution must be offered concerning the use of derivational affixes in building vocabulary. It is not enough to learn the meaning of these affixes and then add them to any base word. Knowing that the prefix *dis-* means 'negation' or 'reversal' does not help in trying to understand the relationship between *appoint* and *disappoint*; the latter no longer means 'to remove from an appointed position'. The derived word bears a very remote relationship in modern English to the meaning of the base word.

The fact that the prefix *dis-* has two quite distinct meanings can be a problem, too. The separate meanings of negation and reversal must be taught in connection with sets of words that are consistent with these two meanings: *dislike*, *disobey*, *disagree* with the negation of the base meaning; *disconnect*, *disown*, *disappear* with the reversal of the base meaning.

An additional problem occurs with lexical items of the third type which contain both internal and external changes in form. These are often derived words that exhibit change in spelling as well as change in pronunciation. Thus, when utilizing the derivational affixes for word building, special care must be taken to point out the most important kinds of sound and/or spelling changes that occur in such pairs as *serene-serenity*, *final-finality*, etc.

Some derivational affixes are much more productive in present-day English than are others. For example, the adverbial suffix *-wise* (usually added to nouns) appears in words like *personnelwise*, *timewise*, and *texturewise*; and the negative prefix *un-* has quite consistently replaced *in-* (and its alternative forms *im-*, *ir-*, *il-*) in the formation of new items such as *uncool* ("that's an uncool remark") and *un-Cola* (referring to a popular soft drink).

WORD FREQUENCY LISTS

Knowing which vocabulary items occur most often is an attractive idea to teachers and to textbook writers; therefore, word lists compiled on a frequency basis may be a useful resource in selecting vocabulary. The best known of these frequency counts, which are based on the written language, are listed below in the order of their publication.

Edward L. Thorndike and Irving Lorge. *The Teacher's Word Book of 30,000 Words*. New York: Teachers College Press, Columbia University, 1944.

Michael West (ed.). *A General Service List of English Words*. London: Longman, 1953.

Henry Kučera and W. Nelson Francis. *Computational Analysis of Present-Day American English*. Providence, Rhode Island: Brown University Press, 1967.

John B. Carroll, Peter Davies, and Barry Richman. *The American Heritage Word Frequency Book*. New York: Houghton Mifflin Company, 1971.

Two other word lists, based on the spoken language, are the following.

Joseph M. Wepman and Wilbur Hass. *A Spoken Word Count (Adults)*. Chicago: Language Research Associates, 1966.

Joseph M. Wepman and Wilbur Hass. *A Spoken Word Count (Children — Ages 5, 6, 7)*. Chicago: Language Research Associates, 1969.

Although word counts may be helpful in discovering whether or not words that appear frequently have been included in teaching materials (thus, they are useful in preparing instructional materials), they can be extremely misleading because they do not differentiate between words of the same form that differ in meaning. Any word spelled the same way is often counted as the same word. Since we know that words may have more than one meaning, simply knowing that a word appears frequently will not tell us which meaning of that word is the most frequently used. For this reason, word frequency lists that contain semantic information (such as that of Michael West) are the most useful.[2]

A recent specialized word count is that of Praninskas (1972) which consists of words that appear frequently in textbooks used by first-year university students. The ten texts utilized in her study represent the disciplines of mathematics, physics, chemistry, biology, psychology, sociology, philosophy, history, literature, and rhetoric. A sample of words from her list is given in the accompanying tabulation. Included in this sample are those words in which the root in its various forms occurred more than 100 times in the excerpts she used from these ten different texts. These words, then, are not limited to a particular field of study but cut across disciplines. Therefore, a close study of the kinds of affixes occurring on these words could be helpful to students.

Another specialized word list is the "Supplementary Scientific and Technical Vocabulary," consisting of 425 words, appended to Michael West's *General Service List*.

Words Occurring Frequently in College Textbooks

Nouns	Verbs	Adjectives	Adverbs
assumption	assume		
complex		complex	
complexity			
definition	define	definite	definitely
definiteness	redefine	definable	indefinitely
		undefined	definitively
element		elementary	
		elemental	
evidence		evident	evidently
		self-evident	
involvement	involve		
method		methodical	

Nouns	Verbs	Adjectives	Adverbs
methodology		methodological	
primitiveness		prime	primarily
		primary	
		primitive	
		primeval	
requirement	require		
similarity		similar	similarly
specification		specific	specifically
specificity		specifiable	

Adapted from Praninskas (1972).

FUNCTIONAL SHIFT

The third category of vocabulary items classified according to form are those that manifest no change in form but exhibit a difference in function. This characteristic is referred to as 'functional shift'. Although many languages use changes in form to indicate differing functions, it seems that very few languages have the option, as in modern English, of utilizing the same form of a word for another, very different, function; e.g., words like *book* and *fish* can be used as either nouns or verbs. Sometimes, however, what appears to be the same written form may have distinguishing features of sound when pronounced. The difference is sometimes one of stress accompanied by a variation in vowel sounds. The words *record* and *separate* provide an illustration of phonological differences that distinguish the functions of each word.

record (noun)	/rékərd/
record (verb)	/rikɔ́rd/
separate (verb)	/sépərèyt/
separate (adjective)	/sép(ə)rət/

OTHER WORD FORMATION PROCESSES

Other processes that operate in the English vocabulary system and result in certain changes in form are those that produce compounds, blends, clipped forms, and acronyms.

Compounds are formed by combining two or more words into one unit with a perceptible lexical meaning. Sometimes these are written as one word (*basketball*); sometimes they are hyphenated (*night-long*); and sometimes they are written as separate words (*day laborer*). The relationship between the individual words that make up a compound is not always the same: e.g., *basketball* can be either a game using a basket and a ball or a ball used in this game with a basket; a *day laborer* is a laborer who works and is paid by the day; and *night-long* is the equivalent of throughout the night.

Blends are formed by combining parts of two words into a newly created form. Often these words enter the language as slang, but many of them achieve regular status in the language: *motel* (a blend of *motor hotel*); *smog* (a blend of *smoke* and *fog*); *brunch* (a blend of *breakfast* and *lunch*).

Clipped forms are abbreviated words. These are usually more appropriate in informal conversation; however, some clipped forms have made their way into standard usage. *Exam* is one of these; another is *sub*, an abbreviated form of *submarine* or *substitute*. An example of an informally used clipped word is *fridge* from *refrigerator* (or possibly the brand name *Frigidaire*).

The use of acronyms seems to be widespread throughout the languages of the modern world, and English is particularly susceptible to this process of adopting the initial sound and letter of words in a phrase to form a separate word. TESOL (pronounced either as /tíysɔl/ or as /tésɔl/) is the acronym for the professional organization of Teachers of English to Speakers of Other Languages. Other examples of this process are SAFE (Sex and Family Education) and NASA (National Aeronautics and Space Administration).

A second type of acronym is that in which the letters are not used to produce a word but are simply pronounced as a sequence of letters with stronger stress on one of the letters: FBI /ef biy áy/ or UN /yuw én/.

Some vocabulary items derived originally as acronyms have become so much a part of the language that their source is sometimes forgotten. There may be persons who are unaware that *radar*, *laser*, and *scuba* were originally acronyms respectively for radio detecting and ranging, light amplification by stimulated emission of radiation, and self-contained underwater breathing apparatus.

Meaning

Lenneberg tells us that "words are not the labels of concepts. . . . They are labels of a categorization process. . . . Words tag processes by which the species deals cognitively with its environment."[3] The classifications and categories resulting from the associations that learners make between a word and the situations in which the word is used are an important aspect of meaning. Thus, without further classificatory information it is quite impossible to give an absolute answer to someone who asks, "What does *principal* mean?" Even without considering the problem of its homonomy with *principle* (a problem which constantly plagues English spellers), there are two possible answers. It may be the adjective meaning 'of highest importance' or the noun designating the head officer of a school. The particular meaning will depend upon which category or classification the word is being associated with.

Vocabulary items carry cultural information. This follows logically from the fact that meaning is closely associated with experience, and culture is the sum total of the experience of the people who share that experience. The ways in which speakers of a language view their experience has a bearing on the way in which they categorize ideas, and certain problems may develop in learning a second lexical system because of the predisposition of the speakers of a language to categorize meanings in a particular way in their first language. This predisposition tends to be carried over into the second language.

German speakers differentiate between two acts of eating, that done by humans (*essen*) and that by animals (*fressen*). The Greek word κερδίζω can be variously translated into English as 'win', 'gain', or 'earn'. Interestingly enough, Spanish *ganar* can also be translated into English in these three ways. Greek πολύ includes the meanings designated by English *too* 'excessively', *very*, and *much*. Distinguishing among these three English words causes considerable difficulty for Greek speakers learning English.

All the above examples are illustrations of Lenneberg's concept of words as reflecting the cognitive categorization developed by the speakers of a particular language; and these relationships are an essential part of the lexical system.

COLLOCATION

One kind of relationship that is useful for learning vocabulary is what British linguists refer to as *collocation*. In its simplest terms it is the arrangement or juxtaposition of words. Words quite often co-occur in close proximity with a high degree of frequency. Learning these collocations will be useful to students. This process of considering groupings of words involves the consideration of the whole context in which a word occurs. Thus, learning the word *car* might involve learning some of the words that collocate with it: *driver, accelerate, stop, seat belt*; *gas (oline), oil, lubrication, service; windshield, brakes, insurance, collision*. Even certain stock phrases such as *check the oil, fill 'er up* could be part of the extended situation in which the item *car* might be introduced. The easiest way for students to learn such vocabulary is for it to be presented in situations that are clearly defined and within the experience of the learner so that there is an unambiguous understanding of what is signified by each vocabulary item.

A more sophisticated type of collocation is that which occurs in the two phrases *put the children to bed* and *put the newspaper to bed*. Both phrases contain the same lexical item *put . . . to bed*, but the meaning of the first is literal and the second figurative. The collocational relationships provide a clue to the difference in the meaning. The literal meaning occurs when the object is animate or is given the characteristics of an animate object (as in the phrase *put the doll to bed*). The figurative meaning occurs when the noun is inanimate. This type of collocation offers a structural clue to meaning, and modern syntactic analysis is providing more and more of this kind of information about the semantic characteristics of English.

An interesting collocation that involves the order in which the same lexical items occur in a construction is that of *parents*, *children*, and *mind* as revealed in the following sentences.

Parents, mind your children.[4]
Children, mind your parents.

In the first sentence *mind* has the meaning of 'watch' or 'take care of', but in the second it means 'be obedient to'. With the first meaning we may also say "Mind your manners" or "Mind your step." The improbability of parents being obedient to children would tend to disallow the juxtaposition of the two nouns in the second sentence while still retaining the meaning of 'be obedient to'.

Collocations occur in another fashion also. Speakers of one language combine words into phrases in ways which may or may not parallel those in another. Mackey compares English phrases containing the word *head* with equivalent phrases in French.[5]

	tête	(of a person)
	chevet	(of a bed)
	face	(of a coin)
	pomme	(of a cane)
head =	bout	(of a match)
	haut bout	(of a table)
	directeur	(of an organization)
	mousse	(on beer)
	rubrique	(title)

Such differences indicate the need for caution to be used in translating phrases from one language to another. It also illustrates the fact that various members of the human species differ in their categorization of their environments.

Another example of this phenomenon is found in the way in which the word *table* is used in English as contrasted with Spanish.

table	mesa
tablecloth	mantel
timetable	horario

table of figures	tabla
turntable (phonograph)	plata
turntable (railway)	plataforma giatoria
turn the tables	volverse la tortilla

Conversely, the Spanish verb *hacer* requires many different translations in English, some of which are the following.

	frío	'to be cold' (weather)
	algo	'to do something'
	algo	'to make something'
	milagros	'to work miracles'
hacer	un papel	'to play a part'
	una semana	
	(que está aquí)	'has been here a week'
	una semana	
	(que estuvo aquí)	'was here a week ago'
	sombra	'to shade'
	Dios hizo la tierra.	'God created the earth.'
	No le hace.	'It makes no difference.'

SYNONYMS AND ANTONYMS

Meanings are often learned through the use of two associative classes that are opposite in nature, namely synonyms and antonyms. Collocations, described above, may include both these kinds of associations (or neither, of course). *Car* and *automobile* may be introduced as synonyms; *stop* and *go* as antonyms. At present considerable emphasis is being given to the use of synonymous constructions. In the attempt to lead students to communicative competence as soon as possible, the rigidly limiting attitude of providing only one way of saying something has given way to the more flexible use of language, and this includes alternative expressions. An early example of this use of structurally different expressions of the same semantic content in instructional materials may be found in Newmark, Mintz, and Lawson.[6]

One of my students (Eric Nelson) has pointed out that the use of synonyms and synonymous expressions is especially important when students have poor pronunciation. If, instead of repeating the misunderstood portion of speech, students use an alternative way of saying something, they increase their chances of being understood.

However, there are traps for the unwary in the use of both synonyms and antonyms. Synonyms may be misleading because there may be differences in usage patterns which make them only partially synonymous. Although the following words are listed as synonyms in *Webster's Third New International Dictionary* (1961), they are certainly not freely interchangeable: *lift*, *raise*, *rear*, *elevate*, *hoist*, *heave*, *boost*. *Rear* is seldom used in present-day English with the meaning of *lift*; *boost* is used in informal speech, often for lifting persons (*Give me a boost over the fence*); *hoist* is generally used for heavy objects, often implying mechanical means (*We will need to hoist the steel to the top of the building*). Thus, great care must be exercised in presenting synonyms. The situations in which they occur often differ, and very few words can ever be used in exactly the same way.

The use of synonyms and antonyms in vocabulary building involves another problem. Some words have two quite different synonyms or antonyms depending upon which meaning of the original word is selected. The opposite of *old* can be *new* or *young*, the former generally correlating with inanimate and the latter with animate objects; however, a friend can be either *new* or *young* depending upon whether age or length of acquaintance is under discussion. Other commonly occurring lexical sets of this kind are the following:

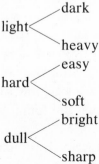

Another word of caution concerning antonyms has to do with the manner in which they are introduced to students. Robert Allen recalls that he was taught the Turkish words for 'upstairs' and 'downstairs' at the same time; and although he can remember both words perfectly, he has difficulty remembering which means which![7] Somehow the meaning for each of these words was not correctly associated with the word. He suggests that in some cases it may be better to introduce opposites in different lessons to avoid the difficulty he encountered.

IDIOMS, PROVERBS, AND CLICHÉS

Idioms, proverbs, and clichés are an essential part of the vocabulary system, and they would have to be learned even if students were not as eager as they often are to learn them.

Idioms are expressions whose meanings cannot be deduced from the sum of the meanings of the constituents. (A foreign student once quite felicitously, albeit erroneously, referred to them as 'ideams'.) These can be quite unusual: *mind your p's and q's*; *no skin off my nose*; *off base*. Sometimes they are very basic to the vocabulary: *look up* 'search for'; *call on* 'visit'; *put up with* 'tolerate'. Such expressions must be taught in appropriate contexts, and their relationship to specific usage levels (where such a relationship exists) must be pointed out.

The sentences below contain a few of the more than fifty idioms with the verb *have* listed in *A Dictionary of American Idioms* (1975). This limited sample may offer some concept of the extensive use of idioms in the language.

> We had it straight from her sister.
> You must admit she has you there.
> I think he has something up his sleeve.
> I have a bone to pick with you.
> I wouldn't have it, if I were you.

Idioms can be very misleading when carried from language to language. Although English *laugh* is more or less equal to French *rire* and to German *lachen*, Mackey points out that English

Hi and Lois

by MORT WALKER and DIK BROWNE

OH, OH! HERE COMES HI, AND DINNER ISN'T READY YET.

HE'S GOING TO BE IN A STEW!

JUST WHEN I THINK I'M GETTING THE HANG OF THE LANGUAGE, SHE PULLS SOMETHING LIKE THAT!

GUESS WHO DROPPED INTO MY OFFICE TODAY. MITCH ZARBA!

WHAM!

I HAVEN'T SEEN HIM SINCE HE AND DODIE BROKE UP.

I HEARD HE WAS HITTING THE BOTTLE PRETTY HARD.

YEAH, HE WAS ON THE SKIDS AND TOOK HIS WHOLE FAMILY DOWN WITH HIM!

BUT HE BECAME AA AND HE'S PATCHING UP HIS HOME LIFE NOW.

AA

BOY! DAD SURE KNOWS SOME WEIRD PEOPLE.

11-21

speakers *laugh up their sleeve* while French speakers *laugh in their beard* and German speakers *laugh in their fist*.[8]

Like idioms, proverbs are an integral part of the language and culture of each society, and language learners should be acquainted with those that occur frequently. Many proverbs contain moral statements which often have a universal appeal, even though they may be expressed in different ways. *Don't count your chickens before they're hatched* and *don't put all your eggs in one basket* are admonitions to caution. Under certain conditions it may be said that *too many cooks spoil the broth*, while at other times *many hands make light work*. English-speaking children are often told to curb their envy of others by the statement *the grass is always greener on the other side of the fence*. As they grow older they learn to *forgive and forget*. They learn that *absence makes the heart grow fonder*, but are also made wary by the expression *out of sight, out of mind*. The caution to *look before you leap* is balanced by the more adventurous *nothing ventured, nothing gained*. (Proverbs often employ this balancing of two grammatical constituents, technically referred to as an aphoristic expression: *easy come, easy go*; *the more, the merrier*.)

Unless students learn these proverbs, they will lack the ability to comprehend not only their lexical significance but also the cultural attitudes on which they are based.

Clichés are also frequently used in speech; and even though native speakers of English are admonished to avoid them, non-native English speakers should learn to recognize them because they are part of the order and organization of lexical items. Students must learn, for example, that English speakers say *black and white* in just that order. They also use similes such as *pretty as a picture*, *strong as an ox*, and *cool as a cucumber*. Expressions such as these are very much a part of the vocabulary system, and they warrant attention on the recognition level even if they are not necessarily taught for production.[9]

Usage

When students learn a vocabulary item, they must also learn under what circumstances it occurs since not every word or phrase may be used appropriately in all situations. Problems may arise if a vocabulary item commonly associated with one style of speech or writing is used in a style for which it is inappropriate.[10] For example, *kids* and *children* have somewhat the same meaning, but *kids* is a term that is normally reserved for informal or intimate speech, and it would be most inappropriate in a formal style of speaking or writing.

There are many variables that influence vocabulary choice, some of which are related to age, regional dialect, social position, sex, purpose, and manner of the discourse.

To illustrate that age may make a difference in vocabulary choice we need only consider the use of the word *phonograph* by an older generation as contrasted with *record player* or *stereo* by a younger generation. Teen-agers have their own vocabulary filled with words having meanings often recognizable only by members of their own age group. At various times in recent years *groovy, boss, bad, mellow* had more or less the same meaning of approval. Disapproval has been expressed in recent teen-age jargon by describing a person as *gross, sad, a turkey*.

Geographical location may make a difference in vocabulary choice because regional dialects are common in English. One of the major distinctions between British and American English is in the area of lexical items: British *lift, bonnet*, and *lorry* are the equivalent of American *elevator, hood* (of an automobile), and *truck*. Within the United States, regional dialects are often characterized by differences in vocabulary items. Variations such as the following tend to be found in certain geographical areas: *frying pan* and *spider*; *rubber band* and *rubber binder*; *turtle* and *cooter*; *green pepper* and *bell pepper*.[11]

Social relationships between speakers may account for differences in the choice of vocabulary. The choice of *How do you do* or *Hi* as a greeting when being introduced signals a particular

HÄGAR The Horrible

by DIK BROWNE

HEY! IT MUST BE TIME TO EAT

WHAT DO YOU WANT TO EAT?

I DON'T KNOW...THERE ARE SO MANY DIFFERENT PLACES TO EAT OUT IN THIS CITY...

FRENCH RESTAURANTS MAKE ME FEEL DUMB — I NEVER KNOW WHAT I'M ORDERING...

Chez COO COO

FOOD'S NICE

FORGET IT

LET'S TRY THIS ENGLISH PLACE. AT LEAST I CAN UNDERSTAND WHAT I'M GETTING!

EVENING, GENTS — WHAT'LL YOU HAVE?

WHAT HAVE YOU GOT?

INKEY—DINKEY... BUBBLE AND SQUEAK... COCK-A-LEEKIE... BANGERS AND BLOATERS... ...TREACLES AND TRIFLES — ROLY POLY OR FIGGIE HOBBIN

WHAT DO YOU SAY?

I THINK THERE'S A CHINESE JOINT DOWN THIS WAY — LET'S TRY IT

5-1 DIK BROWNE

level of formality or informality and something about the social relationship between the speakers. Slang and very casual language is often reserved for peers, and more formal lexical items are chosen when speaking to those who are older or superior in social position.

Differences in sex are also reflected in speech. Vocabulary that may have been traditionally used by women may not be equally suitable for men, and vice versa. Exclamations such as *Oh, my goodness* or *Oh, dear* are conventionally associated with women's language. Words traditionally employed by both men and women are probably more useful for students to learn. For example, adjectives that are neutral in regard to their use by either sex such as *great, terrific, neat* are probably better to teach than what have been thought of as typically feminine adjectives like *adorable, lovely, darling,* and *divine.* It behooves the teacher to take care not to inflict on students vocabulary that has been traditionally associated with a particular sex. However, such differences in the use of vocabulary by male and female speakers are slowly disappearing, and further changes can be expected in the future.

The purpose for which language is used may also result in a difference in lexical items. Politicians are wont to choose their words very carefully because their purpose is to influence their listeners. Thus, a politician may refer to an opponent's plan as *hastily conceived* although the proponent of the plan might describe it as *an immediate answer to a problem.* What one person may consider *making the best of* a situation may be looked at by someone else as *putting up with* something. Thus, in addition to being a reflection of the speaker's perspective, lexical items may be chosen in order to influence the person spoken to.

There are obvious differences between the lexical content of the written and the spoken language; in general, the written language uses vocabulary that is thought of as being more formal. What may appear in speech as *run into* and *get around* may occur in writing as *encounter* and *circumvent.* Thus, the two modes of discourse — speech and writing — necessitate special attention in terms of vocabulary content.

Teaching Vocabulary

Cognate Vocabulary

The existence of cognate vocabulary, that is, words that have similar forms and similar meanings in two or more languages, may be an advantage to some students learning English. English contains many words that are similar in form to those in French, Spanish, and Italian as well as to those in German, Dutch, and other Germanic languages. The Germanic element is that which is native to English; both German and English, and other Germanic languages such as Dutch, are descended from the same branch of the Indo-European family of languages. The Romance element, which entered the English language mainly after 1066 A.D., is represented by borrowings from languages which belong to another branch of the Indo-European family (e.g., Latin, French, Spanish, Italian).

The fact that words like English *deport*, French *déporter*, Spanish *deportar*, and Italian *deportare* exist may give speakers of the Romance languages an advantage in learning English; speakers of German may have a similar advantage with English cognates of Germanic origin. English *ring*, *mouse*, and *long* are cognate with German *Ring*, *Maus*, and *lang*(e). Differences in pronunciation, which are often considerable in cognates, must be taken into account, and for this reason cognates are probably more helpful in the written language than in speech because of such possible phonological differences.

However, cognates may cause problems since they often develop different meanings in the various languages. It is not unusual to hear Spanish speakers say, "I cannot *support* ('tolerate') him" or "She is *embarrassed* ('pregnant')," or to hear French speakers say, "She is a *sensible* ('sensitive') woman." Virginia French Allen (personal communication) tells me that one of her Spanish-speaking students who seemed to get along with her extremely well once sent her a sympathy card — *simpatía* in Spanish means 'congeniality', or 'feeling in tune with' someone.

These errors are caused by what are termed 'false' cognates, words that are similar in form to those in another language but different in meaning. Errors of the most glaring sort, such as those above, should be pointed out to students so that the advantages gained by the existence of true cognates may not be overshadowed by problems created by those that are 'false'.

Receptive and Productive Vocabulary

In addition to the fact mentioned earlier that speakers of a language are constantly adding lexical items to their store, there is another important aspect of the lexical system to be considered. All speakers are able to recognize more words than they actually use on a productive level. Productive vocabulary is that utilized in everyday speech. Receptive vocabulary, on the other hand, although needed for comprehension, is not necessarily essential for production in speaking and writing. Textbook writers in ESL tend to treat all vocabulary equally; that is, they generally imply that students should be able to produce all vocabulary presented. Teachers and students should concentrate on the acquisition for production of those lexical items that will be most useful for everyone. Another kind of attention should be given to the acquisition of receptive vocabulary which can often be comprehended through the use of contextual and collocational clues.

The basic productive and receptive vocabulary does not include specialized lexical items that are needed for a particular job or profession. These are probably best learned in connection with the job or profession itself. The field called English for Special Purposes (ESP) or Scientific and Technical English (STE) puts great stress on the specialized vocabulary connected with various professional or technical fields.

Importance of Vocabulary

Language teachers have sometimes tended to overlook the importance of the lexical system by overemphasizing grammatical and sound systems. This may have resulted from the fact that an individual lexical store cannot be clearly defined because it depends upon the speaker's need and particular experience. It is an 'open' system. The systems of grammar and sounds, on the other hand, can be clearly defined, are much the same for all speakers, and thus are easier to teach.

Lexical items may also have appeared to be of secondary importance because they have sometimes been seen as that which is used to 'flesh out' the structure or to exemplify parts of the sound system. However, without lexicon the major meaning-carrying element in language is missing. Therefore, the acquisition of vocabulary is an integral part of learning a second language.

On the other hand, there are teachers who have tended to overemphasize the learning of words, and the lengthy vocabulary lists in the old language texts bear silent witness to such an approach. The solution here is to strike a happy medium. Students should be exposed to the vocabulary needed to express the ideas they want to communicate. The vocabulary items should not be strictly limited, nor should vocabulary acquisition be stressed to the exclusion of other parts of the language system.

Vocabulary Selection

Teachers will naturally select vocabulary items that will be most useful for their own students, and this will vary from situation to situation. However, the following categories of lexical items appear to be generally appropriate for most students early in their language learning experience (in addition to the simple items needed for classroom activities): numbers (to tell time and age), colors, kinship terms, body parts, articles of clothing, days of the week, months of the year, foods. However, the actual lexical content of any given instructional program is best determined by the topics that students want to discuss.

Vocabulary Building

Exercises related to word formation, synonyms and antonyms, and guessing the meanings of words from contexts are excellent means of increasing the vocabulary. There are texts that are written primarily as vocabulary builders (Franklin, et al., 1968; Barnard, 1971) as well as reading texts with a strong emphasis upon vocabulary or word study (Croft, 1960; Kurilecz, 1969; Saitz and Carr, 1972). Drills on idioms can also be helpful in adding to students' lexical stores (see Dixson, 1971; McCallum, 1970, 1978; Reeves, 1975).

Below are examples of vocabulary exercises from Croft illustrative of English word formation and the relationship between various forms of vocabulary items that can be used to increase vocabulary.

(a) adjective-noun

   She looked at the *important* paper and was impressed by its (*importance*).
   She looked at the *dull* knife and was impressed by its _____.
   She looked at the *clear* water and was impressed by its

   _____.

(b) adjective-verb

   The ropes are *tighter* now; they have just been (*tightened*).
   The houses are *larger* now; they have just been _____.
   The clothes are *damper* now; they have just been _____.

(c) verb-noun

   They *compared* the scores, but I never knew the reason for the (*comparison*).
   They *complained* about the guest, but I never knew the reason for the _____.
   They *preferred* the brick house, but I never knew the reason for the _____.

Kurilecz (1969) bases her word study exercises on short readings. Below are excerpts from an exercise on word formation related to a reading about Leonardo da Vinci.

(able)   Da Vinci showed great _____ in many fields.
(rich)   His art _____ the world.
(splendid) Leonardo always dressed _____.

Learning to guess the meanings of words from the context in which they occur is an important part of reading ability. Norris (1970:196) illustrates this kind of exercise with the following example:

A *dynamic* person can keep Washington affairs from becoming boring. Often, through his activity, he can become well known in a short time.

The best synonym for *dynamic* is
_____ powerless   _____ forceful
_____ athletic   _____ cheerful

Croft (1967) provides an extensive list of phrasal clichés occurring commonly in English which are useful items for students to know. These include pairs with *and* (*comb and brush*), pairs with *or* (*win or lose*), triplets (*how, when, and where*), similes with *as* (*cool as a cucumber*), and similes with *like* (*drinks like a fish*).

Exercises

A. Using the prefixes and suffixes listed below, form as many words as possible with each root. The first item has been partially completed as an example.

un-	-(i)able	-tion	-ize
in-	-al	-ness	-ify
re-	-less	-ment	
en-	-ive	-ity	-ly
	-ent	-ence	

1. form formal, informal, formality, reform, formalize . . . .
2. name _____
3. horror _____
4. note _____
5. differ _____
6. force _____
7. corrupt _____
8. direct _____
9. shape _____
10. product _____

B. This exercise serves to illustrate the fact that what are termed synonyms cannot always be used interchangeably. Fill the blanks with the appropriate word from the following list of synonyms.

bonus	bounty	subsidy	dividend
premium	prize	reward	gratuity

1. The factory employees will receive a _____ this year as part of their Christmas check.
2. The sign in the dining room says that guests are not to give any _____ to the waiters.
3. The town is offering a _____ for every rat killed.
4. The _____ for the best slogan was won by a girl in the ninth grade.

5. The stockholders will receive a _____ because of the increased business that the corporation had this year.

6. The government has granted a _____ to those farmers who produce more than their usual amount of grain.

7. The furniture store is offering a _____ in the form of a discount to customers who purchase merchandise worth $300 or more during this month.

8. The woman received a _____ when she returned the lost dog to its owner.

C. The following are lists of synonyms taken from *The American Heritage Dictionary of the English Language*. Can they be used interchangeably? If not, what information must students have in order to use them appropriately? Which of the synonyms would be more useful for students to learn? Why?

1. annoy, irritate, bother, irk, vex, provoke, aggravate, peeve, rile.

2. moment, minute, instant, second, trice, jiffy, flash.

3. rob, burglarize, filch, pilfer, plunder, loot, ransack, steal, thieve.

4. mix, blend, mingle, coalesce, merge, amalgamate, combine, compound, fuse.

5. familiar, close, intimate, fraternal, confidential, chummy.

D. Guess what single English word has all the meanings listed below. Then supply a context in which it can be used with these various meanings.

1. a muscular organ

2. capacity for sympathy

3. central or innermost part

4. a playing card

5. a game (plural)

6. basis or essence

7. love or affection

E. Add words to the following lexical sets that might usefully collate with them. Notice that different collocations may occur with the same word, depending upon the situation in which it is used.

   1. examination, doctor, nurse ....

   2. examination, school, study ....

   3. books, radio, television............................

   4. books, homework, teacher ....

   5. home, mother, brother ....

   6. home, old people, retire ....

   7. grass, garden, flowers ....

   8. grass, smoke, law.................................

   9. sister, family, brother-in-law ....

  10. sister, church, vow ....

F. Complete the expressions below; then ask persons who speak languages other than English to tell you how they would complete them in those languages.

1. strong as _____	9. cute as _____
2. clean as _____	10. sharp as _____
3. neat as _____	11. roar like _____
4. dead as _____	12. laugh like _____
5. sober as _____	13. sleep like _____
6. slippery as _____	14. swim like _____
7. crazy as _____	15. eat like _____
8. weak as _____	16. bark like _____

G. Ask persons whose native language is not English if their language contains proverbs that express the same ideas as those below.

   1. A bird in the hand is worth two in the bush.

   2. The early bird catches the worm.

   3. All that glitters is not gold.

   4. A barking dog seldom bites.

5. You can't judge a book by its cover.

6. Better late than never.

7. A new broom sweeps clean.

8. Birds of a feather flock together.

9. Beauty is only skin deep.

10. A penny saved is a penny earned.

11. An apple a day keeps the doctor away.

12. Haste makes waste.

13. A stitch in time saves nine.

14. Let sleeping dogs lie.

15. He who hesitates is lost.

16. It's never too late to learn.

17. You can't teach an old dog new tricks.

18. Never put off until tomorrow what you can do today.

H. Pick out the proverbs in Exercise G that are similar in meaning and those that seem to contradict each other.

I. Which of the dialect variants in each item below is most familiar to you? Ask someone from another region or another English-speaking country which alternative he or she prefers.

1. quilt — comforter (a soft, filled blanket or bedcover)

2. divan — sofa — couch — chesterfield (a piece of furniture)

3. dinner — supper (evening meal on weekdays)

4. gas — petrol (gasoline)

5. cottage cheese — Dutch cheese (soft white cheese made from milk curds)

6. afternoon — evening (4 p.m.)

7. bucket — pail (metal container)

8. funny bone — crazy bone (point near elbow that tingles when pressed)

9. kitty corner — catty-corner(ed) — cattywampus (diagonal)

10. firefly — lightning bug (insect that glows at night)

Notes

1. Eric H. Lenneberg, *Biological Foundations of Language* (New York: John Wiley & Sons, 1967) p. 335.

2. For a discussion of word frequency lists see Richard Yorkey's review of *American University Word List* in TESOL Quarterly 10:244–50 (June, 1976).

3. Lenneberg, p. 34.

4. I am indebted to Janet Ross for this example which she saw on a sign in a British park.

5. William F. Mackey, *Language Teaching Analysis* (Bloomington: Indiana University Press, 1965), p. 95.

6. Leonard Newmark, Jerome Mintz, and Jan Ann Lawson, *Using American English* (New York: Harper and Row, 1964).

7. Robert L. Allen, "The Use of Rapid Drills in the Teaching of English to Speakers of Other Languages," TESOL Quarterly 6:13–32 (March, 1972).

8. Mackey, p. 95.

9. For a useful list of clichés see Kenneth Croft, "Some Co-occurrences in American Clichés," TESOL Quarterly 1:47–49 (June, 1967).

10. For a discussion of the variety of styles characteristic of Standard English and other national languages, see Martin Joos, *The Five Clocks* (New York: Harcourt Brace Jovanovich, 1967).

11. I recall how surprised I was when grocery shopping in central Indiana (after returning from several years' residence in Puerto Rico) to see a sign advertising *mangoes*, and how disappointed I was when I discovered that this was a regional term for *green pepper*. (*Mango* as a regional term for green pepper is substantiated by *Webster's Third International Dictionary* for any reader who is as surprised as I was.)

TEACHING ENGLISH
TO SPEAKERS
OF OTHER LANGUAGES

4

Language and Culture

The preceding section of this book contains an overview of the linguistic aspects of English — its grammar, sounds, and vocabulary — knowledge of which is essential for teachers of English to speakers of other languages. But language is a tool of the society that employs it, and the ways in which language is used reflects the culture of that society. This relationship between language and culture forms an important part of the acquisition of a second language because it involves the way in which members of a culture view the world.

Language and Cultural Diversity

The English language contains separate lexical terms for *finger* and *toe*, and this reflects a perception on the part of English speakers that they are distinct parts of the anatomy. Spanish speakers, on the other hand, do not view them as distinct but classify them together, using only one word, *dedo*, for both parts of the body. Speakers of Hopi (a North American Indian language) must choose between two words in their language for what English speakers call *water*. They refer to it as *pāhe* if it is freely running, as in a river or fountain, and as *kēyi* if it is confined, as in a bottle or glass (Whorf, 1940).

A simple contrast of Japanese and English provides an excellent example of the fact that knowledge of language items in itself is not all that is required to use language effectively; organization also plays a role in its use. Ota (1971:122–23) gives the following examples of addresses and dates in Japanese and English which demonstrate that these two cultures organize space and time in quite different fashions.

> In English you start with the smaller units and go toward the larger units like:
>
> Dr. Randal Whitman
> Department of English as a Second Language
> University of Hawaii
> 1890 East-West Road
> Honolulu, Hawaii 96822
> U.S.A.
>
> In Japanese the order is just the opposite:
> U.S.A.
> Hawaii 96822, Honolulu
> 1890 East-West Road
> University of Hawaii
> Department of English as a Second Language
> Dr. Randal Whitman
>
> The date systems obey the same principle.
> In English: 10 A.M., June 11 (or 11 June), 1970.
> In Japanese: 1970, June 11, A.M. 10.

Differences in culture are probably more startling when reflected in different languages, as in the Spanish/English, Hopi/English, and Japanese/English contrasts mentioned. However, there are also cultural differences among speakers of the same language that result in different meanings being applied to the same linguistic form. Variation such as this should not seem surprising when we recall that lexical differences exist within a given language; e.g., the use in English of *frying pan*, *fry pan*, *skillet*, and *spider* as regional variants that refer to the same cooking utensil.

I remember as a child spending summers in a small English-speaking community in Canada and being surprised at the strange way in which members of that community used certain language forms. My brother and I found hilarious their use of *good night* as a polite greeting on the streets in the evening. (Everything that is different is "funny" when you are a child.) We were sure that everyone (this, of course, meant speakers of American English from the Upper Midwest) knew that *good night* was a leave-taking. I was equally taken aback (but by that time more sophisticated in my reaction) as an adult resident of central Indiana to hear *good evening* employed as a greeting as early as two o'clock in the afternoon; I later discovered that this was fairly common practice among speakers of the Midland dialect of American English.

In both of these cases I had known the general meaning of the lexical items *good night* and *good evening*, but I certainly was ignorant of their appropriate use within the communicative situation. In teaching and learning a second language we must be concerned with the communicative use of language since our goal should be to reach what Hymes (1974) terms *communicative competence* or the social use of language. Merely learning lexical items, then, is not enough. We must learn when to use them, i.e., under what circumstances they are appropriate, if we want to truly understand what they mean.

Charles C. Fries was wont to use meals as an example of the way in which language and culture interact in the social situation. The word *breakfast* is fairly easy to understand — 'the first meal in the morning'. But he would insist that one does not fully understand that word unless one knows what the meal consists of, where it is eaten, with whom, and at what time. Is it a large meal, like that served in England? Is it a continental breakfast, or perhaps the bowl of cereal and milk so dear to the hearts of American children, or the cup of coffee swallowed on the run? Is it a meal eaten with the whole family, like the main meal of the day, or is it eaten alone? Is it served early in the morning or late? (Here I am reminded of the large breakfasts I observed on a farm I visited during my childhood. Breakfast was served at about 8 o'clock after the farm workers had already worked for two or three hours.) Is it prepared by one person or does each person in the family prepare his or her own? The full meaning of a given linguistic item will not be grasped unless it is associated with the situation in which it occurs.

Lists of particular cultural features that may differ from language to language may be found in W. P. Allen (1956:17–29), Brooks (1964:90–95), and Fries (1945:58–60). The following are examples taken from these sources as indicated.

Social structure of family groups. Size and relationships of family; marriage, divorce, and remarriage; line of descent. (Allen, 23)

Appointments. How are appointments for business and pleasure made? What are the usual meeting places? How important is punctuality? (Brooks, 92)

Telephone. What phrases and procedures are conventional in the use of the telephone? What is the role of the private telephone in the home? Where are public telephones to be found and how is the service to be paid for? (Brooks, 91–92)

Pets. What animals are habitually received into the home as pets? What is their role in the household? (Brooks, 91)

Verbal Taboos. What common words or expressions in English have direct equivalents that are not tolerated in the new culture, and vice versa? (Brooks, 91)

For the child: places and time of play; stories that are told and pictures that illustrate these stories; segregation of sexes in schools; teachers (men or women). (Fries: 58–59)

Motions and gestures in social situations. Shaking hands — how frequently and who extends hand first? Introductions. (Fries: 59)

Practices accompanying eating. Spoken formulas. Methods of using eating utensils. ('American forks' are quite noticeable in Europe.) Water with meals. Tea, coffee, wine, beer, cocktails, liqueurs. Attitudes toward various beverages. 'Soft drinks'. (Fries, 60)

Language as a Reflection of Culture

The belief that there is a very close relationship between language and culture has long been held by anthropologists, and American linguists with strong interest in non-European languages, like Edward Sapir, have emphasized the interplay between language and the culture it reflects. There is strong support among linguists for statements like the following from Sapir.

> Language does not exist apart from culture, that is from the socially inherited assemblage of practices and beliefs that determines the texture of our lives. (1921:221)
>
> Human beings do not live in the objective world alone, nor alone in the world of social activity as ordinarily understood, but are very much at the mercy of the particular language which has become the medium for their society. . . . The fact of the matter is that the "real world" is to a large extent unconsciously built up on the language habits of the group. . . . We see and hear and otherwise experience very largely as we do because the language habits of our community predispose certain choices of interpretation. (1929:209)

Cree (an Algonquian language of North America) provides an interesting basis for speculation about the possible relationship between language and the culture it reflects. Cree specifies a definite order in the use of verb prefixes that show person: second person ('you') always precedes first person ('I' or 'we'), and both of these precede third person ('he', 'she', 'it', 'they'). Geary (1943:150) speculates on the relationship of this particular order to Cree culture:

> It seems to be a sociological trait among the Algonquian-speakers, equivalent to our idea of 'politeness.' But whereas, in English, it is considered impolite but not ungrammatical to say "I and you" it seems that in Algonquian this would also be ungrammatical!

Also in support of this contention that language reflects culture, Ervin-Tripp (1964) reported on an experiment with Japanese and English speakers to test her hypothesis that "as language shifts, content will shift." In this study Japanese-

English bilingual women were asked to complete statements that they heard and read in both languages. The responses of one woman, which were typical of the others, were as follows:

1. When my wishes conflict with my family . . .
   (Japanese) it is a time of great unhappiness.
   (English)   I do what I want.
2. I will probably become . . .
   (Japanese) a housewife.
   (English)   a teacher.
3. Real friends should . . .
   (Japanese) help each other.
   (English)   be very frank.

In this study the specific language employed seemed to mirror a particular cultural view since the content of what was said varied with the language being used.

Trudgill (1974) provides another kind of example of the effect of the social or cultural environment on language. He points out that a society's kinship system is revealed in its kinship vocabulary; distinctions that are important in a culture are reflected in the lexicon of the language of that society. He says, for example, that the distinction between maternal and paternal aunt is not significant in English-speaking culture; therefore, no special term is required as it may be in other cultures. He also provides the following example from Russian of the way in which social change affects language.

> During the period from 1860 to the present day the structure of the Russian kinship system has undergone a very radical change as a result of several important events: the emancipation of serfs in 1861, the First World War, the revolution, the collectivization of agriculture and the Second World War. There has been a marked social as well as political revolution, and this has been accompanied by a corresponding change in the language. For example, in the middle of the last century, *wife's brother* was *shurin*, whereas now it is simply *brat zheny*, *brother of wife*. Similarly, *brot*.*er's wife*, formerly *nevestka*, is now *zhena brata*, *wife of brother*. In other words, distinctions

that were formerly lexicalized, because they were important,
are now made by means of phrases. The loss of importance of
these particular relationships, and the corresponding linguistic
changes, are due to the fact that social changes in Russia have
led to the rise of the small, nuclear family. (28–29)

Sapir's influence on Benjamin Lee Whorf was considerable,
and Whorf's study of the differences between the structures of
European languages and Hopi convinced him that speakers of
these various languages conceptualize reality in different ways;
but more than this, he believed that these contrasting views
resulted from differences in language structures. He stated his
belief this way (Carroll, 1956:235): "Facts are unlike to speakers
whose language background provides for unlike formulation of
them." In other words, he hypothesized a causal relationship
between the structure of a given language and how speakers of
that language view reality. His thesis is sometimes referred to as
that of "linguistic relativity." Although most people accept
Sapir's view — that people who speak different languages view
the world differently — they are less ready to accept the causal
relationship proposed by Whorf, which says that the structure of
the language is responsible for these views.[1]

The current campaign against the use of sex-biased language is
premised on the Whorfian thesis that language shapes thinking.
Many feminists believe that by changing language forms (using
sex neutral pronouns, for example) cultural attitudes can be
changed. Others tend to believe that attitudes must be changed
first; then language changes will follow (as with the social
changes that occurred in Russia, mentioned above).

Learning a Second Culture

In learning a second or foreign language one must try not to
carry over cultural views from the first language. As Fries points
out (1945:58): "If one wishes to master a foreign language so that
he may understand with some completeness the native speakers
of that language, he must find some substitute for the kind of

background experience he has in his own language." The acquisition of this communicative competence with its understanding of the cultural viewpoints and attitudes reflected in the appropriate use of language is probably more easily accomplished if the language is being learned in an environment where it is the principal language. Language learners are then immersed in the culture and have the opportunity for first-hand observation of the situations in which the language is being used. If the language is acquired where direct observation of the culture of the language is not possible (e.g., English as a foreign language in Europe), teachers will have to provide specific cultural information. This can be done in various ways: through pictures, films, magazines, literature, descriptions of their own experience in English-speaking countries, and the like. But truly learning the language must go hand in hand with an understanding of the cultural setting in which it is used.

In order to interpret culture to speakers of other languages, it is essential that teachers be consciously aware of cultural behavior which is sometimes so automatic that it is unnoticed. For example, English speakers alphabetize books on shelves from left to right because this is the way they read, and they may assume that this is the way it is always done. As a matter of fact, a colleague of mine had a foreign graduate assistant who very conscientiously alphabetized all of her books on the shelves from right to left!

Gumperz (1964) says, "The more we know about a particular society, the more effectively we can communicate in it." Christina Paulston, a Swedish-English bilingual, provides an illustration of how communication can sometimes break down because of cultural misinterpretation of language. Her description of an experience she had in Sweden, after having been away from that culture for many years, illustrates the fact that even though the linguistic forms may be readily understood by those interacting in a conversation, they can be interpreted differently because of cultural differences.

In Sweden, we celebrated Thanksgiving by having my immediate family and friends for a traditional turkey dinner. I was busy in the kitchen and came belatedly into the livingroom where my sister-in-law had just arrived. In impeccable Swedish I asked her politely, "Do you know everyone?" Any native American would correctly interpret that to mean that I wanted to know if she had been introduced to those guests she had not previously met. She looked at me sourly and said, "I don't know everyone, but if you are asking me if I have greeted everyone, I have." Fussed as I was and in such an archetypical American situation, I had momentarily forgotten that proper manners demand that Swedes do not wait to be introduced by a third party, but go around the room, shake hands with everyone and say their name aloud to those they have not previously met. Any child knows that, and my sister-in-law felt I had reprimanded her for bad manners, her faulty sharing of a systemic set of social interactional rules. Clearly, the meaning of an interaction is easily misinterpreted if the speakers don't share the same set of rules, as in this example of non-effective communication where the same surface structure carried different social meaning. (1974:351)

A somewhat different example of communicative difficulty due to misinterpretation of what would usually be considered straightforward linguistic forms comes from an Arabic culture. William Slager (personal communication) told me that Egyptian culture prohibits speakers from saying "no" to any polite request. No matter how impossible it may be to carry it out, it would be considered extremely impolite to refuse; therefore, every request is answered affirmatively, even if the speaker has no intention of complying. One simply has to learn to read other signs in order to know whether the "yes" is truly affirmative or a polite answer that really means "no."

The Social Use of Language

Hymes (1962, 1974) stresses the need for an "ethnography of communication" that includes in the act of communication a consideration of setting, participants, topic, and purpose, in addition to form. Appropriate interaction among these factors, Hymes says, results in communicative competence, which he describes in this way:

> Within the social matrix in which it acquires a system of grammar a child acquires also a system of its use, regarding persons, places, purposes, other modes of communication, etc. — all the components of communicative events, together with attitudes and beliefs regarding them. There also develop patterns of the sequential use of language in conversation, address, standard routines, and the like. In such acquisition resides the child's *socio*linguistic competence (or, more broadly, communicative competence), its ability to participate in its society as not only a speaking, but a communicating member. (1974:75)

Although Hymes here refers to the child learning a first language, the same communicative competence should be the goal when acquiring a second language. There is general agreement, however, with Virginia French Allen's comment (personal communication) that total learning of the social uses of language is probably less essential in EFL situations since "the learner is less likely to communicate directly with native speakers."

Knowledge of how a society uses languages involves the concepts of acceptability and appropriateness. Obviously a grammatical choice must be made, but is the chosen language form one that is acceptable to native speakers as appropriate for the particular situation? There are, then, both grammatical and social restraints on what a person says. Gumperz (1964:138) states succinctly, "Grammatical restraints relate to the intelligibility of sentences; social restraints to their acceptability."

In teaching and learning a second language, much of the time is spent on practicing grammatically correct language. Less emphasis is usually placed on demonstrating which of the correct forms are appropriate in a given situation. But for non-native speakers of a language this information is as important as knowing the correct grammatical form. A word of caution is in order here, however. In the early stages of language learning, students should be encouraged to use the language (appropriately or not) just to establish the fact that they *can* use it. Too much emphasis on appropriateness may result in an oversensitivity to what is considered correct and produce a fear of speaking at all.

Style of speaking or writing can vary from extremely formal to intimate. Joos (1961) says there are five styles in English and indicates that most speech falls somewhere in the middle range of these five, in what he refers to as ''consultative'' — the normal style for conversation — and ''casual'' — that used by close friends and acquaintances. He points out that a speaker can shift from one style, or register, to another within a single conversation; but politeness requires that such a shift involve no more than two neighboring registers.

The age or sex of participants in a communicative situation often defines the style or register used, and these factors very often affect linguistic content. For example, a conversation between teen-agers would undoubtedly contain different words and idioms than a conversation between adults; and lexical items used by women often differ from those used by men. Lakoff (1973) mentions that women are able to make many more color distinctions than are men (in terms of identifying them by name). She also points out that the following adjectives when employed to express approbation or admiration belong exclusively to women: *adorable, charming, sweet, lovely, divine.*

The use of slang, or other items characteristic of an informal speech style, by the non-native speaker often leads to an expectation of nativelike control of the language. After all, the listener reasons, this person must know the language really well to be able to handle such idiomatic language. Often these informal bits of speech are isolated items that a learner absorbs without realizing that they are characteristic of a particular style. An example of such mixing of registers occurred in the speech of a foreign graduate student in a final oral examination for the master's degree, a rather formal situation. He was describing a study he had carried out with pupils in a public school in his own country, and he referred to the subjects in the study alternately as *kids* and *children*. It was obvious that he thought these were equivalent terms. When I later pointed out the difference in their use, he admitted that he had never known this.

Usually, it is better for non-native speakers to adhere to slightly more formal levels of language, thereby avoiding giving an impression of greater fluency than they actually possess. Also, the use of a more formal style is often a signal that the speaker is not a native speaker and that the listener should not expect complete control over the language and its appropriate use.

Nonverbal Cultural Devices

A discussion of the appropriate use of language within a given culture would not be complete without mention of certain nonverbal characteristics of communication, such as gestures and what Hall (1966) terms "proxemics," the use of space in communicative encounters. Those who have observed conversations between Arabic speakers realize that they stand much closer to each other than Americans do when talking together. An English speaker talking to an Arab tends to draw away when the Arab assumes a normal conversational stance. When seated, English speakers lean toward the person they are talking to when they want to express interest in what is being said. (See Hall, 1966, and Clark, et al., 1977, for photographs of various speaking stances in English communicative situations.) An interesting discussion of seating arrangements, another use of space, can be found in Brislin (1974).

Body motion, gestures, and signs are culturally determined. Birdwhistell (1970) says, "We have found no gestures or body motions which have the same social meaning in all societies." For example, nodding or shaking the head to indicate "yes" or "no," respectively, does not apply universally. As a matter of fact, in Eskimo they work in exactly the opposite fashion (Farb, 1974:233).

Murdock et al. (1945:4) in their outline of cultural materials list the following categories of gestures and signs which, of course, may vary from culture to culture:

expressions of affection, aggression, derision, modesty, humiliation, fear, and other emotions; facial expressions; suggestive gestures; greetings; obeisances; signs (beckoning, warning, affirmation, negation, indications of size and shape); numerical signs, nervous habits and postures.

Another nonverbal aspect of communication is the use of touch. This, too, differs from culture to culture. Keating (1976:12) reports the following distinctive use of touch across cultures.

In a preliminary exploration of tactile behavior, Jourard (1966) observed pairs of individuals chatting in college shops located in different countries and recorded the frequency of touching. Over an hour-long sitting for each pair, the scores were: London, 0; Gainesville, Florida, 2; Paris, 110; and San Juan, Puerto Rico, 180.

Cultural Taboos

Just as the knowledge of appropriate gestures and body motion is necessary in acquiring communicative competence in a second or foreign language, taboos must also be adhered to. As might be expected, not all cultures agree on what is taboo. There may be verbal taboos — expletives or 'dirty words' (which, of course, many speakers hasten to learn so they can be avoided!). Such words or phrases, though not allowed in ordinary conversation, may be permitted under certain circumstances (in sexually segregated groups, for example). There may also be subjects that one avoids mentioning — areas of silence. Asking someone the cost of an article, for instance, is avoided in American culture unless the person asked is a very close friend. And, according to Pearson (1977:297), among some North American Indians the correct response to bad news is thoughtful silence.

A taboo among Mazatec Indians who consider themselves susceptible to witchcraft is reported by Pike (1956). She tells of asking a little girl her name; the girl immediately countered by asking Miss Pike her name. After getting a response, the little girl replied, "My name is the same as yours. My name is Eunice." Mazatecs hesitate to reveal their names to strangers, who are considered witch doctors, because witch doctors are thought to be able to converse with demons and (for a price) request that a spell be cast on someone. However, without a specific name, the demons are unable to identify the person they have been called upon to harm. For this reason, Pike says, "The really clever thing to do is to turn the witch doctor's evil design back upon himself; and that is why I have so frequently been told, 'My name is Eunice'!"

Culture Shock

Although all cultural differences are not as marked as some of the above examples, even momentary misunderstandings may arise when cultural wires are crossed. I recall my own reaction to the practice of strangers asking *"Quien habla?"* ("Who is speaking?") when I answered the telephone during my first stay in a Spanish-speaking culture. I had been taught that such a question was impolite, even boorish; and my initial negative reaction to this very common (and, after all, very useful) question resulted from applying the telephone conventions of my own culture to another.

'Culture shock' is often experienced by those who find themselves surrounded by speakers of another language. Notice, however, it is not merely *language* shock but the shock of a difference in everything that impinges on the behavior of persons speaking that language that produces this uncomfortable initial reaction. The total culture is different, and language is only one aspect of that difference. As many have found out from first-hand experience in a foreign country,

> it is probably not the differences in physical landscape, climate, religion, dress or even food which bring[s] about the strongest sense of confusion. More often, it is the assumptions underlying everyday life, shared by members of a society by virtue of constant interaction from birth, assumptions which are so much a part of culture that they are not even consciously held. (Watson, 1974:59)

An understanding of what constitutes these assumptions is an essential part of acquiring communicative competence in another language.

Exercises

A. What are some of the cultural stereotypes that are often used to differentiate speakers of American English from speakers of other languages or from speakers of British English? For example, we are often considered to be gum-chewing, materialistic people who are slaves to time. Do you agree with this? What is the source of such stereotyping?

B. What are some of the major taboos in English-speaking culture? Ask speakers of other languages about taboos in their culture.

C. The words designating sounds that animals are said to make are thought to be somewhat imitative. English dogs say "bow-wow," cats "meow," pigs "oink-oink," and donkeys "hee-haw." Ask speakers of other languages what sounds their animals make. Are they the same as those in English? [It is interesting to note that Eeyore, the donkey in Milne's *Winnie-the-Pooh*, has a name that represents the British rendition of *hee-haw* ("eeyaw") — without "h" sounds and with the final "r" in the spelling unpronounced.]

D. *Buen provecho* and *bon appétit* are common expressions in Spanish and French culture, respectively. Ask a Spanish or French speaker to describe the situations in which these occur. Do we have an equivalent expression in English?

E. Find out how to signal "come here" in several different cultures.

F. How are birthdays celebrated in different cultures?

G. For a short period of time observe carefully the gestures you use in conversation and classify them in relation to the social use of language. For example, to emphasize ideas do you use gestures together with or in place of words? Do you use any gestures either together with or in place of words of affirmation or negation like *yes* or *no*?

H. Are eating utensils used in all cultures? What kinds are there? Are they employed in exactly the same way? How do you ordinarily eat bananas or pears — with or without utensils? How is silverware placed on the table in your home? In other homes you have visited? Are there generalizations about the placement and use of eating utensils in American culture that would be helpful to those from another culture?

I. How do you show by gesture how tall a person is? Do you use the same gesture to indicate the height of an animal? Ask members of other cultures these same questions.

J. If you are able to observe speakers of several different languages in a relaxed and informal situation, replicate Jourard's experiment concerning tactile behavior (see page 155).

K. What are the hesitation forms in other languages which are used like English "uh . . . uh . . ."?

L. Over a short period of time observe your use of space (proxemics) in conversations with others. Is it the same with all speakers? If not, on what basis does it differ?

M. If you have lived or traveled in another country (with or without knowledge of the language spoken there), what were the most unsettling intercultural communication problems you encountered?

Note

1. For an enlightening discussion of the Sapir-Whorf hypothesis and examples of studies that tend to support Whorf's thesis of linguistic relativity, see Hoijer (1954) and Kluckhohn (1961).

5

Current Trends and Issues in Language Teaching

Good teachers always want to make use of the most effective method of teaching and the best instructional materials available. Teachers of English to speakers of other languages are no exception. However, the search for the best method is reminiscent of the search for the Holy Grail; indeed, at times it has appeared that proponents of certain pedagogical methods have been just as fanatic. Although the search for the 'one best method' has been as devoutly pursued as that in the chivalrous quest, it has also been as frustratingly unsuccessful. That this discussion has been going on for some time is evidenced by the appearance of Otto Jespersen's *How to Teach a Foreign Language* in 1904 and that of Harold Palmer in 1917 with the title and lengthy subtitle *The Scientific Study & Teaching of Languages: A Review of the Factors and Problems Connected with the Learning and Teaching of Modern Languages with an Analysis of the Various Methods Which May be Adopted in Order to Attain Satisfactory Results*. Marckwardt (1965) describes what is often thought of as a rather modern approach toward language teaching that appeared as long ago as 1622 in the *Grammaire Angloise* of George Mason but which is in effect a form of pattern practice:

> Give me my doublet — hosen, shooes, pointes, cloake. . . .
> Will you your bootes? — spurres? boot-hosen? . . . Bring me a
> cleane towel — napkin, handkerchief. . . . God be praised, I
> am ready.

Why are there differing views of what may or may not be an effective method of teaching a second language? Where have these various methods come from? Why is there no one best method? These questions will be addressed in this chapter. The discussion is not meant to be exhaustive, merely indicative of current trends and issues in teaching languages, with particular reference to English as a second or foreign language.

Language Teaching as Related to Linguistics and Psychology

Wardhaugh (1968) has rightly observed that language teaching involves at least three disciplines: linguistics, psychology, and pedagogy. Linguistics provides information about language in general and about the specific language being taught; psychology describes how learning takes place; and pedagogy blends the information from linguistics and psychology into a compatible 'method' of presentation in the classroom. Since the disciplines of linguistics and psychology have changed their theoretical viewpoints from time to time, pedagogical methods reflecting these disciplines have also changed. Therefore, the answer to the question posed above — ''Why is there no one best method of second language teaching?'' — is, at least in part, that too little is known with assurance about what language is and how it is learned, and too little is known about the best way to teach. What may today seem the best means of teaching a second language may not remain so in the light of new findings in the fields of linguistics and psychology.

Let us now look at the major changes that have occurred in linguistics and psychology that bear upon pedagogical matters. Since the beginning of the century, three major approaches to linguistic study have been discernible: the *traditional*, the *structural*, and the *transformational-generative*. These have been more or less paralleled in language teaching pedagogy by the *grammar-translation* method, the *audio-lingual* method, and the *cognitive code-learning* method.

The traditional linguistic approach was based on an analysis of the written literary language in which grammatical descriptions tended to be prescriptive in tone; and the rules were generally stated in terms of Latin grammar.

The structural approach, which flourished in the 1940s and 50s and which reacted strongly against the traditional emphasis upon the written language, placed major stress on the empirical analysis of speech data. Structuralists described many non-Indo-European languages, emphasizing the great differences among languages, and they accepted the behavioristic attitude that language is learned behavior, that the mind is a *tabula rasa* (a blank tablet) upon which language is engraved through habit-forming practice.

In the late 1950s and early 60s the transformational-generative linguists, epitomized by Noam Chomsky (1957, 1965), turned the study of linguistics around once more. Their approach differs from that of the structuralists in several ways: it proposes 'rules' for generating sentences which are expressed in an abstract formalism similar to that of mathematics and logic; it searches for the universal characteristics of languages, emphasizing the similarities between languages rather than their differences; and it views the ability to learn language as an innate characteristic of man, thereby returning to a rational view of the universe, eschewed by the structuralists but held, in the main, by traditionalists.

Learning theory in the early study of psychology emphasized the importance of mental discipline, and meaning and memorization. One of the early approaches to learning is that of Edward Thorndike, which stressed the association of ideas and transfer of learning. Then came behaviorism or stimulus-response psychology, most often associated with B. F. Skinner, which supports the concept of learning through reinforcement and conditioning. The behaviorists hold that conditioning is of overriding importance, and they strongly support the concept of overlearning, that is, constant practice until responses to particular verbal cues are automatic. The more recent cognitive psychol-

ogy, exemplified by Jean Piaget's studies in language development, focuses on the inherent capabilities of the human mind and
its creative power. For this reason, cognitivists are characterized as mentalistic, in contrast to behaviorists who are often
referred to as mechanistic.

Language pedagogy reflects a blending of the linguistic and
psychological theories popular at a given time. Thus, *grammar-
translation* was reinforced by the emphasis of the traditionalists
on written language and the then current acceptance on the part
of psychologists of the importance of mental discipline. A strong
reaction against this emphasis upon the written language in traditional linguistic studies and against the grammar-translation
methodology laid the foundation for the *direct method* which
concerns itself primarily with the spoken language and pays little
or no attention to grammatical rules. Only the language being
learned is used in the classroom in this approach, which has
never been closely associated with any particular 'school' of
linguistics. Habit formation as essential to learning, an accepted
tenet of behaviorism, combined with the description of linguistic
patterns provided by the structural linguists, resulted in the
popular 'pattern practice' of the *audio-lingual* method. As
structuralism has given way to a transformational-generative
base in linguistics and as behaviorism has been challenged by
cognitive psychology, the *cognitive code-learning* approach has
emerged, in which more attention is paid to the reasoning
process and the formulation and application of rules.

The outline below summarizes the characteristics of second
and foreign language teaching in relation to the three periods of
linguistic theory.

Traditional: Use of a Latin model for grammatical explanations;
emphasis on reading and writing rather than on speaking; learning about language through grammar-translation rather than
learning to use the language for communication; language learning as a mental discipline with memorization of vocabulary lists
and grammatical paradigms given high priority.

Structural: View of the human mind as a *tabula rasa* on which language is engraved through conditioning; major attention paid to spoken language; audio-lingual approach with emphasis on practice of forms and arrangements rather than on meaning content; avoidance of errors; inductive approach in practice; emphasis on contrastive analysis of native language of the learner and the language to be learned as a means of predicting or accounting for speaker errors.

Transformational-Generative: Recognition of the innate capacity of humans to learn language and to create utterances never heard; errors accepted as a natural part of the learning process and a means of discovering students' learning strategies; more attention paid to the meaning of what is being learned than formerly; reasoned application of rules through a deductive approach.

Contrastive Analysis and Error Analysis

One of the most vociferous controversies in recent years in the application of linguistics to language teaching has concerned the place of contrastive analysis — the detailed comparison and contrast of the language of the learner with the language to be learned (the target language). Wardhaugh (1970) describes two hypotheses of contrastive analysis: the 'strong' and the 'weak'. The strong hypothesis takes the position that a contrastive study will enable one to *predict* points of difficulty in learning because of differences between the two languages (Lado, 1957). As a consequence, those supporting this strong hypothesis believe that teaching materials can be written which will be extremely effective in overcoming such difficulties (Fries, 1945). The weak version of contrastive analysis does not advocate its use as a predictive tool but simply to explain the source of problems which occur. However, from the failure of contrastive analysis to explain certain errors made by learners of a second language, as pointed out by Ritchie (1968), has come a tremendous interest in 'error analysis', now a fertile field of research (Corder, 1967;

Dulay and Burt, 1972; Richards, 1971, 1974). Schachter (1974), on the other hand, has demonstrated that the study of errors provides insufficient evidence for abandoning contrastive analysis because of the 'avoidance phenomenon' inherent in error analysis: language learners will not make errors on what would have been predicted by contrastive analysis to be difficult items because they will simply avoid using the construction altogether.

Selinker (1972) has taken another approach to those errors that cannot be immediately accounted for by contrastive analysis. His 'interlanguage' thesis is that there are several stages in the acquisition of a second language (interlanguages) which can be observed. Such developing stages reveal the nature of the language learning process and at the same time exhibit errors made in the acquisition process that are not related to interference from the native language (overgeneralization of target language 'rules', for example).

Linguistic theory has not yet reached the point where linguistic descriptions of all languages are easily available and in such a form as to permit absolute contrastive analysis. What seems sure, as Ferguson (1968) has stated, is that "contrastive analysis is basic to all linguistics since only by this approach can a general theory of language ('language universals') be constructed and only with at least implicit contrastive analysis can a particular language be fully characterized."

A Balanced Approach

Theories of linguistics and psychology are not what the teacher actually takes into the classroom; language teaching is much more than a mere blending of these theories. Learning depends upon many variables which cannot be controlled, such as the age of the students, size of class, motivation of both students and teachers, the training of the teachers, the personality of the teachers, and so forth. Thus, no one approach can be expected to produce the same results in all cases; nor should one approach be used to the total exclusion of another. The most effective aspects of the grammar-translation, audio-lingual, and cognitive approaches can usually be seen in all classrooms in which learning is taking place.

In defense of an eclectic approach, Hammerly (1975:17) notes that an absolute choice between a deductive and an inductive approach is unnecessary:

> Following the current fashion maybe ignores one important fact: that certain structures are most amenable to a deductive approach while others — many others — can be learned very well by an inductive approach.

and Bolinger (1968:41) decries the reliance on linguistic theory which has tended to produce the pigeonholing of language teaching into various 'methods'. He says,

> A professional is entitled to a mind of his own. He can be grateful for linguistic controversy precisely *because* it gives him a choice. . . . Teaching, like life, has its own criteria by which it integrates for its own needs, and it should not bother language teachers whether they are clean enough to draw straight theoretical lines around.

Carroll (1971) has synthesized the most useful aspects of various psychological theories into what he, as a psychologist, terms the *cognitive habit-formation* approach, accommodating the reasoning aspects of language acquisition to the essential practice necessary for language learning. He also points out that misunderstandings have arisen in the application of psychology to language learning (1971:111).

> On the *formation* of habits, the audiolingual theory assumed that practice and repetition were the crucial factors. But it was found long ago in psychology that practice and repetition are not crucial to learning, although they have certain roles to play. *Successive* repetition of the same response is, in fact, generally the wrong way to "stamp in" a habit; there are few kinds of learning where this is effective. Evocation of the response on a number of aperiodic, widely-spaced occasions, with interpolation of different material in the intervals, is a

much more effective method of strengthening a habit, but such a method has been insufficiently employed in pattern drills.

Carroll's approach seems to have gained wide acceptance among teachers who desire a less mechanistic approach but who also feel the need for habit-forming activities.

Innovations in Language Teaching

Stevick (1976:104), who has made outstanding contributions to the language teaching profession, has confessed to deserting the pedagogical territories of Audiolinguia and Cognitia for Terra Incognita, in which he has found new perspectives on language teaching not limited to the application of linguistics and psychology. In his pedagogical travels he has encountered two quite different approaches to language learning which he finds effective: Community Language Learning and The Silent Way.

Community Language Learning provides a strong incentive for students to communicate in order to belong to the 'community' of students in the group. In this method students are seated in a circle and ask questions or make comments in their native language on any topic of interest to them. The teacher (counselor-teacher in this approach) translates these questions or comments into the target language (the language being learned) and the students repeat them. The sentences that develop in this fashion are analyzed by the teacher, and by taking notes of the teacher's analysis students develop their own reference text. This method is an application of a more general approach to the learning process called Counseling-Learning (Curran, 1972), in which the 'counseling response' on the part of the teacher plays an essential role. Stevick says of this role:

> This response from the teacher may take different forms, depending upon circumstances. If we are willing to learn it, and to explore its uses in our work, I believe that it can prove to be a key concept in a psychodynamic view of foreign language teaching. (1975:72)

Gattegno's Silent Way, which Stevick has also found to be a viable means of teaching language, involves the manipulation of colored rods and the use of color-coded wall charts, demanding at times quite complex uses of language without the oral intervention of the teacher, who remains silent except for the initial modeling of new words.

Stevick has perhaps exerted the strongest influence today on the language teaching profession in attempting to induce teachers to accept what he calls "a new way of seeing." He warns that this is not to be an abandonment of old ways or necessarily the development of new ones, but "something simpler and profoundly more difficult," which he identifies at one point (1975) as "a psychodynamic view" of teaching. He emphasizes that the personal relationship between students, as well as the personal relationship between the teacher and the students, is of utmost importance; and he says it is vital to place "principles of learning" (looking at the teaching-learning situation from the point of view of the student) before "principles of teaching" (looking at the situation from the point of view of the teacher).

It is clear, then, that attitudes toward language teaching are changing. More attention is being paid to preparing teachers to be flexible in their teaching, to accept alternative ways of teaching, and above all to place more emphasis upon the teacher-student relationship and its effects on the learning process.

An early voice crying for change in method, and pleading for more communication and less mechanical drill in language teaching, was Clifford Prator (1965), who delineated a manipulation-communication scale, looking away from the purely systematic practice of patterns to the use of language in a more meaningful way. That early article and other writings since then (cf. Paulston and Bruder, 1975, 1976) have led teachers to the conclusion that although practice is necessary and drills remain an essential part of the language classroom, they no longer must be mechanical and meaningless. The best classroom activities are those that are contextualized; they are not merely simple repetitive exercises made up of long lists of unrelated sentences illustrating a particular linguistic form or arrangement of forms. The goal *within* the language classroom today is to prepare the student to use the language *outside* the classroom.

There is nothing so very new in all of this. Jespersen's (1904) *How to Teach a Foreign Language* placed great emphasis upon questions and answers as a means of eliciting the use of language by students. These could be teacher-student conversations or student-student exchanges. Although his questions and answers were often based on reading material, his admonitions are also pertinent for oral exercises as long as the content is kept within the experience of the student.

> If this question-exercise is used and all its possibilities for variation exhausted in the right way — with liveliness, tact and constant consideration for the pupils' standpoint — it gives ample and abundant opportunities for the teacher not only to talk to, but with, the pupils in a foreign language; and notice that it is not "talking to the pupil in a language he does not understand" — this fear is often expressed by those who have misgivings as to the advisability of conversational exercises at an early stage — but from the very beginning nothing is said which the pupil cannot be required to understand and to answer intelligently in the same language. (105)

It should be noted that Jespersen is concerned with what the Counseling-Learning approach terms 'counseling response' when he states that the exercise should be used "with liveliness, tact and constant consideration for the pupils' standpoint." However, in keeping with Stevick's statement that teachers need not dispense with the old ways, we find that attention is still being paid to dialogues (Rigg, 1976), vocabulary (Richards, 1976), and translation (Taylor, 1972).

Emphasis upon the Learner

It seems clear that the perspective is shifting from teaching to learning and from the teacher to the learner. Studies of the learner's language, the learner's errors, and the role of language input by teachers and others with whom the learner comes in contact have elevated the learner to a much more crucial position in the language teaching process. This emphasis upon the learner's point of view is reflected in Wilkins's (1976) 'notional syllabuses', which are based on communication-oriented categories which are useful to students, such as expressions of time and location, approval and disapproval, concession, and personal emotions. Wilkins does not imply, however, that the use of notional syllabuses will preclude the need for grammatical content.

> It is taken here to be almost axiomatic that the acquisition of the grammatical system of a language remains a most important element in language learning. The grammar is the means through which linguistic creativity is ultimately achieved and an inadequate knowledge of the grammar would lead to a serious limitation on the capacity for communication. A notional syllabus, no less than a grammatical syllabus, must seek to ensure that the grammatical system is properly assimilated by the learner. We do not express language functions in isolation. . . . What we can express through language still depends on, among other things, how far we have mastered the grammatical rules that underlie the production of utterances. (66–67)

The desired objective for English-as-a-second-language students in an English-speaking country is for them to be able to use the language as native speakers use it, since they will be surrounded by native speakers of English. Therefore, the purpose is what Lambert (1963) calls *integrative*: that is, these learners intend to become an integral part of the society that uses English as a medium of communication. Stevick (1976) refers to this as *receptive* learning, which involves matters of attitude and emotion rather than materials and techniques. Although the objective in learning English in a non-English-speaking country may not be as all inclusive — what Lambert has referred to as *instrumental* rather than integrative — it still aims at communicative competence of a certain level.

Language teaching is an exciting, dynamic field of endeavor; and dynamism by its very nature portends change. The end result of the changes going on in this field at present is a new perspective, one that tends toward less dogmatism and more flexibility. Therefore, it behooves the second-language teacher to be prepared to handle situations as they arise. No one method can be said to be better than another in any absolute sense. What everyone seems to be saying is that it is the teacher who makes the crucial difference. Carroll (1971:113) puts it this way:

> In language teaching, as in other kinds of instruction, probably the critical factor in success is in managing the learning procedures of the student in such a way that at any given stage of learning the student is learning just what he needs to learn, being given the appropriate strategy for that learning to take place, and being properly reinforced in that learning. Any extreme, one-sided theory of language teaching tends to distract the teacher from his task and make him neglectful of certain essential operations in teaching. This is perhaps one of the reasons why comparisons between different teaching methods and procedures are seldom productive of any large average differences favoring one method or another.

Close (1977:183) says that teachers should beware of "banners and bandwagons" which fanatically espouse one or another method, and he offers the following advice:

> In this human world, I suppose that banners and bandwagons are inevitable; but let us keep them in their place. Certainly every 'method', from the Direct to the Notional, that I have mentioned . . . has made an important contribution to the science-and-art of English-language teaching. What we ourselves may need is more of the 'breadth of understanding' that will help us to keep it all in balance and to find the right method for each particular occasion.

Teachers have individual personalities and abilities; students are of different ages and have differing interests. Effective teachers, no matter what their 'method' may be, are those who think of the student as the most important ingredient in the teaching-learning process and adapt their approach to students and to circumstances. As I have said elsewhere (Robinett, 1977:43),

> The success of second language teachers is ultimately measured by how well their students have learned to communicate in the second language. I believe that success can best be attained by teachers who possess a sound knowledge of their subject matter and express warmth, sensitivity, and tolerance in imparting their knowledge.

There is no one method of achieving this success.

Exercises

A. If possible, observe several language classes. Were they all taught in the same way? If they were, why do you think that was so? If not, what was the reason for the difference? Can you classify the method(s) being used as any of the following: grammar-translation, direct, audio-lingual, cognitive habit formation? What techniques were employed (drills, games, dialogues, role playing, etc.)?

B. If you have been a language teacher for several years, has your method of teaching changed since you began? The techniques you have used? If so, how? If not, why not? (Obtaining consistently good results could be one reason for not changing, couldn't it?)

C. Obtain a set of compositions that non-native speakers of English have written and analyze the types of errors they contain. Are they the same kinds of errors native speakers of English of comparable age and experience would make? List the errors that seem to be caused by interference from the student's native language (if you happen to know something about that language). Do you have any explanation for any of the other errors?

D. If you wanted to imitate a German accent (or that of some other language) in English, as actors sometimes are required to do, how would you go about it?

E. Is the following exercise deductively or inductively organized?

> Pronounce the plurals of the words listed below. Add /əz/ if the final sound in the word is any of the following: /s, z, š, ž, tš, dž/; otherwise, add /z/ if the final sound is voiced and /s/ if the final sound is voiceless.

1. class	4. dog	7. girl
2. cat	5. dish	8. book
3. bench	6. chair	9. cup

F. Find an example of a deductively and an inductively organized exercise in a language-teaching textbook. Why do you think they were done in that particular way? Would it have been better to have presented them differently?

6

Acquiring
Second Language Skills

What does learning a second or foreign language actually entail? Although little is known with certainty about the nature of second language acquisition, a growing interest in the field, as evidenced by such publications as that of Brown (1976) and the survey article by Cook (1978), bodes well for a better understanding of the process. At any rate, the end result of second or foreign language learning is the ability to comprehend and produce the second language in its spoken and/or written form. This, in turn, involves the acquisition of some or all of the receptive and productive skills traditionally categorized as listening, speaking, reading, and writing. In this chapter we will examine these skills closely in an attempt to determine what they comprise; in the following chapter (Teaching the Communication Skills) we will outline specific techniques for teaching the various receptive and productive skills.

As we have stated previously, the grammatical, sound, and lexical systems of language do not exist autonomously; they are aspects of a unified whole by means of which the peculiarly human system of communication operates. Just so, the four language skills are interlocked and interdependent, although for particular reasons some learners may desire only a reading or a speaking knowledge of the language. It is interesting to note that various studies have shown that students tend to learn what it is they are taught (Carroll, 1966; Scherer and Wertheimer, 1964). If they receive instruction in speaking, they learn best to speak the language;

if they are taught primarily to read, they learn best to read. Thus, any method that tends to emphasize one or the other of the language skills will tend to result in greater learning of that skill.

For pedagogical purposes one or the other of the various skills may be emphasized separately in order to give students practice in those in which they are especially deficient. However, each of the skills demands a synthesis of linguistic and cultural knowledge necessary for interpreting language (comprehending it through the ear or the eye) or transmitting it (producing it in speech or in writing). Figure 3 shows the interrelation of the various means through which language operates in the communicative situation. It should always be remembered that spoken and written language — two distinct modes of communication — are not exact equivalents; we will return later to a discussion of the differences between them.

Interference from the First Language

In acquiring the ability to communicate in a second language, interference from the first or native language plays a part. Thus, in the early stages of acquiring English, Spanish speakers tend to pronounce *thing* as *sing* and *thank* as *sank*. The explanation for this is that (non-Castillian) Spanish contains no sound which is the equivalent of /θ/, the initial consonant sound in *thing*; therefore, these Spanish speakers substitute for that initial sound the one in their own language that seems most similar: /s/. Comparisons of the phonological systems of various languages with English explain many other substitutions that speakers of specific languages consistently make in pronouncing English. Although there is some controversy about the absolute predictive power of a contrastive analysis of the native language and the language to be learned, there is little doubt that the phonological system is most susceptible to this kind of interference; it is therefore the aspect of language to which contrastive linguistic information can probably be applied most productively.

In light of interference theory, speakers of other languages will

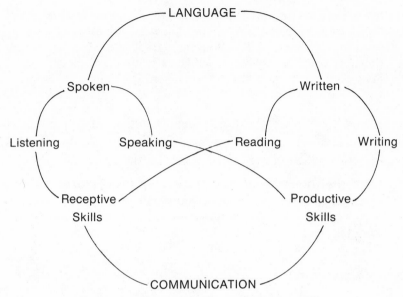

Figure 3. Interrelation of communication skills.

have varying degrees of difficulty in recognizing the significant features of the English phonological system. This is true not only of the segmental features (the vowels and consonants) but also of the suprasegmental or prosodic features (stress, intonation, rhythm).

G. D. Allen (1975), in a discussion of perceptions of rhythmic patterns in various languages, refers to a study by Jakobson, Fant, and Halle (1969) in which they found that speakers of different languages, when listening to sounds grouped together rhythmically, perceived these sounds in ways that conformed to the rhythmic patterns of their own languages. They made the following observations:

> Interference by the language pattern affects even our responses to non-speech sounds. Knocks produced at even intervals, with every third louder, are as groups of three separated by a pause. The pause is usually claimed by a Czech to fall before the louder knock, by a Frenchman to fall after the louder; while a Pole hears the pause one knock after the louder. The different perceptions correspond exactly to the position of the word stress in the languages involved; in Czech

the stress is on the initial syllable, in French, on the final and in Polish, on the penult. When the knocks are produced with equal loudness but with a longer interval after every third, the Czech attributes greater loudness to the first knock, the Pole, to the second, and the Frenchman, to the third. (Jakobson, Fant, and Halle, 10–11)

Although not all experiments bear out these findings, Allen points out that where attention is paid to listening in the "speech mode," this reaction may be general; he then observes (84):

Rhythm functions mainly to organize the information-bearing elements of the utterance into a coherent package, thus permitting speech communication to proceed efficiently. Rhythm therefore does not carry much *linguistic* information, other than helping to signal the language of the speaker; without rhythmic organization, however, the linguistic message would be difficult to transfer.

Lack of control of English rhythm makes speakers of English from India difficult for other English speakers to understand; their timing is so different from that of standard speakers that it is not easy to comprehend the content of what they say. This has little to do with their basic linguistic competence, but from the point of view of actual language performance they do not conform to what native speakers have come to expect as an intelligible norm.

Difficulty in orienting to the 'set' of a second language causes difficulty in aspects of the language other than the sound system. Students whose native language calls for word order which is different from that of English or which, unlike English, utilizes many inflectional changes in words to designate different functions must have practice in orienting themselves to English grammatical signals; in other words, they must learn the 'rules' that govern the English language. Lack of control, either receptively or productively, over such signals may well interfere with communication.

Acquiring the Receptive Skills

Let us now consider each of the language skills separately (listening, speaking, reading, and writing), discussing their essential characteristics and what must be mastered to become fluent in their use. The order in which we choose to treat the various skills is probably not important. We could follow the traditional sequence of listening, speaking, reading, and writing; or we could begin with the productive skills (speaking and writing) and then deal with the receptive skills (listening and reading). Since most texts, no matter in what order they describe the various skills, have tended to place more emphasis upon the productive skills, we have deliberately chosen to discuss first the receptive skills of listening and reading, not because they are *more* important than the others, but because this sequencing may demonstrate that they are *equally* important in learners' attempts to develop communicative competence in the language. This sequencing is not to be interpreted as the order in which skills necessarily should be acquired. As has already been mentioned, the purpose for which the language is being learned will dictate the emphasis given particular skills and probably also the order in which they should be introduced. However, learning one skill seems to reinforce the learning of another.[1]

The terms 'productive' and 'receptive' should not be equated with 'active' and 'passive' as has sometimes been done in the past. As we will see, there is just as much activity in the exercise of receptive skills (listening and reading) as in that of their productive counterparts (speaking and writing); the activity is simply internal and not directly observable.

Listening

The skill of listening with comprehension is an essential part of communication and basic to second language learning. The goal of the listening skill is to enable the learner to perceive the second language in the way native speakers perceive it. To do this, as V. F. Allen (1966) has pointed out, there is a need for listening practice that is not the usual kind of mimicry or memorization exercises often used in classrooms and in language laboratories. The listening practice she describes is that in which the student "is to listen with full attention to something that interests and challenges him; he is to get at the meaning of what he hears, and then produce a response that shows he has understood."

What are the characteristics of English that the listener must become familiar with in order to "get at the meaning of what he hears"? Obviously, they involve the grammar, sounds, and vocabulary of English. What peculiarities of the language might be bothersome to a non-English speaker? We will begin with examples from the sound system because it is this 'noise' that first strikes listeners' ears. Clearly, listeners must be able to identify the intonational devices of the language (for example, rising intonation is often, but not exclusively, a signal of a question). They must be aware of the means by which emphasis or contrast is signaled (stressed versus unstressed words), and the significant contrasts in sounds (/p/ and /b/; /iy/ and /i/; etc.).

At the same time, the listener must be alert to such grammatical signals as those indicating tense (*-ed* endings or irregular past forms of verbs); number (*-s* endings or irregular plural forms of nouns); modificational relationships (*chocolate milk*, *milk chocolate*); questions and negatives (with or without the auxiliary *do*); sentence coordination and subordination.

While attending to the signals both of the sound system and of the grammatical system, listeners must simultaneously process the meanings of the lexical items in the utterance. For example, they must be aware that *dog*, *cat*, and *mouse* refer to animate but nonhuman beings; that *listen* and *hear* are similar but different aspects of one of the five senses; that *pitcher* can refer to a container for liquids or to a specific player in the game of baseball; and that the idiom "little pitchers have big ears" does not refer to either of the *pitchers* just mentioned.

In addition to these linguistic prerequisites for listening comprehension, there is the need for understanding the culture of English speakers. Language always occurs within a cultural and social setting of some sort, and it must be interpreted in the light of this social and cultural environment. Listeners must realize, for example, that they are not being insulted when people who are not close friends call them by their first names; this behavior is a reflection of the relative informality of the culture of the United States.

Differences between the spoken and written language are considerable in English and will be discussed in detail in the section in this chapter dealing with reading. However, we should mention here that if learners have been exposed only to written language, the first contact with the spoken language can be a shock. There are countless stories of those who, having actively pursued the study of English in their country (with little or no access to spoken English), are absolutely unable to understand anything when first hearing native English speakers talk.

Since listening is an essential factor in achieving communicative competence, it deserves its fair share of specific attention in the second language curriculum. Allowing for practice in listening calls attention to its importance in the language acquisition process and provides students with structured practice in this receptive skill before they are plunged into the 'real' world. Activities for developing this skill will be dealt with in the following chapter, but a few of the problems involved in listening comprehension must be mentioned here.

Two of the most important characteristics of spoken English are the reduction of vowel quality in words occurring in the stream of speech and the use of contractions. These processes were discussed in Chapter Two (The Sound System), but the following examples will serve as a reminder of the differences in pronunciation in words and phrases like *him*, *do not know*, *might have* when they occur in isolation or within the stream of speech.

Did Jim give *him* the book?   /him/ becomes /im/
I *don't know*; he *might've*.   /duw nat now/ becomes
                                     /downt now/ or /dǝnów/
                                     /mayt hæv/ becomes
                                     /máytǝv/

The presence of WH words (*who*, *which*, *when*, *what*, *where*, etc.) should alert listeners to the possibility that they may be directly or indirectly asked to respond to an utterance. Below are some direct and indirect questions that might evoke the responses in parentheses.

Who was there? (I don't know.)
I wonder who was there. (I don't know.) or
(I do, too.)
I'd certainly like to know who was there.
(So would I.) or (I would, too.)

Students also need to listen for stress, which often pinpoints the important components of a message (Shillan, 1967).

I lost my cáp yesterday. It was my réd cap, the one I álways wéar.

Listening should have as one of its objectives the development of the ability to predict what may be expected next in the stream of speech. This includes the concept of collocations of words, that is, sets of vocabulary items with some type of semantic relationship. The term *collocation* as used by British linguists implies that certain words have the mutual expectancy of other words. Part of the meaning of *dark*, for example, is its collocation with *night*. From the point of view of vocabulary, then, this calls for the development of vocabulary sets that collocate with each other so that when listeners hear one word in the set, they are prepared to expect others in the set. For example, when they hear the word *bank*, they can also expect to hear words or phrases like the following, which are commonly associated with it in one of its meanings: *deposit*, *withdraw*; *money*, *cash*; *checks*, *travelers' checks*; *teller*, *manager*; *checking account*, *savings account*; *interest*; *loan*; and, perhaps, even *free gifts*. From the point of view of grammar, the likelihood of certain items occurring with others is also to be expected. Very commonly a noun follows a definite or indefinite article, and an adjective or adverb regularly follows the adverb *very*. Likewise, when the situation calls for a conditional utterance (*if* . . .), listeners should probably expect to hear in the next phrase one of the modal auxiliaries (*may*, *might*, *could have*, *should have*, etc.).

> If he arrives on time, we can (might, should, etc.) . . .
>
> If he had arrived on time, we could have (might have, should have, etc.) . . .

The attitudes of speakers toward what they are saying is sometimes revealed to listeners through linking words and phrases such as *but*, *however*, *as a consequence*, etc.

> The washing machine is out of order, but (the speaker is not worried) the repairman is coming right away.
>
> The washing machine is out of order; and (the speaker is worried) the repairman won't be able to come for a week.

When people actually speak to each other, they do not enunciate each word clearly; they do not always speak in complete sentences; they *do* falter, repeat themselves, interrupt themselves, and in general do not conform to the usual language samples in textbooks. The following two examples illustrate this point. These are taken from a radio program in which the commentator (the first example) reads a prepared introduction of the second speaker (second example), who then, quite obviously, proceeds to speak extemporaneously.

> Energy — oil, gas, electricity — is going to be in short supply for a long time; and whatever energy is available will cost a lot more. With these facts in mind, architects and engineers looked again at the buildings they had designed and found them wanting. One study showed that the average energy use for buildings put up in the late 1960's was more than twice that of structures built fifteen years earlier. In other words, in many cases the newer the building the more energy it uses. R——— S——— has analyzed energy consumption for the American Institute of Architects.
>
> Building costs are usually separated from operating costs, and if you've had any experience with a, let's say, a suburban school referendum, you'll know that the only question there is how much is that going to cost, not how much is it going to cost to run. Same thing is true with office buildings. Many of them

are built for a very fast sale and turnover, and the builder's only concern is to build as inexpensively as he can, get rid of it, and leave the problems to whoever comes later.

Note that the definite article *the* is omitted,from the phrase *same thing*, and that the utterance ''you'll know that the only question there is'' can be ambiguous when reading the sentence. However, when heavy stress is placed on *there* (as was the case in the spoken version), that word can only be interpreted as the adverb of place and not the expletive. Therefore, it is not ambiguous when heard. Opportunities to listen to samples of 'real' language, like the second example, will better prepare students to listen for these differentiating clues and enable them to react more quickly to the spoken language.

Typical classroom activities often do not provide students with the kind of listening practice necessary to cope with 'real' language. Henzl's study (1973) of foreign language classroom speech shows rather conclusively that teachers have a particular way of talking in their classes and that the classroom provides fertile ground for inflicting such 'teacher talk' on students. She found that teachers tend to simplify their language and limit their vocabulary to the particular social situations common to the classroom. (See also Gaies, 1976, and Steyaert, 1978.) Teachers, in reality, should take particular pains to avoid such simplification and to provide opportunities for students to hear the kind of language that will prepare them for situations outside the classroom. If the teaching is taking place in a non-English-speaking country, the teacher should try to anticipate the kind of English the students will hear when the opportunity arises for them to be in an English-speaking country.

In summary, listening involves the simultaneous processing of linguistic and cultural information, and necessitates specific practice in digesting such information.

Reading

Most descriptions of reading imply that there are two distinct stages in the process: that of relating the graphic symbols (in

English, the alphabetic representations) to sounds in the spoken language and that of extracting meaning from these graphic symbols. Wardhaugh (1969:133) takes issue with this view of reading.

> There is little reason to suppose that there are two such discrete, non-overlapping stages. Reading is instead an active process, in which the reader must make an active contribution by drawing upon and using concurrently various abilities that he has acquired.

What are these various abilities that are inherent in the reading process? Wardhaugh describes them specifically.

> When a person reads a text, he is attempting to discover the meaning of what he is reading by using the visual clues of spelling, his knowledge of probabilities of occurrence, his contextual-pragmatic knowledge, and his syntactic and semantic competence to give a meaningful interpretation to the text.

Although the process of extracting meaning from the printed page is not directly observable, an attempt has been made to discover what happens internally by observing external indications of the reading process, that is, by observing eye movements. Research done by Oller (1972) and Oller and Tullius (1973) using Eye Movement Photography shows that it is neither regressions nor fixations that slow down reading rate in readers of English as a second or foreign language but *length of fixation*. This suggests that the longer fixation is needed to process the semantic and syntactic information with which readers are being bombarded. These findings tend to dispel the oft-held notion that students need practice in developing the habit of making fewer fixations per line. Oller and Tullius summarize their findings thus: "It appears that the core of the problem for the non-native reader is essentially one of central processing rather than peripheral skill."

A discussion of Wardhaugh's "visual clues of spelling," "knowledge of probabilities of occurrence," "contextual-pragmatic knowledge," and "syntactic and semantic competence" may lead to at least some understanding of this "central processing."

"VISUAL CLUES OF SPELLING"

The use of "visual clues of spelling" necessitates learning the letters of the alphabet and the spelling patterns that English uses to symbolize sounds and sound combinations as a preliminary step in the decoding process of reading. Although English is alphabetically symbolized, which means that it utilizes the principle of a letter to represent a sound, there is relatively poor 'fit' between sound and graphic symbol. Although there is sufficient evidence to dispute the idea that English spelling is chaotic, nonetheless, in English there is not the one-to-one relationship between sound and symbol that is characteristic of languages with better 'fit', such as Finnish or Spanish. Spelling clues in English are complex. Consider, for example, word pairs such as *bit-bite*, *mad-made*, and *not-note*, in which the 'silent' *e* signals a change in vowel sound.[2]

One of the most obvious difficulties for non-native speakers in using spelling cues appears when the students' language is not alphabetically represented. J. Ronayne Cowan (personal communication) thinks that Persian students may have more than the usual difficulty in reading English because of conditioning by their own orthography which is nonalphabetic and written from right to left.

"PROBABILITIES OF OCCURRENCE"

The importance of vocabulary has always been emphasized in teaching reading. Selecting vocabulary through the use of word frequency lists such as those of Thorndike and Lorge (1944), Michael West (1953), or Carroll, Davies, and Richman (1971), or inserting word glosses or vocabulary lists is common practice in the preparation of reading materials. However, Wardhaugh's reference to "probabilities of occurrence," in addition to mere frequency of occurrence, includes the concept of semantic collocations, which has already been mentioned in relation to the listening process. The British use of the term is generally limited to vocabulary, but in a larger sense the "probabilities of occurrence" may include syntactic signals of subject-verb word order, nouns following prepositions, and the like.

This concept is akin to the idea of "expectancy" described by V. F. Allen (1973) as the students' ability to guess what should come next in connected discourse. Syntactic items such as sequence signals (conjunctive adverbs, pronouns, etc.) play an important part in providing such expectancy clues.

The effective use of cloze procedure is certainly dependent upon the concept of "probabilities of occurrence" or "expectancy." Although this procedure has most often been associated with testing, it is equally effective as a teaching device. (See for example, the text by Newmark, et al., 1964.) This procedure forces students to utilize their total linguistic competence. Here again we may be witnessing a means of developing or helping to develop the "central processing" which seems to be part of the reading skill.

"CONTEXTUAL-PRAGMATIC KNOWLEDGE"

The fact that students can read something orally does not mean that they understand what they have read. To make sense of it they must have some practical knowledge of the context of what they are reading. A lack of contextual-pragmatic knowledge bedevils us all. A page of quantum mechanics is as frustrating to me as a page of Chinese, with one difference: I can 'read' the quantum mechanics (that is, I can mouth the words, at least until I reach the very involved symbolic representations); but in Chinese I have not even reached the first level of reading, the ability to translate the characters into their spoken form. With Chinese I lack the ability to react to visual clues. With quantum mechanics I lack pragmatic knowledge.

Morris (1968) says that we often stop short of providing students with this contextual-pragmatic knowledge.

> The major weakness in the reading of ESL students at the secondary level is the fact that, in all too many instances, the initial reading step is performed: the child decodes the symbols and produces the word — and stops. The word fails to trigger *anything* because the concepts it represents to us and to the author do not exist for the child, or they exist in a limited, vague form.

Teachers can prepare students for what they are asked to read. This means explaining cultural concepts with which students may be unfamiliar — a kind of cultural reading readiness, so to speak.

The hypothesis that presenting cultural information beforehand would improve reading comprehension was tested by Gatbonton and Tucker (1971). They found that providing students with cultural concepts, which were implicit in the reading but which Filipino students did not possess, significantly improved their performance on tests of reading comprehension.

It has sometimes been thought useful to present cultural information through reading, but this can be done most effectively when students have reached a point in their reading when this is *all* that is being required of them, that is, they are being asked only to absorb new information, not to puzzle out structures and meanings (Fries and Fries, 1961).

"SYNTACTIC AND SEMANTIC COMPETENCE"

In addition to possessing the ability to 'crack the code' of the writing system (i.e., to interpret the written symbols as meaningful items in the language just as listeners learn to interpret the spoken symbols) it is also taken for granted that reading comprehension depends upon a knowledge of the syntax and semantics of the language. Without a knowledge of grammar and vocabulary, the reader will react to the written page as if it were nothing but a sequence of meaningless words strung together. Furthermore, we have already pointed out that some pragmatic knowledge of the content is necessary to comprehend what is being read.

But why is it that students who have a basic understanding of the syntax and semantics of the spoken language still have trouble reading? And this is exactly what happens to countless nonnative speakers (to say nothing of native speakers). This is especially true at the advanced level where students have gone beyond reading only what they produce orally. A major source of difficulty seems to stem from differences between the spoken and written forms of the language. The misconception that writing is merely 'speech written down' has long since been dispelled, and most people are now willing to agree that speech and writing are two different but related performance models of a given language. There are, in fact, people who may learn one model and not the other. Also, linguists sometimes speak of 'reducing' a language to writing, which implies that something may be omitted in the process.

Reading what is written is in some ways easier and in some ways more difficult than comprehending what is spoken. Norris (1970:23) lists the following features of ease in reading as compared to speech: (1) written forms often differentiate homophones and word junctures that are obscured in speech; (2) dialectal variations in spelling and syntax are few and minor; (3) expository writing makes use of a more limited range of sentence types than speech; (4) writing is permanent, not transient in time; (5) written English provides more background information than does informal speech; and (6) writing does not distract readers by requiring them to formulate a verbal response.

On the other hand, Norris (22) also lists the features of difficulty in reading as compared to speech: (1) words and phrases known orally may not be recognized in print; (2) vocabulary and usage not commonly heard in speech are encountered often in reading; (3) writing uses word order, lexical variation, and other signals to make distinctions signaled in speech by sentence stress, pause, and intonation; (4) writing uses long complete sentences — sentences that employ complex embedding, nominalization, and other syntactic devices; and (5) contextual clues to meaning are necessarily limited to the written text and cannot be derived from the nonverbal situation.

Commenting on the difference between speech and writing, V. F. Allen (1973) mentions transposed elements, prepositional phrases in initial position (often with inverted subject and verb), and participial constructions. She provides the following as examples of these constructions.

Although most people deplore it, the use of graffiti is wide-
spread.
Of special interest to teachers is the Language Methodology
Center.
Funded by the Office of Education, the project will begin on
March 1.

Twaddell (1973) points out that an important distinction needs
to be made between two kinds of reading comprehension: one
where understanding must be absolute (laboratory instructions,
Internal Revenue Service instructions), and the other where
educated guesses will suffice. The latter type seems not to be
emphasized in the teaching of reading, but the ability to accept
vagueness in meaning or of being satisfied with 'getting the
general effect' is necessary for rapid reading.

Povey (1967) provides a humorous illustration of this type of
vague comprehension in an anecdote about a student reading the
story of Rip Van Winkle. The student was disturbed because he
did not know what a sycamore tree was (under which Rip osten-
sibly slept for twenty years). Povey suddenly realized that *he* did
not either; but he also realized that it did not really matter. The
general concept of 'tree' was all that was needed to understand
the story.

The type of reading ability required for comprehending technical writing has received considerable attention lately (Cowan,
1974; Ewer and Hughes-Davies, 1971; Richards, 1976; Widdowson, 1972). This kind of research on the occurrence and frequency of occurrence of specialized syntax and lexicon in technical and scientific writing will surely provide useful insights for
teaching reading in specialized areas.

Lackstrom, et al. (1970) identified differences in the use of
tenses, in the use of definite and indefinite articles, and an abun-
dance of 'stative' passives as special characteristics of technical written English in contradistinction to the spoken language.

Cowan's work reveals some interesting data.

From our very limited analysis of medical texts we already
have indications that certain structures, embedded questions

for example, occur with such low frequency that it would be pointless to emphasize them or even teach them at all.[3]

When discussing the lexical component in technical English, Cowan makes a distinction between technical and subtechnical items. Technical vocabulary is that which is essential to a given discipline and necessarily learned as a by-product of study within that discipline; e.g., *cellulose*, *molecule*, *carbohydrate*, *photosynthesis*. Subtechnical vocabulary, on the other hand, is not discipline-specific but comprises items that are, according to Cowan, "context independent words which occur with high frequency across disciplines"; e.g., *function*, *inference*, *isolate*, *basis*, *presuppose*, *simulate*.

Having now looked at the process of reading, we come to the conclusion that it involves something of a global attack by readers on the printed page just as the listening process involves simultaneous processing of linguistic and cultural information. Clearly, readers draw upon all the abilities delineated in Wardhaugh's definition of reading for what Oller and Tullius call "central processing" and what Eskey (1973) calls "creative synthesis."

Acquiring the Productive Skills

Speaking

Having considered the receptive skills (listening and reading), we now proceed to a discussion of the productive skills, dealing first with speaking. Speaking can be thought of as a mirror image of the listening skill and one for which the same linguistic and cultural knowledge is required. However, it is only a partial image since it involves the added problem of pronunciation, the articulatory production of sounds.

The sounds of speech that are generally assumed to be the basis of pronunciation are the consonants and vowels; but pronunciation also includes the especially important covering patterns of language, the suprasegmental features of stress, pitch, juncture, and rhythm. If students concentrate only on the individual sound segments of English (the *th* sounds, for example), they may produce accurate renditions of these individual sounds but still be grossly misunderstood if the 'tune' of the language is inappropriate. The teacher must, therefore, emphasize all the elements of the sound system in teaching pronunciation: vowels, consonants, semivowels or glides; word and sentence stress; intonation or patterns of voice pitch; juncture or pause; and the characteristic combinations of stressed and unstressed syllables in discourse which produce the rhythm of English.

Statements have often been made that listening should precede speaking, that aural discrimination is a prerequisite for accurate oral production. However, Brière's study (1966) revealed this to be a false assumption, at least insofar as it relates to the discrimination of unaspirated and aspirated /t/ on the part of native speakers of English. They produced the difference more accurately than they recognized the difference in their early attempts.

In Chapter 2 we discussed in detail articulatory techniques for the production of speech sounds in English, including matters of stress, intonation, and rhythm. There is no need to repeat that material here. The vowel charts and face diagrams, such as those in Chapter 2, exemplify the ways in which the articulatory aspects of speaking can be illustrated. However, there are problems associated with speaking that are related to the teaching of pronunciation, so a word about them seems to be in order. First, it has been said that pronunciation is an unpopular subject with teachers (Morley, 1975). It has been my experience that teaching pronunciation is unpopular only with those teachers who are inexperienced in teaching it and those who have had inadequate training in phonetics. Such teachers are unable to diagnose and treat pronunciation problems, and thus become frustrated in their teaching. Teachers, like most human beings, want to succeed at what they are doing; and improving pronunciation in a second language is sometimes a very difficult task.

Morley also makes the comment that many teachers consider pronunciation a bore. If pronunciation is taught through the use of minimal pair distinctions alone (and, unfortunately, this is common practice), it can be boring. But pronunciation should be integrated into all aspects of the language. Although it is most commonly associated with listening and speaking, it can also bear on reading and writing. The orthographic system, the use of punctuation, and differentiation of homographs are related to pronunciation.

It does not matter, in most cases, what aspect of pronunciation is treated first, except that it is my belief that stress and intonation should probably be heavily emphasized early since they provide the distinctive 'tune' of the language. Without control over these elements of the sound system, speakers may be unintelligible even if they produce individual sounds well.

An important aspect of developing speaking skill is the matter of classroom atmosphere. This includes aspects of the affective domain that bear upon learning. In the 1975 Office of Civil Rights guidelines for compliance with the Lau vs. Nichols Supreme Court decision, which requires school districts to provide equal educational opportunities for pupils from non-English speaking backgrounds, the statement is made that "an ESL program does not consider the affective nor cognitive development of the students" at the elementary level and is, therefore, inappropriate. It has been my experience that this is not true. In the late 1940s I wrote an editorial for *Language Learning* entitled "The Importance of Classroom Atmosphere" which reflected the concern of many teacher-trainers with the affective and cognitive development of students. Statements made in that article show that attention was being paid to many of the affective variables that are now recognized as playing a role in language acquisition.

Yorio's classification (1976) of affective variables that influence language learning includes anxiety. Let me quote from my nonrecent editorial to show that teachers have been interested in this domain for many years (Wallace, 1949:73).

> Unless the student feels very much at home with his teacher and with fellow students, he will not be able to achieve the freedom necessary for learning to produce sounds that are strange to him.

> To achieve this free and wholesome atmosphere it is necessary
> for the teacher . . . to give each student a feeling of satisfac-
> tion in attaining some goal, however small, during each class
> hour; to prevent the student from being embarrassed in any
> way; to be as patient as possible with the student's mistakes; to
> encourage those who are having great difficulty.

Another variable Yorio mentions is "self-consciousness."
What did the editorial have to say about that?

> Many students can be corrected time and again without being
> embarrassed, but others must be handled carefully. (74)

Another variable, referred to by Yorio as "ego permeability,"
I prefer to call "challenge level." What was said about that?

> Some [students] can throw themselves into the experience of
> language learning and forget their self-restraint or pride; others
> find this difficult and often impossible. The teacher, in each
> case, needs to discover the utmost capacity of the student in
> this regard and hold the student responsible for this capacity.
> This will provide a goal for each individual which will not be
> beyond his reach. (74)

At this point it seems appropriate to mention Rivers's (1976)
distinction between "natural" and "normal" uses of language in
the classroom because it relates to this matter of self-
consciousness. She says that what we teach in class is the "normal" use of language, the language patterns that conform to
everyday use. The "natural" use of language, on the other hand,
may be very idiosyncratic; it is a much more personal, subjective
use of language. She points out that anxiety and self-
consciousness may develop when we use this kind of language.
The natural use sometimes occurs when students are asked personal questions which may embarrass them. The normal use,
Rivers says, is more objective and less threatening. She admits
that in class, depending upon the relationship between teacher
and students, natural use can occur. But she believes it is best
developed outside the classroom. At any rate, it can only be
used when students are well acquainted with what it is they are
asked to talk or write about. She cautions teachers in regard to

the "natural" use of language in this way: "Some of us, with some classes, will see the flowering of 'natural language use' if we are psychologically willing and prepared for the change in relationship which it brings."

The old adage "Practice makes perfect" is often heard in connection with learning skills of all kinds. Language learning is frequently thought of merely as a motor skill, like tennis or golf. However, we now know that language learning is a cognitive process; reasoning is involved. Therefore, it follows that students cannot be taught a finite set of motions (in this case utterances) which can then be used in that same form in any and all situations. They must learn cognitively to adapt what they have acquired to unique situations. The more practice they have in this kind of adaptation, the better they will be able to operate outside the classroom. To this end, students must be given opportunities to use normal English under many different circumstances.

Writing

Writing bears the same relationship to reading as speaking does to listening; therefore, much of what has been discussed in this chapter concerning reading will also pertain to writing. However, just as speaking differs from listening in that it necessitates the articulation of sounds, so writing demands the production of orthographic symbols, not just their interpretation.

The term *writing* is ambiguous since it is used to refer both to the mechanical act of penmanship and to the very complex process of composition. We will discuss both types of writing in this chapter.

The first stage in the writing process is basic: everyone who wants to do any kind of writing must learn control of the graphic symbols that represent the sounds of the language. Older generations of English speakers remember the hours spent in the elementary grades perfecting their handwriting. Nowadays, not so much emphasis is placed on penmanship; and for the past twenty or twenty-five years pupils in schools in the United

States have been taught manuscript writing (printing) before being introduced to the normal cursive script, which usually does not occur until the end of the second or the beginning of the third grade.

The way in which individuals form letters of the alphabet varies, but always within certain acceptable limits. Just as a too great variation from the accepted norm in the articulation of sounds can cause a breakdown in oral/aural communication, a person's handwriting can become a source of misunderstanding if it differs too much from the agreed upon standard. Lack of clarity in distinguishing the letters *a* and *o*, for example, can cause confusion between words like *an* and *on* or names like *Dan* and *Don*.[4]

The distinction made in English between lower case and capital letters is not one that occurs in all writing systems. In alphabetic systems like English, however, the use of a capital letter is a clear indication of a proper noun or the beginning of a sentence. Lack of such a distinction can be a source of ambiguity, as in all-capital newspaper headlines. The headline CHOOSE BLACK FOR TEAM is ambiguous in three ways. If the word *black* would normally be capitalized, the headline would mean that a person named Black had been selected; if the word would not normally be capitalized, it could then mean either that a member of the Negro race had been chosen or that the team color was to be black.

Writing involves an understanding of the problems caused by the poor 'fit' between English sounds and letters. Such texts as those of Allen, Allen, and Shute (1966), Fries (1962), and Prator and Robinett (1972) contain useful information regarding the relationship between spelling and sound in English. Students of any age should be encouraged to learn English spelling patterns and not be given the impression that English spelling is totally inconsistent. However, the fact that spelling 'bees' are such a common occurrence in English-speaking educational systems is evidence of an inherent difficulty in English orthography.

Spelling words as they are pronounced or pronouncing words

as they are spelled can cause problems. The word *sesame* in the expression "Open Sesame" has been pronounced /siyseym/ by native speakers of English who have never heard it before. Spelling pronunciations are commonly employed by non-native speakers upon first encountering a word in writing not previously heard: e.g., *vegetable* as ve-ge-*table*.

Interesting dialectal differences are often revealed by spelling. What is usually referred to as a certain make of car (*Chevy*) was once identified in an Indiana newspaper as a *Chivy*; such a spelling reflects the Midland U.S. dialect tendency to replace the sound /e/ with /i/ in certain positions in words.

Spelling also reveals interesting dialectal pronunciations in other languages. Caribbean Spanish speakers, such as Puerto Ricans, confuse /l/ and /r/ in certain words. I found two examples of this dialect peculiarity in Puerto Rico. One was written on the wall of an Indian cave, a tourist attraction on the north shore of the island, where a name had been scratched; instead of the usual *Ricardo*, it appeared there as *Ricaldo*. The second example appeared in a newspaper advertisement for frozen foods where *arroz con gandules* ('rice with gandules') was printed as *arroz con gandures*.

The acquisition of certain mechanical abilities is the first stage in the communicative skill of writing; this includes the ability to put down on paper words, phrases, and sentences, leaving spaces between words, and starting sentences with a capital letter and ending with some mark of punctuation. Once students have mastered these conventions of writing, the next stage comprises learning to write compositions: developing sequences of sentences into paragraphs and arranging these paragraphs into a unified whole. It should be pointed out that not all native speakers of English master this second stage of writing. This stage depends upon learning to use language differently. Willis (1967:9) states the difference in this way:

> Good writing is much tighter, less wordy, and more logical in structure than casual speech. . . . Casual speech is likely to use more sentence units, or simpler parts within a long sen-

tence, than good writing. The written language uses *expansions* of the simpler spoken sentence, since the writer has more time to think about what he is doing.

The rhetorical conventions of composition (rules of punctuation, paragraphing, and the logic of organization) seem to be related to the specific culture of which the language is a part (Kaplan, 1966). Perhaps too much has been made of the particular kind of logical development used in English composition, but it seems to be true that many non-English speakers have had little or no training in expository writing. The concepts of unity (organizing paragraphs around one topic) and coherence (arranging ideas in logical order) are espoused in all English composition textbooks. Exercises showing how these concepts can be developed will be found in the next chapter where grammatical and lexical items used in expository writing to produce logical and unified paragraphs will also be discussed.

Seliger (1972) points out that chronological sequencing and cause and effect sequencing seem to be universally understood; they can, therefore, be efficiently used in the early stages of writing as a basis for organizing discourse into paragraphs and whole compositions. Certainly, much expository writing utilizes these two kinds of organizational patterns.

For the purpose of further discussion of the process of writing, let us now turn to the comments Wardhaugh made about the reading skill, since they are equally important from a productive as well as a receptive perspective. The "visual clues of spelling" as utilized in writing signify the ability to spell, not just being able to interpret what has already been spelled for readers. As previously mentioned, this is no mean feat in English; and, although there are specific spelling patterns in English, native speakers of the language constantly refer to dictionaries, particularly for the spelling of unaccented portions of words.[5]

Applying Wardhaugh's "probabilities of occurrence" to writing, we see that writers must have at their command sets of vocabulary items, collocations of semantically related words. In addition to such vocabulary items, writers must be familiar with words and phrases that are useful in rhetorical organization. For example, in a paragraph in which comparison and contrast is being used as a rhetorical device, writers soon discover the usefulness of words and phrases like *however*, *nevertheless*, *on the contrary*, *similarly*, *in like fashion*, *likewise*, and grammatical constructions identified with expressions of comparison: *-er than*, *more than*, *as* ——— *as*, etc.

Since writing is a means of communicating ideas, the "contextual-pragmatic knowledge" which Wardhaugh deems essential to reading comprehension is also required on the part of writers; simply stated, they cannot be expected to write intelligently about something they know nothing about. The perennial assigning of a composition about "My Summer Vacation" to students returning to school each autumn, though unimaginative, is understandable in light of the fact that students must have knowledge of the subject they are writing about. The practice of making writing assignments based on subjects that have been read about or discussed beforehand is a good one for this very reason.

A knowledge of the syntax and semantics of English is as necessary for writers as it is for readers. One of the reasons beginning students are prone to plagiarize the writings of others is that they lack the syntactic and semantic knowledge of a native speaker. Even though non-English speakers may understand the content of what they want to write about, they may not have learned the syntactic and lexical items necessary to express their ideas well. They, therefore, prefer to copy the words of another, which seem so much more accurate and elegant than their own.

On the other hand, those who have acquired good control over the syntax and semantics of conversational English may still have difficulty in writing because of differences in the two modes of communication (already discussed in the section on reading in this chapter). Furthermore, for those writing on scientific subjects, studies have already shown (Huddleston, 1971; Cowan, 1974; Lackstrom, et al., 1970; Selinker, et al., 1976) that there are differences in the way in which English structures are employed in the English of science and technology and in literary English; and the use of technical and subtechnical vocabulary (Cowan, 1974) constitutes an important distinction between scientific and literary styles of English writing.

Learning a Second Culture

The very nature of the relationship between language and culture ensures that learning a language includes learning the culture of the people who speak that language. An understanding of culture is a necessary part of all the skills: comprehending references that occur in speech and writing ("He's as wise as Solomon."); being able to use the language appropriately (knowing the different connotation of *kids* and *children*); interpreting the figurative use of language ("She concentrated feverishly."); and conforming to cultural norms in speaking and writing (knowing what is taboo in both media).

Nonverbal communication is as important at times as the actual words employed. The use of kinesics (body language), gestures, and space in conversing with others plays a part in the communicative act. Research on nonverbal communication reported by Birdwhistell (1970), Key (1975), and Taylor (1976) provides useful information for those involved in either teaching or learning English as a second language.

Summary

We reiterate our assumption that although language can be subdivided into various skills for purposes of analysis and for teaching, in the long run the knowledge necessary for communication is not easily divisible; furthermore, each skill seems to call upon this cumulative knowledge. The kind of second language learning which seems most useful is that which avoids an overemphasis upon analysis and works toward a synthesis of knowledge.

Exercises

A. English-speaking children in their early acquisition of the language sometimes use forms like *throwed* and *foots* although they have never heard such forms. What do errors like this tell you about the language learning process?

B. Record a portion of a radio or television interview program and analyze it for problems speakers of other languages might have in comprehending it. Are all the utterances complete sentences? Do you find any examples of the use of language that does not conform to textbook rules you are familiar with?

C. The following exercise (adapted from one developed by Professor William Howell, Department of Speech-Communication, University of Minnesota) illustrates the "expectancy" clues exhibited by stress and intonation. Notice the difference in the two readings of the first part of each item, depending upon whether you select (a) or (b) to complete the sentence. To test your ability to distinguish which of the two items will follow, have someone else read the first part of the sentence, selecting either (a) or (b) as the completion without letting you know which one they have selected, and you then guess which should be the concluding sentence.

  1. I believe that,
    (a) but there is something else I do not believe.
    (b) I need no further facts.

  2. Your plan is not bad,
    (a) but it is not particularly good, either.
    (b) as a matter of fact, it is very good.

  3. My wallet is here,
    (a) but my checkbook is gone.
    (b) but her wallet is gone.

  4. He's a slow reader,
    (a) but he's a careful reader.
    (b) but he's a fast talker.

5. Did he turn in the report,
   (a) or is it still not in?
   (b) or did someone else do it?

D. In reading our own language we often run across words that are completely unfamiliar to us, but we can sometimes guess their meaning from the context. Are you familiar with the word *objugations*? Can you guess its meaning as it appears in the following sentence? "He told me the same story that I had heard from Mary, but much garlanded with objugations" (from John Buchan, *The Three Hostages*).

E. If you did not know the meaning of the underlined words in the excerpts below, what contextual clues might help you to guess their meaning?
   From John Buchan, *The Three Hostages*

   1. "It was almost dark when at last, after several false *casts*, I came to Palmyra Square."
   2. ". . . the meadows were full of shimmering grey flocks of *fieldfares* on their way north."

   From Theodore H. White, *The View from the Fortieth floor*

   3. ". . . you sign first, where it says President, Chairman of the Board.
      Warren took out his pen and *scratched*."
   4. "Then they could see Warren *loping* back across the street to fetch them. It was the lope of a man who likes to run."

   From Theodore Dreiser, *Sister Carrie*

   5.   "Hurstwood sat and read by his *radiator* in the corner. He did not try to think about his need of work. This storm being so terrific, and tying up all things, robbed him of the need. He made himself wholly comfortable and toasted his feet."

F. What do the following attempt to communicate?

dawg   verrrrrrry interesting   Ah don't mahnd.
purty   INexpressive not UNexpressive   Pahk the cah.
enuff

G. How might the following conversational utterances appear in formal written language?

1. She likes it, and he does, too.

2. The man who you talked to on the phone is here.

3. I'm the one who will have to finish the job, aren't I?

H. Explain what you would say in the three situations below if you were unable to respond affirmatively because you had to be out of town. How would your responses differ?

1. Your best friend has invited you to a party.

2. Your aunt (who is quite elderly) has asked you to drive her to the dentist's where she has an appointment.

3. Your employer's wife has sent you a formal written invitation to a large dinner party at their home.

I. Analyze your handwriting. Does it conform to general handwriting rules? What idiosyncratic differences does it present which might cause difficulties for a non-English speaker?

J. If you have learned a second language, what was most difficult for you in the process? Can you speak it? Can you read it? Can you write it? Can you understand it when it is spoken to you? If the answer is "no" to any of these questions, do you know why this is so?

K. Ask several non-native speakers of English (of different language backgrounds, if possible) to read the following paragraph. List their errors in pronunciation. Did they all make the same errors? Do you know of anything in their native language that might account for the errors they made?

1   I was swimming in the Mediterranean sea one day when
    I saw a large fish coming toward me at great speed. His
3   jaws were wide open, and I was directly in his path. There
    was no way to avoid him. I made myself as small as possi-

5 ble and passed through his jaws into his stomach. The
place was dark but warm. I kept thinking of how to get out
7 of my prison, and at last I hit upon an idea. I began to hop
and jump and dance around within the darkness. This
9 movement inside of him seemed to disturb the fish, for he
raised his head high up out of the water. He was seen by
11 some men in a fishing boat who quickly harpooned him.
I was congratulating myself on my good luck when I
13 heard the sailors talking about cutting the fish up to pre-
serve the oil. I had seen the long knives that they used,
15 and I wondered if I, too, was going to be cut up with the
fish. But my luck held. They started cutting from the tail
17 end, and before they reached the place where I stood I
called out in a loud voice to be saved from this black hole.
19 Imagine their great amazement when they saw me walk-
ing out of the fish! I told them the whole story, and to this
21 day I don't think they really believed it.

Did they use a spelling pronunciation for any of the words in
this paragraph? Most of the words conform to the usual spelling
patterns in English (e.g., *swim*, *fish* as contrasted with *knives*).
However, there are a few words that are irregular in their
sound-spelling representation (*one*, *imagine*). As a spelling-
sound exercise, list all the words that are spelled with the same
vowel letters and see what correlation there is between spelling
and sound.

Notes

1. A pilot study carried out by S. M. Ziahosseiny at Pahlavi University in Iran (reported in Research Notes in *TESOL Quarterly*, March, 1977) shows that students who
were given listening tasks in a language laboratory developed a reading competence
superior to the group that did not receive such listening practice. The transfer of learning
from listening to reading was quite evident.

2. An interesting study by Corcoran (the basis for an M.A. thesis at UCLA) dealing
with the possible relation between native and non-native speakers' awareness of the
presence of these 'silent' *e*'s is reported by Hatch (1978). Corcoran found that when
asked to cross out *e*'s on a printed page native English speakers do not do as well as
non-native speakers; they tend to skip over these letters when they appear in noncontent
words and to cross out with more accuracy those in stressed syllables. The relationship
here between the acoustic signal and the written symbol is undeniable. The fact that a
native speaker can slur over these 'silent' *e*'s to the extent that they are not consciously

perceived may be part of what lies behind the difference in rate of reading between native and non-native students.

3. Cowan (personal communication) believes it necessary to define approaches to teaching reading in terms of the educational setting in which it is taught. He designates at least three such approaches: (1) reading taught as part of a program emphasizing total communicative competence; (2) reading taught as a single skill with little or no emphasis upon speaking and listening comprehension; and (3) reading taught in a bilingual situation. In the above quotation he is referring to his second approach when he says, "even teach them at all."

4. As one whose penmanship tends to vary greatly from the standard, I can testify to the fact that poor handwriting can cause a breakdown in communication. I once was blessed with a secretary who learned to 'decipher' my handwriting in much the same way that archaeologists are wont to unlock the secrets of ancient inscriptions. She was even known to interpret my own handwriting to me (once it had gotten 'cold').

5. Evidence of the problem that native speakers have with spelling appeared in a recent letter which I received from a colleague in which *warrant* appeared as *warrent*. I often use the dictionary to assure myself of the correct spelling of words containing the suffixes *-ible*, *-able*; *-ance*, *-ence*.

7

Teaching the Communication Skills

The preceding chapter deals with the skills involved in learning another language; this chapter will discuss ways in which the teacher can facilitate that learning. The concept of the teacher as facilitator is one which views the teacher as providing somewhat controlled activities at the initial stage of learning but as continually relaxing those controls until the student, as Rivers (1972) describes it, "is talking off the top of his head."

It should be clear from the outset that students should practice *using* the language. They should be told that no stigma is attached to making errors. On the contrary, errors often reveal the learning strategies employed by students, and teachers can adapt their teaching to such strategies. For example, if students are making errors that are the result of overgeneralizing certain rules in the language, the teacher can emphasize those items which do not follow the particular rules.

Examples of drills and exercises appropriate for the various levels of proficiency — beginning, intermediate, and advanced — will be provided to illustrate the communication skills of listening, speaking, reading, and writing. The ultimate goal of all these activities is to lead students toward the attainment of communicative competence in the 'real' world.

Manipulation to Communication

The movement away from a total use of tightly controlled practice toward the introduction of more communicative exercises in teaching a second language was given particular impetus by Prator's description (1965) of a manipulation-communication scale for classroom activities. Stating that "true communication implies the absence of external controls," he recommended that language instruction be composed of cycles of activities "so arranged as to constitute a gradual progression from manipulation to communication." He defined these two end points on his scale in this manner:

> We may define communicative classroom activities as those that allow the student himself to find the words and structures he uses. The other type of activity, in which he receives the words and structures from teacher, tape, or book, may be called — for want of a better word — a manipulative activity. In this sense, an example of pure manipulation would be a drill in which the students merely repeat sentences after the teacher. An example of pure communication would be a free conversation among members of a class. (141)

Prator's four-point scale commences at one end with activities that are completely manipulative, moves to those that are predominantly manipulative, on to those that are predominantly communicative, and finally reaches those that are completely communicative. He strongly suggests that the teacher devise activities that impel students toward the communicative end of the scale as soon as feasible. Furthermore, he recommends that this progression from one end of the scale to the other be attempted *at every level* of activity. So often, actual communication in a second language has been thought to be the prerogative of advanced students only. If Prator's suggestion is followed, exercises at the predominantly communicative point on the scale could be introduced into the classroom from almost the beginning stages. Thus, in a given class period it is conceivable that activities devised for learning a particular item could be sequenced so as to progress from manipulation to communication.

Somewhat similarly, Paulston (1971) classifies structural drills as mechanical, meaningful, and communicative on the basis of what determines the form of the response. A mechanical drill depends solely upon the teacher's direction for a response. A meaningful drill is still dependent upon the teacher but can also involve a particular situation, reading, or something that is common knowledge on the part of the whole class. For free or communicative activities the students themselves determine the response, offering information about themselves and their 'real' world outside the classroom.

Although there has been a suggestion in the recent past of a strict dichotomy in language teaching between habit-forming and rule-giving activities (Saporta, 1966), with an accompanying criticism of language drills, there is general agreement that practice is a necessary component of language learning (Ney, 1968; Brown, 1969; Schutz and Derwing, 1978). Bolinger (1968:40) states the case for drills in strong terms.

> Teaching something involves more than the initial grasp of a rule. That may of course be taught by deductive presentation. But being given a rule is like being introduced to a stranger; we may be able to recognize him on later encounters, but cannot be said to know him. Teaching a rule involves not just the phase of grasping but the phase of familiarizing. . . . We have to return to the lowly origin of drills, which was in the humble setting of the classroom before anybody thought of dressing them up in behaviorist philosophy. We have pragmatic reasons for retaining them, and retain them we should. This says nothing of *the limitless need for improving them.* [italics mine]

Drills, or the kinds of activities that Prator refers to as manipulative, provide the practice that leads to fluency; they offer students an opportunity to mouth difficult sequences of sounds or to become familiar with the order of sentence elements which often differs from that in their own languages. However, drills need not be a mindless activity. We should note carefully Bolinger's comment regarding "the limitless need for improving them."

A classification of grammatical drills was provided in Chapter 1. Examples were given which attempted to illustrate a student-centered approach to drilling in which the teacher may act as initiator of the drill but rapidly withdraws, giving responsibility to the students for the actual use of language in carrying out the practice. The drills may still be manipulative, but they try as much as possible to reproduce 'real' language.

Each skill can be practiced mechanically. Listening can be sharpened through the use of aural discrimination exercises that employ minimal pairs of words or sentences (*beat-bit*; *he beat it-he bit it*); speaking can involve conversion exercises (*he asked a question-did he ask a question*); reading comprehension can be checked through questions demanding a simple repetition of information exactly as it appears in the reading selection; and writing can be as simple as copying sentences or paragraphs, or converting a paragraph of questions into statements. Manipulative exercises are useful as a first step in practicing the language, but they should always be viewed as a means to an end, not an end in themselves. They are simply a way of familiarizing students with the forms and arrangements of language items so that when students are ready to communicate something on their own, they will already have had some practice in articulating the linguistic items necessary to do so. However, classroom activities should never consist of mechanical, manipulative drills alone. An example of how classroom activities can progress from mechanical to meaningful drills and then to partially communicative activities is provided below in a series of drills on comparative expressions. (Adapted from an exercise written by Darlene Kunze, Program in English as a Second Language, University of Minnesota.)

T = teacher
S = student

Mechanical Drill (a simple substitution drill)

(a) T: John is taller than Bill.   S: John is taller than Bill.
      old
      big   John is older than Bill.
      young   etc.
      short
      small
      heavy

(b) T: John is the tallest.   S: John is the tallest.
        old   John is the oldest.
        big   etc.
        young
        etc.

Meaningful Drill

Figure 4. Teacher draws the stick figures on the blackboard and labels them with name, age, and weight.

Who is taller, David or John? John is. (John is taller than David.)

T: older — Susie — David   S₁: Who is older, Susie or
                                  David?
                             S₂: David is. (David is older than
                                  Susie.)
    shorter — Susie — Mary   S₃: Who is shorter, Susie or
                                  Mary?
                             S₄: Susie is. (Susie is shorter
                                  than Mary.)
    younger — David — John   etc.
    heavier — David — Mary

Who is the oldest? Wilt is. (Wilt is the oldest.)

T: shortest   S₁: Who is the shortest?
                             S₂: Susie. (Susie is.) (Susie is
                                  the shortest.)

heaviest	S₃: Who is the heaviest?
	S₄: John. (John is.) (John is the heaviest.)
youngest	etc.
tallest	

Communicative Drill (a response drill)

(a) T: (asks two students)
     Would you please
     stand up?
     (asks another student)
     Who is taller?   S₁: ——— is. (——— is taller than ———.)

                     S₂: (asks two other students)
                         Would you please stand up?
                         (asks S₃)
                         Who is taller?
                     S₃: ——— is. (——— is taller than ———.)
                                 etc.

(b) T: (asks three students)
     Would you please
     stand up?
     (asks another student)
     Who is the tallest?   S₁: ——— is. (——— is the tallest.)

                     S₂: (asks three students)
                         Would you please stand up?
                         (asks S₃)
                         Who is the tallest?
                     S₃: ——— is. (——— is the tallest.)
                                 etc.

(c) T: (asks several students
     how old they are and

how much they weigh)
(asks another student)
Who is the oldest/ S_1: —— is. (—— is the
youngest/heaviest? oldest/youngest/heaviest)

S_2: (asks another student a
[Care should be question not asked by the
exercised in using this the preceding student)
exercise since Ameri- Who is the oldest/youngest/
can culture has a taboo heaviest?
about revealing age S_3: —— is. (—— is the
and weight under cer- oldest/youngest/heaviest.)
tain circumstances, espe- S_4: (asks several other students
cially among adults.] how old they are and how
much they weigh)
(asks another student)
Who is the oldest/youngest/
heaviest?
etc.

Another example of how one can proceed from a manipulative activity to a freer kind of exercise is taken from Harding, Delisle, and Escorcia (1969). The first series of drills, though manipulative, allows practice on alternative ways of saying the same thing; the second exercise presents short dialogues in which students are given some freedom to choose among these alternatives.

Manipulation Drill (can be a repetition or simple substitution drill)

some	I'd like some eggs, please.
a few	I'd like a few eggs, please.
a dozen	I'd like a dozen eggs, please.
a half-dozen	I'd like a half-dozen eggs, please.
any	I'm sorry, there aren't any left.
any at all	I'm sorry, there aren't any at all.
none	I'm sorry, there are none left.
none at all	I'm sorry, there are none at all.

any	Do you have any milk or any cream?
some	Do you have some milk or some cream?
a few bottles of	Do you have a few bottles of milk?
a dozen bottles	Do you have a dozen bottles of milk?
some — any	We have some milk, but we don't have any cream.
some — any at all	We have some milk, but we don't have any cream at all.
any — some	We don't have any milk, but we have some cream.
any at all — some	We don't have any milk at all, but we have some cream.

Communication Drill (a dialogue in which alternative forms may be used where words appear in parentheses)

A1: I'd like (some) eggs, please.
B2: I'm sorry, there aren't (any) left.
A1: Do you have (some) milk or (some) cream?
B2: We have (some) milk, but we don't have (any) cream.

A3: I'd like (a few) eggs, please.
B4: I'm sorry, there are (none) left.
A3: Do you have (a few bottles of) milk?
B4: We don't have (any) milk (at all), but we have (some) cream.

Instead of *eggs* in the above exercise various fruits could be substituted (*oranges* or *lemons*). The substitution of *grapes*, *pears*, or *cherries* would necessitate the substitution of *pound* for *dozen*. If *tea* or *coffee* were substituted for *milk* and *cream*, a correlative substitution of *packages* and *cans* would be necessary in place of *bottles*. Such substitutions would, of course, add variety to the drills at the same time teaching the appropriate partitive or descriptive expressions that correlate with the particular word (*a pound of grapes*; *a pound of coffee*; *a package of tea*; *a can of coffee*).

Practicing the Communicative Skills

In discussing activities for practicing the individual communicative skills we will begin with listening. However, practicing each skill reinforces the others, and classroom activities planned in such a way as to include attention to more than one skill provide variety as well as reinforcement. It is incumbent upon the teacher to select the kinds of activities most useful for particular students and in conformity with the agreed-upon curriculum.

Listening

Since the goal of listening is comprehension, it is essential that listening activities attract and hold the attention of students so that, no matter what their age, they are motivated to listen carefully. Listening practice is especially important in classrooms where English is taught as a foreign language, that is, in situations where English is not the language of the country and where opportunities for hearing English outside the classroom are few. Students in such environments often learn to read and write English, and even to speak English, but they frequently have great difficulty comprehending English spoken to them.

The first step in teaching the listening skill is to accustom students to the 'noise' of the language. This early stage is best accomplished by what Nida (1953:101) referred to as "selective listening."

> In general, one of the greatest problems in language learning is the abundance of strange data which is thrust at us more rapidly than we can assimilate it. We get nowhere if we attempt to take it all in at once. We must concentrate on certain features at a time, and in order to do this systematically and efficiently, we should employ selective listening.

This "selective listening" can be as specific as teaching the discrimination of sounds, both in words and sentences:

| washing | She's washing the car. |
| watching | She's watching the car. |

Or it may be the discrimination of structure words that are usually unstressed and thus difficult to hear accurately:

It's in the box.	Give him the book.
It's on the box.	Give her the book.
Are they large ones?	Yes, they are.
Are there large ones?	Yes, there are.

Specific features that cause problems in comprehension for speakers of other languages are those that are related to English stress and rhythm: (1) neutralization of vowels in unstressed syllables to /ə/: *for* (/fɔr/ becoming /fər/; *geography* /džiyágrəfiy/ and *geographic* /džìyəgrǽfik/; (2) contractions: *isn't, can't, she's*, etc.; and (3) loss of consonant sounds in such words as *he, her, them, of*, etc.: *give 'er the book*; *a cup a' coffee*; *tell 'em everything*. These reductions can also cause misinterpretations of words like *in* and *and*, both of which are often reduced to /ən/ or /n/ (a syllabic consonant in which the vowel of the syllable is included in the consonant sound itself).

DOONESBURY   by Garry Trudeau

Exercises which demand that students listen specifically for these 'reduced forms' in speech are necessary since the forms differ from the way they appear in writing and the way they are pronounced in isolation. This difference causes special difficulty for students who have been introduced to the language through the written word as well as for those who are unaccustomed to such a discrepancy between spoken and written forms in a language.

Taped exercises can be used to provide listening practice on these reduced forms. One such set of exercises, developed by Bird (1975), concentrates on the following frequently occurring syntactic items: verb + *to*, modal auxiliaries, adverbials, pronouns, and auxiliary *do* in questions and negatives. Examples of the kinds of reductions heard on these tapes are given below.

> I'm *going to* /gənə/ talk about New York City.
> They *can* /kən/ see us later.
> How *about* /bawt/ later?
> Tell *them* /əm/ to stop by.
> Where *do* /də/ you live?

Teachers sometimes contribute to the difficulty that students have in comprehending speech outside the classroom because of the use of 'classroom English' or 'teacherese', a kind of language that does not reflect the language of the 'real' world. Teachers try to simplify structures and vocabulary, to pronounce the language very clearly, and in various ways to facilitate comprehension artificially (with the best intentions). If students are constantly 'spoon-fed' the language in this fashion, they will not be prepared for actual spoken language outside the classroom. Therefore, teachers, whether native speakers of the language or not, must avoid this kind of 'teacher talk' and provide opportunities for students to hear samples of actual language usage. The more formal type of English, which in many cases is the type that English teachers cling to, must not be the only variety to which students are exposed.

Young children learning English develop comprehension rapidly, especially children who learn the language orally before being introduced to reading and writing in English. They enjoy listening to stories; and an excellent means of building comprehension skills in small children is by storytelling, especially if the stories are illustrated by pictures and gestures on the part of the teacher. Bumpass (1963:90–130) has an excellent, detailed description of the presentation of "The Three Bears" for young children.

Games, too, can be just as effectively used for listening practice as for speaking (Dorry, 1966; Lee, 1965; Finocchiaro, 1964:105–12). Simon Says is a popular listening game for young children, and Bingo can be adapted in various ways for all ages (Dobson, 1974:117–18).

Older students, particularly those who have been introduced to the language through writing rather than speech, or at least have had the written form provided simultaneously, often have great difficulty recognizing the spoken forms. Dictation exercises can be a great help in this case. Undoubtedly, more attention should be paid to dictation as a technique for teaching listening comprehension although it is most often used as an exercise in writing. While Sawyer and Silver (1961) and Sutherland (1967) emphasize the importance of dictation in teaching writing, they also remark that dictation helps students discover what it is they do not hear accurately. One of the most effective aspects of dictation results from the immediate feedback provided if the dictation exercise is corrected as soon as the exercise is completed.

It is only fairly recently that specific textbooks have appeared that are intended to develop listening ability (Morley, 1972; Plaister, 1976). There is also some evidence that writers of general textbook series are paying more attention to this aspect of language learning by providing directed practice on listening comprehension (Porter and Sharp, 1977; *English for Today*, third edition, forthcoming).

It is well known that anyone living or traveling in a foreign country often hesitates to use the telephone; the reason, obviously, is that telephone communication depends upon aural comprehension. One of the easiest ways to develop students' confidence in using the telephone is to ask them to call numbers that provide recorded messages. Students do not have to respond, so they feel less insecure. The next step is to assign an exercise that requires them to telephone for some specific information (bus schedule, prices of symphony tickets, public library hours, etc.) and to report this information to the class. In the United States, telephone companies often provide special equipment (called *teletrainers*) to be used in the classroom so that students may learn how to use the telephone. Many colleges and universities have recorded messages for information about services provided by the institution. Most large cities also have numbers to call for time, weather, bus schedules, etc.

The use of taped materials (recordings of dialogues or of radio and television programs) or films can provide excellent opportunities for students to increase their listening comprehension of 'real-life' language. Radio commercials can be used effectively as models of typical spoken English. They can be taped and played several times while students try to guess at words and phrases they cannot understand, drawing upon their knowledge of the language to fill in the gaps that occur as they listen for the first time. This kind of 'expectancy' practice develops their total communicative ability. The following is an exercise based on a radio commercial that is used with young adults at the intermediate level. Note that speaking and writing activities can also be provided based on what is essentially a listening exercise.

Listening Comprehension Exercise (Radio Commercial)

(Adapted from an unpublished paper by Jennifer Hurwicz, "Twelve Commercials to Be Used in Teaching Listening Comprehension," Program in English as a Second Language, University of Minnesota, 1976.)

Taped commercial:

1   D———'s Jewelry is holding a half-million
    dollar diamond jewelry sale just in time for
3 the holidays. One-fourth to one-third off the
    regular price on men's and women's rings;
5 wedding rings, cocktail rings, earrings, pendants,
    too. In addition, you can save twenty-five
7 percent on diamond engagement and wedding rings;
    they've got a fine assortment to choose from.

9 And you can use their "thrifty plan," even if
  you don't have a regular D———'s charge, and
11 defer your first payment till February. The
  Diamond Spectacular at all D———'s fine jewelry
13 departments. Check it out.

Vocabulary Study

assortment	defer payment	one-third off
thrifty	holding a sale	check it out

Comprehension

1. How much is marked off the regular prices on men's and women's jewelry?
2. Must the first payment be made immediately? (Note: This commercial appeared in December.)
3. What holidays do you think are being referred to in this commercial?

Discussion

1. In the United States, when a couple becomes engaged to be married, it is customary for the man to buy the woman an engagement ring, which she wears as a symbol of their engagement. Do you have tokens of engagement in your country? If so, what are they? Do you think a woman should help to choose her own engagement ring?
2. What do you think of being able to defer your payment on goods, using the so-called 'time payment' plan?

Exercises

1. Two of the sentences in this commercial are not complete sentences; make them into complete sentences.
2. Write a commercial similar to this one, but make it for a furniture sale. Be sure to include the percentages off, particular items for sale, how payments can be made, and where the sale is taking place.

Listening activities should include those that train students to identify types or varieties of English, from the most formal to the most informal. This is an important part of comprehension since clues to levels of formality indicate what kind of language students should use in their responses. Students need to learn to identify idioms, phrases, and sayings that are characteristic of the various levels of speech. The best way to do this is to consciously watch the situations in which they occur and the kinds of people who employ them. If the situation is a formal one and the speakers are of a certain social stature, it is to be expected that the language forms being employed are fairly formal. Speakers conversing informally with their social equivalents are probably using speech that is not formal. Teachers should make very clear to students the situation in which certain language items should be used, if they are not generally appropriate. The ability to make appropriate choices in speech is first developed by practice in identifying the various varieties in listening exercises.

Rivers (1966) emphasizes the need for listening practice throughout the language learning experience.

> Above all, it must be clearly borne in mind by teacher and student alike that listening comprehension is not a skill which can be mastered once and for all and then ignored while other skills are developed. There must be regular practice with increasingly difficult material.

Godfrey (1977) supports Rivers's contention and describes the role played by the listening skill in teaching advanced students to comprehend discourse relationships.

It is clear to most teachers that the types of listening activities possible in the classroom are limited only by the ingenuity of the individual teacher.

Speaking

For some time now great emphasis has been placed on oral practice in language teaching. However, classroom exercises have tended to be mechanical drills meant to develop automatic, errorless responses to set patterns; these drills have often been referred to as 'pattern practice'. Without overlooking the importance of drills in learning another language, it is now agreed that such practice should be made meaningful. This can be done if care is taken to develop or select proper instructional activities.

The first rule of thumb in eliciting speech from students is to ensure that they have something to talk about that interests them. Early in their experience classroom objects — desks, chairs, pens, pencils — may be useful to talk about; however, such vocabulary should be learned quickly and then relegated to its utilitarian level as soon as possible. Students find that talk about the classroom soon palls.

Young children will pay close attention to language that is correlated with toys — cars, animals, houses — which can be manipulated as if they were real objects. *Starting English Early* (1967), a film illustrating the teaching of English to young children whose first language is Spanish, is filled with examples of activities that hold the interest of small children and elicit speaking on their part.

Games provide an excellent way to elicit speech; and they can be as effective with adults as with children, if judiciously used. There are also now available recorded songs written especially for teaching English to speakers of other languages (see bibliography).

Hok (1964) lists the following as forms of oral exercises: dialogues; games, play acting or role playing; conversations based on reading material, an oral account, visual aids, or shared experiences such as field trips. Dobson (1974) offers a number of suggestions for activities for adults that will provide practice in speaking.

Oral activities can be tightly controlled or more or less 'free', in the sense that they simulate communicative situations outside the classroom. Controlled or guided speaking exercises include the following: oral drills — the manipulative structure drills described in Chapter 1; memorized dialogues, which can be two-line or relatively complicated, longer exchanges; answering of questions based on assigned readings, which can range from answers couched in exactly the same words as appear in the reading passage to answers that require rearrangement of words and restatement of ideas; games; and songs.

Less guided activities are those for which the teacher can prepare students but over which there is no direct control. These can be role plays; panel discussions of items of topical interest (perhaps something pertaining to the school or the community); descriptions of happenings to themselves or to others; retelling of news items from radio and television; reporting information that students have acquired by telephoning.

Attention should be paid to problems in pronunciation when teaching speaking. All pronunciation problems may not be as dramatic as one reported to me recently: a physics professor who is not a native speaker of English expounded for some time on a topic which everyone in the class understood as "Kennedy orgy" but which turned out to be *kinetic energy*! Errors that interfere with communication should be corrected as soon as possible. (Specific techniques for teaching pronunciation have been described in Chapter 2, The Sound System.

Oral practice becomes meaningful to students when they have to pay attention to *what* they are saying. In other words, mere mechanical exercises can be produced with little attention to meaning; students are paying attention to *how* the utterance is stated. The ultimate goal is to develop thinking language users, speakers with whom we can communicate and who can communicate with us. Therefore, the teacher should devise exercises that force students to think about what they are saying at the same time they are saying it.

Dobson (1974:9) makes an erroneous assumption when she states that it is rather difficult to begin conversation activities in the classroom because "the student has adjusted to a passive role during the manipulative phase of language learning and is unprepared for the active role demanded in conversation practice." If the manipulative exercises have been meaningful — that is, if students have had to think about what they are saying as well as how they are saying it — they will have been participating actively. We should, for just this reason, accept Prator's advice to cycle classroom activities in such a way that even from the initial stages students are moved along the continuum from manipulative to communicative activities in learning each particular item. Then there will be no need for this adjustment from 'passive' to 'active' roles; students will be active participants from the very beginning.

Dialogues continue to be a popular form of oral drill in the classroom. They simulate conversation, giving students a sense of using actual language. If well done, they can be very like real communication. Certainly they are useful in teaching vocabulary items and structures appropriate for specific situations, but they should be used for more than just a mere exemplification of structure or vocabulary; they should serve a useful purpose in the overall scheme of enabling students to communicate ideas, and students should know exactly what that purpose is.

V. F. Allen (1958:100) makes the very useful observation that dialogues need not be creative gems. Plain, ordinary language is most practical for students. In discussing the preparation of dialogue material, Allen says that a materials writer sometimes goes to either of two extremes.

> Either he is so conscious of the student's limitations that he makes his characters talk like a poor translation of Esperanto, or — more commonly — he writes the way one would for a sophisticated American reader, and shuns clichés. Yet clichés are precisely what the student needs to learn. A first step, then, in learning to write such material is to resist the temptation to be clever and creative. A smart retort may give the *teacher* a flattering opinion of the writer's wit, but what the *student* needs is the banal response that eight out of ten Americans would utter in the situation portrayed.

Allen also points out that in their planning teachers should take into consideration the subjects that students want to talk about. Farid (1976) recommends the use of student-improvised dialogues; and Rigg (1976) recommends that teachers use student errors as a basis for preparing dialogues that will correct these errors.

In all practice it is essential to identify utterances with situations so that the meaning is clear. Thus, "Good morning" uttered as the teacher enters the room in the morning is learned and understood from the situation. Other language items (words, phrases, and longer utterances) can be introduced through the use of objects or pictures.

An approach referred to as "situational reinforcement" is employed in a textbook series in which actions and objects are related by situation to the language used to discuss them. Below are examples of this approach. This kind of oral practice 'reinforces' the relationship between the situation and the language being learned.

Situational Reinforcement Exercise

From Eugene J. Hall, *Situational Reinforcement, Orientation in American English.* Text 2. Washington, D.C.: Institute of Modern Languages, 1970, pp. 19–20. Reprinted by permission of the Institute of Modern Languages, Inc.

Listening Practice

He's getting a coke.

He's getting it from a vending machine.

You can get coffee from a machine.

You can get candy from a machine.

You can get stamps from a machine.

You can get sandwiches from a machine.

You can get cigarettes from a machine.

Response Sequence

1. What's he doing?
   He's getting a coke.
2. Where's he getting it?
   He's getting it from a vending machine.
3. What else can you get from a vending machine?
   You can get coffee from a machine.　candy/stamps/
   sandwiches/cigarettes

4. Is there a coffee machine in the building?   candy/cigarette/

Yes, there is.   stamp

There's one downstairs.

Experienced teachers, as well as inexperienced teachers, who are desirous of teaching *communication* will be able to think of many ways in which students can participate in lively, meaningful, and useful oral activities.

Reading

Just as listening has as its goal the comprehension of the spoken language, the ultimate goal in reading is to comprehend the written language. The ability to decipher the spoken symbols (the sounds of the language) is paralleled in reading with the ability to decode the written symbols. Learning to read a second language is made easier if students already know how to read in their first language; they have already learned the process of relating graphic symbols to the language which they speak. Reading a second language, however, involves deciphering a set of graphic symbols (which may or may not be similar to those in their own language) and relating them to a language in which they are not fully competent.

For those who do not already know how to read in their first language, there is a basic principle to be observed in the beginning stages of teaching reading: material to be read should be limited to the vocabulary and grammatical structures that are already within the linguistic experience of the students; that is, they should have been practiced orally first. This initial stage in learning to read is the process of connecting spoken language to writing. Enrichment of vocabulary and grammatical structures through reading should be left until a later stage in the reading program.

This initial stage of recognizing visual symbols (alphabetic representation in English) takes time, especially, as has been mentioned, for those who have not already learned to read in their first language. Such seemingly simple differences between lower case and capital letters can be troublesome, especially when they are quite different in shape:

A	a	E	e	L	l
B	b	G	g	R	r
D	d	I	i	T	t

English poses orthographic problems since there is not a one-to-one correlation between the sound and the written symbol. However, there are strong patterns of spelling which should be capitalized upon.[1] These patterns should be pointed out to students systematically so that they become acquainted with the many consistencies in spelling, even those that seem not to follow the accepted concepts of spelling patterns, like those illustrated below in which the final 'silent' *e* is still very much an indication of a spelling-sound correspondence.

hat	hate
pet	Pete
sit	site
dot	dote
cut	cute

In beginning reading classes, students can be asked to read words, sentences, and short dialogues after they have been practiced orally. Fries and Fries (1961:378) point out that this should not be just "saying the words" but reading "with expression"; that is, students must indicate by their reading that they understand what they are reading.

> This reading "with expression" is giving not only the sound patterns that make up the separate words but also supplying the tone sequences, the stresses, and the pauses that mark the word groupings that signal the total range of meanings. This is the productive reading that is real reading as distinct from just saying the words.

After the decoding process has been acquired, the next stage is to lead students to the comprehension of material that has not been practiced orally beforehand. After all, one of the major purposes of reading is to broaden the knowledge of the reader —

to learn something new. Thus, reading involves the acquisition of new vocabulary and an understanding of grammatical structures that may differ somewhat from those usually learned in speaking (*had he known the truth . . .* instead of *if he had known the truth . . .* or *extraordinary though it may be, we . . .* instead of *though it is extraordinary, we . . .*).

At this point the teacher must devise means of teaching students how to get meaning from the written page. Care must be taken not to accept rote recitation of what is on the page as an indication of real comprehension of content. Many things enter into comprehension: the students' grasp of the subject matter of the reading, their understanding of the vocabulary used, their knowledge of the cultural content implicitly or explicitly expressed, and their ability to cope with the grammatical structures in the passage.

Although the decoding process is essential, teachers should leave that aspect as soon as students have grasped the essentials of sound-symbol relationships and can read "with expression." Smith (1971) and others in the reading field warn against too much attention to the decoding process and urge teachers to stress the development of "expectancy" ability, which was discussed in the preceding chapter.

WORD STUDY

Certain assumptions can be made about the grammatical structures students know at a given time in an English program, and readings can be selected that will not include grammar which is beyond their competence to handle. On the other hand, reading material can be prepared or selected to highlight particular grammatical constructions that may or may not be known to students beforehand (V. F. Allen, 1953, 1957; Kurilecz, 1969). However, the lexical content must be understood in order for reading comprehension to occur. Therefore, vocabulary or word study should be part of any reading program. Exercises related to word formation, synonyms and antonyms, and guessing the meanings of words from contexts are excellent means of increasing vocabulary. There are texts written primarily as vocabulary builders (Franklin, et al., 1968; Barnard, 1971) as well as reading texts with a strong emphasis upon vocabulary or word study (Croft, 1960; Kurilecz, 1969; Saitz and Carr, 1972). Drills on idioms can also be helpful in preparing for reading (Dixson, 1971; McCallum, 1970, 1978; Reeves, 1975).

Examples of vocabulary exercises may be found in Chapter 3 (The Vocabulary System).

READING COMPREHENSION

In his excellent article on the techniques and procedures for teaching reading, Norris (1970) suggests five types of questions that may be formulated in an attempt to develop reading comprehension. Norris has hereby provided a useful refinement of the Stage One and Stage Two questions for teaching reading comprehension outlined by Gurrey (1955). Norris's questions are sequenced in such a way as to follow (whether purposely or inadvertently) Prator's recommended progression from manipulation to communication. These five types of questions, starting with the easiest and moving toward the more difficult, are differentiated on the basis of the way in which students respond. The classification is as follows (199–200):

Type 1: The question itself contains information from the reading sufficient for the answer.

Type 2: The question is answerable with information quoted directly from the reading selection.

Type 3: The question is answerable with information acquired from the reading selection, but not by direct quotation from a single sentence.

Type 4: The question is answerable from inference or implication from the reading; the information is not stated explicitly in the selection.

Type 5: The answer requires evaluation or judgment relating the reading selection to additional information or experience of the reader.

Below is a reading selection and suggestions for vocabulary study and comprehension questions to implement the reading in the classroom. This selection is probably most appropriate for teen-agers or adults, but the principles illustrated could be applied with any age group. It is assumed that this reading selection would be used at the intermediate level. (Adapted from an exercise written by Susan Voldahl, Program in English as a Second Language, University of Minnesota.)

Where Blue Jeans Began

Adapted from *Parade Magazine*, supplement to the *Pioneer Press*, St. Paul, Minnesota, November 24, 1974.

Most young people who wear them don't know where blue jeans come from. They believe they were originated by Levi Strauss of San Francisco in the 1848 days of the gold rush.

Denim originated in Southern France, in the city of Nimes, a textile center with a weaving history which goes back to the 16th century. About 450 years ago English merchants began importing a blue cotton cloth from Nimes which was called "Serge de Nimes." Over the years *de Nimes* became "denim."

It was Levi Strauss, a German immigrant from Bavaria, who took bolts of denim with him to San Francisco in the late 1840's, sold the tough cloth first for tents, then made them into pants, reinforcing the pockets with rivets.

The "jeans" half of "blue jeans" also comes from Europe, from Genoa, Italy, where the Genoese sailors wore trousers of blue canvas. *Genes* is the French word for Genoa; thus *Genes* became *Geanes* to the English. Later the Americans adapted *Geanes* to *jeans*.

Vocabulary and Grammatical Explanations

Before students can be expected to comprehend the passage, difficult vocabulary and structural items need to be discussed. This selection lends itself well to several types of word study. First, several items can be grouped since they are related to clothing or the manufacture of clothing: *trousers*, *textile*, *weaving*, *cotton*, *cloth*. The words *tough*, *rivets*, and *reinforce* can all be related to the concept of 'strength'. The partitive expression *bolts of* can be introduced to explain how cloth is sold by the manufacturer, and the further explanation could be provided that *yards of* cloth are sold to individuals. Reference is made to the *gold rush*; this could be discussed and related to the section of the country in which San Francisco is located. Word formation patterns in English can be pointed out with examples from the reading passage: *originate*, *origin*, *originator*; *immigrant*, *immigrate*; *re-in-force*. Stress patterns on English noun compounds could be illustrated with *góld rùsh* and *blúe jeàns*. For more sophisticated students, the difference between the active and passive use of *originate* might be explained (denim *originated*, blue jeans *were originated*).

Comprehension Questions

Next come the various types of comprehension questions geared to the level of reading that students have already achieved. The questions below follow Norris's classification. Not all students would need to begin with questions of the first type; and all students might not be competent to discuss questions of Types 4 and 5.

Type 1: a. Do most young people know where blue jeans come from?

b. Does the "jeans" half of "blue jeans" also come from Europe?

c. Did Genoese sailors wear trousers of blue canvas?

Type 2: a. Where did denim originate?

b. Who took bolts of cloth to San Francisco?

c. Where does the "jeans" of "blue jeans" come from?

Type 3: a. Where does the word *denim* come from?

b. What was denim first used for in the United States?

c. Why were rivets used on pants?

Type 4: a. Why was denim used for making pants?

b. Why do you think that "blue jeans" became the popular name for pants made of blue denim rather than "blue denims"?

c. Do you agree, after reading this article, that Strauss should *not* be considered the originator of blue jeans?

Type 5: a. Are blue jeans popular in your country?
          b. Do you wear blue jeans? If so, why do you like them?
          c. Do you think that blue jeans are appropriate to wear everywhere?

INTENSIVE AND EXTENSIVE READING

The reading done in the classroom is usually carefully guided and *intensive*. It is necessary preparation in order for students to do more rapid, *extensive* reading. In addition to the features discussed above, reading necessitates the ability to grasp the central idea of a paragraph or article and to scan material to find the main ideas. Harris (1966) provides exercises for practice in extracting the central idea or scanning for specific information, all part of intensive reading. Such ability is necessary if students are to be able to read extensively on their own with ease.

Many reading textbooks combine exercises on vocabulary, grammar, dictation, and composition with reading comprehension activities. This again illustrates the fact that the acquisition of one skill can be useful in acquiring another. The combination of all these skills will, of course, lead to greater fluency in extensive reading.

SELECTION OF READING MATERIAL

Reading material selected for class work should not be too difficult. Haskell (1977) suggests that administering a simple cloze exercise (deleting every fifth word from the first 250 words in a reading passage) can indicate the level of difficulty of a particular selection. If many students in a given class can fill in correctly (exact word scoring) less than 43 percent of the blanks, the passage is too difficult and should not be used with those students. If they can correctly supply over 53 percent of the words, they can read the passage well enough to understand it on their own; therefore, class time is not required to read it. Scores from 43 to 53 percent indicate that the passage is about the right level of difficulty for use in class. Although Haskell states that this interpretation of scores may need to be adjusted to individual situations, he finds that it gives an accurate indication of the level of difficulty of a reading selection.

Reading material should also be chosen on the basis of what interests the readers.[2] Baudoin et al. (1977) recommend non-prose reading material as being very effective: menus, newspaper articles, road maps, excerpts from almanacs, etc. Short selections on up-to-date topics are probably more attractive to students than longer selections of a more abstract content. The short selections in Pimsleur and Berger (1974) and the *SRA International Reading Laboratory* (1969) have great appeal for low intermediate, young adult readers.

One of my colleagues (Mark Landa) suggests that materials for reading should have problem-solving tasks built into them as a means of motivating reading. Information of an 'authentic' nature could be provided in the form of want-ads, television listings, catalogs, menus, maps, etc. which students are then asked to scan and read intensively to solve whatever problem was presented.

Reading that illustrates cultural behavior is often of interest to students, but the cultural content should be discussed beforehand to avoid confusion in the minds of students. Historical selections interest some students but bore others. Selections with some feature of suspense often motivate poor readers, who persevere just to find out what happens. Maintaining variety in reading material is probably one of the best solutions to the problem of providing selections that appeal to all students. For a general discussion of selecting and writing reading materials, see Suturia (n.d.).

Writing[3]

We come now to writing, which incorporates many of the abilities in using language that have already been discussed. Certainly a knowledge of grammatical structures is necessary for writing; and an understanding of the orthographic system (the relationship between sounds and written symbols) is as impor-

tant here as it was in the reading process — perhaps more so
since it must be productively employed.

Writing parallels speech, as we have pointed out previously,
and just as oral practice is necessary to become fluent in speaking a language, practice in writing is prerequisite to mastering
the skill of writing. A succession of exercises in writing can be
devised which resembles that used in practicing oral language.
Imitative practice (copying) in the early stages of learning to
write leads through progressively less structured activities to a
freer type of writing: composition.

A distinction needs to be made between writing and composition. Paulston (1972) states succinctly, "Writing is the activity
and the composition is the objective." Slager (1966) defines
composition as "writing beyond the sentence." Writing refers to
the physical act — copying and composing single sentences. We
are concerned here with both aspects of the writing process: the
physical activity and the composing process which leads to the
final product, the composition.

HANDWRITING

Writing a second language is more easily learned by those who
already know how to write in their first language. However, if
students do not already know how to write or if their own writing
system is not alphabetic, the teacher must provide exercises in
handwriting (forming script letters). This is necessary for the
same reason that it is necessary to learn to identify letters in
print. Unlike print, however, which is fairly standardized, there
is often great variation in writing styles. Students will need some
kind of handwriting guide to use as a model; it should contain
both small and capital letters. The guide should also include
Arabic numerals, which are sometimes formed differently by
speakers of various languages. Punctuation could also be included, since punctuation rules differ from language to language.
The handwriting guide below illustrates the necessity for writing
on the line (rather than between the lines as Arabic and Persian
speakers tend to do).

Handwriting Guide

Letters

Numerals

/ 2 3 4 5 6 7 8 9 0

Punctuation

. " " ? ! ' , ; : di =

vided

The ability to read the handwriting of others should also be developed since individual differences in handwriting (like differences in speech habits) can cause problems. Students can be given samples of different handwriting and be asked to identify certain letters. Those that are most frequently confused or misidentified are *t* (*t*, *r*), *r* (confused with *v*: *r*), *o* (confused with *a*: *o*), *n* (confused with *u*: *u*), *g* (confused with *y*: *y*). The tendency for some to imitate printing as they write should also be pointed out; written capital letters very often are formed more like printed capitals than the script form: A (**A**), F (**F**), L (**L**), Q (**Q**), Z (**Z**).

Writing and Composition

Adequate control of syntax and vocabulary is necessary in order to put ideas into writing. Writing also demands a familiarity with spelling patterns which can be developed through specific practice on spelling-sound relationships. Since native speakers of English have considerable trouble with spelling (witness the time spent on spelling 'bees' in British and American schools), it should not seem strange to devote time to spelling when teaching English to speakers of other languages.

In addition, students must learn to follow the general rhetorical principles typical of English composition, which include the logical organization of sentences within a paragraph, the linking of sentences within paragraphs, and the organization of the whole composition. Kaplan (1966) points out that rhetorical principles are probably not universal but language specific; therefore, what may constitute the basis for rhetorical organization in English may be different for other languages.

Danielson (1965:143) describes clearly the kind of writing that is usually done at the various levels of proficiency.

> At the elementary level in second-language learning, students usually begin writing sentences based on constructions and vocabulary items they have previously heard, spoken, and read. After that comes the writing of paragraphs and simple compositions, still primarily based on material learned through oral practice. At the advanced level, students have generally acquired sufficient control of structure, vocabulary, and the mechanics of writing to write freely on a wide range of topics with a minimum of error. Major attention can be given to organization and presentation of material and stylistic matters. The students at the intermediate level are somewhere between these two points. The problem is to get them from one point to another.

She then describes exercises suitable for students at the intermediate level. This kind of activity is usually referred to as guided writing or controlled composition, which will now be discussed in some detail.

GUIDED WRITING OR CONTROLLED COMPOSITION

Although there are some (Erazmus, 1960; Brière, 1966) who have recommended that students write as much as possible without being overly concerned about errors, there is now general agreement that some step-by-step procedure should be followed in the early stage of writing. The first stage in such a series of graded steps leading students to the ultimate goal of free composition is guided writing or controlled composition, which is defined by Slager (1966) as the kind of writing that "students can follow with reasonable expectation of success."

Dacanay (1963), Rojas (1968), and Paulston (1972) provide suggestions for exercises at this early stage such as the following: copying, completion, answering questions, dictation, and substitution. Praninskas (1965) mentions the following kinds of manipulations in controlled writing: direct statements to be changed to reported statements, third person reports to be expressed in the first person, and passive voice constructions to be made active.

These are guided writing exercises, beginning with the simplest and working toward the more complicated. All of these exercises assume that students have already successfully completed the first stage of writing, that is, they are able to copy simple sentences and to write them from dictation.

Robinson (1975) finds copying exercises that include grammatical manipulation an effective technique for reinforcing the teaching of the English tense system. In this type of guided writing she says, "Grammar, embedded in the structure of each sentence in the paragraph, becomes not a subject, but a tool." The following examples are manipulative, as are most guided writing exercises; but in addition to grammar drill, they offer practice in writing that is easily corrected either by the students themselves or by the teacher.

> Directions: Change the following paragraph of questions into a paragraph of affirmative statements.
>
> Are there many lakes in the state of Michigan? Are there also many parks? Do these lakes and parks provide many opportunities for outdoor activities in the summer? . . .

A somewhat less mechanical type of guided writing is developed in two stages by Robinson. In exercise (a) students are asked to change a paragraph of questions into negative statements, thereby supplying the true information on which the second exercise is based. Exercise (b) involves meaningful practice since students must remember the information from the preceding exercise.

(a) Directions: Change the following two paragraphs of ques-

tions into two paragraphs of negative statements.

Is Canada south of the United States? Is the Pacific Ocean
east of the United States? Does the Mississippi River run east
and west? Are the Rocky Mountains of the West older than the
Appalachian Mountains of the East?

Do most farmers in Florida grow wheat? Do most farmers in
California grow corn? Are oranges and grapefruit the chief
crops in New England? (Robinson, 1975: 14–15)

(b) Directions: Make true statements in response to the two
paragraphs of questions below, using your
knowledge or referring to your A7 paper [the
exercise above].

Is Canada north or south of the United States? Is the Pacific
Ocean east or west of the United States? Does the Mississippi
River run east and west or north and south? Are the Rocky
Mountains of the West younger or older than the Appalachian
Mountains of the East?

Do American farmers grow a wide variety of crops? Do most
farmers in Florida grow wheat, or do most farmers in Florida
grow oranges? (Robinson, 1975: 15–16)

Although the above exercises appear in paragraph format,
they cannot be considered practice in composing paragraphs
since they do not contain elements necessary for the development of the paragraph as a rhetorical unit (topic sentence, illustrations or comparisons, etc.). They are simply manipulative
drills to allow students practice in writing. However, writing
exercises can be developed that will illustrate paragraph composition. The following exercise from Robinson is an example of
the creation of such a paragraph model, once the directions have
been followed.

Directions: Change the following paragraph into statements.

Are young women selecting different careers these days?
Do some now prefer driving trucks to waiting on tables? Do

others choose to combine marriage with a career? Are some
women, who in former times might have been nurses or teachers, now becoming doctors or lawyers? . . .

Model paragraphs excerpted from literary works are often
used as a basis for writing practice with upper intermediate students. This is illustrated in the following exercise from Paulston
and Dykstra (1973:19) where students must pay attention to the
implications of changes they are asked to make in the model.

Irving Howe, *T. E. Lawrence: The Problem of Heroism*
   The hero is a man with a belief in his inner powers, a
confidence that he moves in rhythm with natural and historic
forces, lifted above personal circumstances. . . . For better
or worse, the hero as he appears in the tangle of modern life is
a man struggling with a vision he can neither realize nor aban-
don, "a man with a load on his mind."

Situation: Describe the personality of heroes.
Assignment: Rewrite the entire passage, changing *hero* to
              heroes. Change the pronouns, nouns, verbs, and
              determiners wherever necessary.

Situation: Describe the hero as he was in earlier times.
Assignment: Beginning *The hero was a man* . . . rewrite the
              entire passage in the past tense. Change *modern*
              to another word.

Situation: Describe the hero as he was.
Assignment: Beginning *The hero has been a man* . . . rewrite
              the entire passage in the present perfect tense.

   The excerpt from "T. E. Lawrence: The Problem of Heroism" was first
published in *The Hudson Review*, Vol. xv, No. 3 (Autumn, 1962) and is re-
printed by permission of the author. The exercise utilizing the excerpt is from
Controlled Composition in English as a Second Language by Christina Bratt
Paulston and Gerald Dykstra, New York: Regents Publishing Company, 1973.
Reprinted by permission of the publisher.

Many textbooks for teaching composition to speakers of other
languages are based upon grammar, and in these texts writing
exercises are correlated carefully with the grammatical structures needed in order to write about certain topics. Wishon and
Burks (1968) is such a text; and although the following exercise
is meant to give practice in writing, it also reinforces learning of

the comparative and superlative forms of adjectives and adverbs.

> Use the positive, comparative, and superlative form of the adjective or adverb in parentheses. Rewrite the entire paragraph.
>
> Some of the (interesting) inventions ever made occurred in the nineteenth century. A shaving stick was invented that was (good) than any other one and that wasted (little) soap than the earlier models. A Connecticut inventor worked (hard) and (fast) than his neighbors and finally produced the (good) mousetrap in the country. (Wishon and Burks, 1968:75)

As a first step away from strictly guided writing, still working within the confines of particular grammatical structures that students are able to control, assignments can be made in such a way to allow students a freer hand in writing. Two ways of making assignments that will elicit these already learned structures follow.

> (1) By specifying the grammatical construction to be used.
> (Based on an exercise written by Joyce Biagini, Program in English as a Second Language, University of Minnesota.)
> (a) Write a paragraph describing places you have visited. Include such things as historical monuments, museums, geographically important sites, or other things you have seen in your travels which seemed outstanding. Use the present perfect tense (have + past participle) where appropriate.
> (b) Pretend that you have just bought a new house which is much larger than your present house. Think of all the things you have to buy or don't have to buy and write a paragraph about them. Use each of the following words at least once.
> For things you have to buy:
>
> | a little | many |
> | some | a few |
> | much | a lot of |
>
> For things you don't have to buy:
>
> any
> no
> not many

(2) By supplying a topic sentence, as in the example following, that reinforces the learning of a specific grammatical construction (in this case, the conditional). (Based on an exercise written by Mark Landa, Program in English as a Second Language, University of Minnesota.)

As the fulfillment of a life-long ambition, you have just completed a trip by car from Minneapolis to San Francisco. Think of at least five things that could have gone wrong to interfere with the trip. Write these in "if . . ." cluases. Write the corresponding solutions to the problems in the main clauses. In other words, what would you have done if these things had happened?

Topic Sentence:

I had been thinking about my trip from Minneapolis to San Francisco for so long that I had solutions for almost any problems that might have arisen. (If I had run out of money . . .)

Free Composition

Praninskas (1965:146) says that it is erroneous to believe that once students have the ability to write sentences that they have heard or read they are ready for free composition.

We don't write themes by joining a number of conversational statement patterns with a lot of transitional glue such as *however*, *inasmuch as*, and *because of the fact that*. Prose style sentences are different from conversational sentence fragments. They are usually more precise, and they frequently express relationships which are more complex than those expressed by single sentences in speech. Furthermore, they are combined into paragraphs in ways that complement and supplement each other.

The structural signals, mentioned by Praninskas, that are used to express relationships between parts of sentences, such as *although* and *unless*, and those that link sentences or paragraphs, such as *however*, *nevertheless*, *on the other hand*, must be learned like any other lexical item. Unlike native speakers of English, who already know their meaning but may not know exactly how to use them in composition, speakers of other languages will know neither their meaning nor their use in composition. Acknowledging just such a lack, B. Taylor (1978) offers suggestions for teaching cause-effect relationships and comparison-contrast relationships in writing, and the kinds of structure words necessary for such expressions. He stresses the fact that paragraphs using cause-effect and comparison-contrast organization require sentence-level training in the syntactic structures used in such expressions. Students must learn the specific structural requirements for the use of transitional words or phrases such as *because, however, consequently; also, likewise, on the other hand*. In summary, he has the following to say about the similarity of paragraph development using chronological, cause-effect, and comparison-contrast organization.

> The fundamental organizational principles of these three kinds of paragraphs are basically the same, then. That organization is one which involves systematically dealing with one point and then moving on to the next. This is true of chronology, of giving reasons, and of presenting similarities and/or differences. Once a student is equipped with the syntactic knowledge necessary to write cause-effect or comparison-contrast statements, and is introduced to this basic principle of organization, simple paragraph writing of this kind should not present any great methodological difficulty.

One technique for developing the ability to sequence ideas within a paragraph and to learn the use of linking or transitional words is through the use of scrambled sentences which students are asked to reorder in logical sequence (Slager, 1966; Horn, 1977). The following is an example of a reordering exercise from Horn (121):

> You are to arrange the sentences in good order to make a coherent paragraph. First find the sentence that seems best for the topic sentence. Then look for signals (sentence links) that show how the other sentences fit together. Number the sentences in the order in which they should come in the paragraph.

_____The White House is a very large building.

_____His official home is called the White House.

_____Some of the rooms are open to the public.

_____The President of the United States lives and works in a special residence.

_____It contains reception rooms, offices, and rooms in which the President's family lives.

Reprinted by permission of Newbury House Publishers from *Composition Steps* by Vivian Horn, Rowley, Mass.: Newbury House, 1977.

This exercise assumes that instruction has already been given on items that signal reference, i.e., pronouns and connectors such as *however*, *the first*, *later*, and so on.

Another technique for teaching rhetorical organization and the ways in which various sentences are related to each other is by using model passages for analysis and imitation. The following exercise (Ross and Doty, 1975:173) is based on such a model (not reprinted here).

> Note the methods by which the ideas in the paragraph on history are related to each other: by repetition of a term (sentence 2, "a series of *events*"; sentence 3, "these *events*"), by previous reference (sentence 8, "*two* histories"; sentence 9, "The *first* is . . ."), and by transitional words and sentence connectors (sentence 3, "Nevertheless"; sentence 4, "but"). Analyze the passage for other transitional devices by answering the following questions.
>
> 1. How does the author relate sentence 5 to sentence 4? Sentence 6 to sentence 5? Sentence 7 to sentence 6?
>
> 2. What word relates sentence 8 to everything that has been said up to that point?
>
> 3. How are sentences 11 and 12 related to sentence 1? How does the author make this relationship clear?
>
> (Exercise 9 (p. 173) from *Writing English*, Second edition by Janet Ross and Gladys Doty. Copyright © 1965, 1975 by Janet Ross and Gladys Doty. By permission of Harper & Row, Publishers, Inc.)

This exercise also demonstrates the useful device of numbering sentences within a model passage for easy reference.

In order to write compositions, students must have something to write about. Morley and Lawrence (1971) suggest that films can be an excellent prelude to writing. Brooks (1964) suggests that students be asked to retell in their own words something they have read. After the reading has been thoroughly discussed in class, they will have learned to use the appropriate vocabulary and structures to retell the story; then, they will be prepared to write the story. This same technique can be used in preparing for writing an evaluative essay. An article can be discussed beforehand and then a critical composition written.

A specific technique useful at this point is the *dicto-comp* (Ilson, 1962; Wishon and Burks, 1968). The teacher reads a passage to the students who are then asked to write as much as they can remember of the passage. This is a dictation exercise to the extent that students remember exactly what the teacher has read, and it is a composition exercise to the extent that they use their own words in retelling the content of the passage. Ilson (301) points out that the dicto-comp prepares students to handle real-life communication.

> People learning a foreign language must for a long time express complicated ideas in a simple way. In so far as the students who work on a dicto-comp are unable to reproduce exactly what they hear, they must re-phrase the content of the passage using structures and vocabulary items within their active control — just as they will have to do in real life when recounting others' ideas, or their own.

From this point on, the kind of writing instruction given to speakers of other languages parallels closely that given to native speakers. They must learn various kinds of paragraph development: by example, by comparison and contrast, by explanation, by definition, and so forth. Ross and Doty (1975) and Lawrence (1972, 1975) provide exercises for developing the organizational skills in composition writing. An exercise from Lawrence (1972:93) demonstrates the stages through which students are led in enabling them to write a paragraph using comparison and contrast. Students have previously practiced the vocabulary and structures needed in statements of comparison and contrast. Then, with the information provided in the following exercise, they can intelligently compare and contrast information regarding news media.

Comparison and Contrast (News Media)

A. Examine the following data.
   1. In 1969 there were approximately 1,750 newspapers (written in English) in the United States.
   2. There were 328 morning papers and 1,443 evening papers.
   3. There were 578 Sunday papers.
   4. The daily papers had a circulation of around 62,500,000.
   5. The Sunday papers had a circulation of around 49,500,000.
   6. In 1960 there were 116 million home radios in the United States.
   7. In 1960 there were about two million TV sets in the United States.
   8. In 1968 there were 216 million home radios in the United States.
   9. In 1968 there were 64½ million black and white TV sets and 20 million color TV sets.
   10. The population of the United States in 1960 was 179 million; in 1969 it was 202,700,000.

B. On the basis of these data, write THREE statements of CONTRAST.

C. On the basis of these data, write THREE statements of COMPARISON.

D. Write a paragraph of COMPARISON and CONTRAST about the availability of news media to the U.S. population.

Outlining is an essential aspect of the composition process since it necessitates laying out the content in an organized fashion. It can clearly illustrate the use of certain rhetorical devices, such as the development of a theme by definition or by cause and effect. Outlining should not be overemphasized, to the point of substituting it for the actual writing of a composition, but it should be stressed as one of the means by which a good composition can be developed.

At the advanced level of writing, grammatical difficulties arising from students' errors are usually so varied that spending time during the class period discussing a given grammatical structure with the entire group would be an inefficient use of time. An individualized approach is generally more effective at this level. It is much more profitable for students to spend class time in actual writing and for the teacher to move around the class giving individual help as needed on grammatical problems as well as on those of spelling and rhetorical organization.

THE MECHANICS OF WRITING

The mechanics of writing — spelling, capitalization, punctuation, paragraph indentation, syllable division — must be systematically taught. Since languages have their own rules for these mechanical aspects of writing, it must not be assumed that if students know how to write they will know the English rules for punctuation, capitalization, and so forth.

Punctuation is sometimes pointed out when grammatical constructions are introduced, especially when it provides a clue to such constructions. (See, for example, Rutherford, 1975.) Following are examples of the use of commas with nonrestrictive relative clauses, appositives, direct address, quotations, and preposed adverbial clauses. These uses of the comma could be usefully practiced when the construction is taught.

My great grandfather, who was unusually tall for a man in the early nineteenth century, had a special bed made to accommodate his height.

My great grandfather, a captain in the Union Army, was unusually tall.

My father once asked him, "Grandpa, do you think I will ever be as tall as you are?"

For a man in the early nineteenth century, my great grandfather was unusually tall.

Most textbooks for teaching writing to speakers of other languages contain specific information about the use of punctuation (e.g., Wishon and Burks, 1968; Ross and Doty, 1975; Baskoff, 1971); and some grammar texts also provide punctuation rules (Danielson and Hayden, 1973; Praninskas, 1975).

Horn (1977) suggests a way of developing better spelling and punctuation habits through what she calls "copyreading." She provides a paragraph in which there are no punctuation marks and a few errors in spelling and capitalization. Students are then asked to identify the errors and supply the punctuation. This kind of exercise undoubtedly impresses upon students the need for accuracy in spelling and punctuation, and makes them better monitors of their own writing mechanics.

CORRECTING COMPOSITIONS

When students reach the point where they are assigned free compositions, the question arises of how to correct them. Although it is essential that errors be pointed out, the dreaded 'red-penciling' so typical of composition correction — reminiscent of the blood that students have figuratively shed in the process of writing the composition — is frustrating to both students and teachers. One solution to the dilemma of how much and what kind of correction to offer is the checklist approach toward correcting compositions suggested by Knapp (1965) and Robinett (1972). Knapp's checklist is designed for intermediate and advanced students; Robinett's is more appropriate for "the level just beyond guided or controlled writing, when students are just 'trying their wings' in composition." (Both checklists are reproduced on the following pages.)

COMPOSITION CHECKLIST

Date _____

Name _____

Focus _____

Outline

A clear thesis statement that can be supported or proved
Three or more useful supporting points

Text of the Composition

Complete sentences
Mechanics give a clean, orderly impression
> The title:
>> is correctly capitalized
>> indicates the subject clearly
>
> Adequate margins: __ left side, __ right side, __ top, __ bottom
> clear indentation for paragraphs
> Clear, easy-to-read handwriting or typing

Logical development of one idea in a paragraph
> A topic sentence that gives the idea/thesis of the paragraph
>> A clear controlling idea in the topic sentence
> Supporting statements that focus on the controlling idea
> Clear relationship or transition between sentences

Suitable introductory paragraph
> Arouses the reader's interest
> Indicates the central idea
> Suggests how the subject will be organized/handled

Suitable concluding paragraph
> Relates aspects of the subject that have been developed separately
> Summarizes in relation to the central idea
> Reestablishes the relation to the reader's interests

Desirable Qualities

This is a list of desirable aspects that can often be found in well-written compositions. Not every composition would have all of them, but in general they are marks of good writing. They are numbered so that they can be referred to easily.

1. Good selection of detail to suggest larger meaning
2. Careful, correct use of expanded vocabulary
3. Examples of artful phrasing
4. Correct punctuation to develop the meaning of sentences
5. Good use of parallel structure in series
6. Good use of phrases or clauses to tighten or modify the expression of an idea

[This is a recent revision by Donald Knapp of the original checklist that appeared in his article, "A Focused, Efficient Method to Relate Composition Correction to Teaching Aims," in *On Teaching English to Speakers of Other Languages* ed. by Virginia F. Allen. Copyright © 1965 by the National Council of Teachers of English. Reprinted by permission of the publisher and the author.]

Name_____

Composition_____

Program in English as a Second Language
University of Minnesota

COMPOSITION GRADING CHECKLIST

AGREEMENT

____ subject and verb do not agree

____ pronoun and referent do not agree

ARTICLES AND DETERMINERS

Omission   Incorrect Use

____ a   ____

____ an   ____

____ the   ——

____ others   ____

CAPITALIZATION

____ omission

____ incorrect

COMPARISONS

____ use *like*

____ use *the same as*

____ use *different from*

____ use *-er*

____ use *more — than —*

____ use *the -est*

____ use *the most —*

CONTENT

____ incorrect information

____ awkward: needs rewording

____ cannot understand your meaning

DOUBLE NEGATIVE

____ avoid double negatives

FORMAT

____ improper heading

____ improper size paper

____ not written in ink

____ no title

____ improper left margin

____ improper right margin

____ indent for each paragraph

NOUNS

____ should be singular

____ should be plural

____ improper form

____ mass noun (should be singular)

PARAGRAPHING

____ begin new paragraph

____ no new paragraph

PENMANSHIP (Handwriting)

____ handwriting interferes with communication

____ avoid non-English symbols

PREPOSITIONS

Omission   Incorrect use

____ in   ____

____ on   ____

____ at   ____

____ to   ____

____ of   ____

____ others   ____

PUNCTUATION

Omission   Incorrect Use

____ period .   ____

____ question mark ?   ____

____ exclamation point !   ____

____ comma ,   ____

____ colon :   ____

____ semicolon ;   ____

____ apostrophe '   ____

____ hyphen -   ____

____ quotation marks " "   ____

____ underlining _____   ____

____ others (dash, parenthesis, etc.)   ____

SENTENCE

____ incomplete sentence

____ two sentences run together

SPELLING

____ incorrectly spelled

VERBS

____ tense incorrect

____ form incorrect

____ do not use *to* after a modal

____ do not use *-ing* after *to*

_____ use *to* + *verb* form
_____ use plain form
_____ use *-ing* form
_____ incorrect sequence of tenses

VOCABULARY
_____ form incorrect
_____ item incorrect
_____ word(s) omitted
_____ unnecessary word(s)

WORD DIVISION
_____ divide words at syllable

boundaries
_____ write as one word
_____ write as two words

WORD ORDER
_____ observe SVO Place Time
word order
_____ incorrect question word order
_____ incorrect included question
word order
_____ change word order as indicated

This checklist was published originally in an article entitled "On the Horns of a Dilemma: Correcting Compositions" in *Studies in Honor of Albert H. Marckwardt*, edited by James E. Alatis, Washington, D.C.: Teachers of English as a Second Language, 1972. Reprinted by permission of the publisher.

When one uses the "Composition Grading Checklist," compositions are corrected only for selected items. These particular items are marked on the students' papers but not corrected. They are then clearly designated appropriately on the checklist so that students can see exactly what kinds of errors are being made. Students are then asked to correct their own errors and are directed to appropriate sources for help. Often students are asked to rewrite their compositions making the corrections as indicated. This approach concentrates on correcting a few items at a time, thereby avoiding the discouragement so often resulting when all errors are marked. At the same time, students can be made aware of resources (particular textbooks or even specific drills in textbooks) that will aid them in correcting their own errors, thereby providing a positive learning experience.

TERM PAPERS

Some ESL textbooks include instruction in term paper writing (Robinson, 1975; Ross and Doty, 1975; Yorkey, 1970), although at this stage of writing many students are able to use texts prepared for native speakers. Even though they may still have some problems in writing, they have arrived at a point where they not only can compete with native speakers, they are one step ahead of many native speakers: They can communicate competently *in writing* in a *second* language!

Culture as Part of Communication

As was pointed out in Chapter 4, Language and Culture, knowledge of the culture is easier to acquire when the language is being learned in the country in which it is employed as the usual medium of communication. Students are immersed in the culture of the language they are learning, and the actual use of the language is closely entwined with the culture it reflects. In an environment where English is a foreign language, cultural information usually must be specifically selected and introduced within the classroom, perhaps through pictures or films.

At a fairly advanced level, much cultural information can be garnered from fiction and drama written in English. Just as Mark Twain's *Huckleberry Finn* and Sinclair Lewis's *Main Street* provide present-day readers with a view of the American social situation of former times and of particular geographical regions, modern works of fiction and drama can be a source of information about American culture for speakers of other languages.

Contextualized activities of many kinds are an excellent means of teaching culture. The use of cartoons (Fowles, 1970), newspapers (Blatchford, 1973), and field trips (Wissot, 1970) offers many opportunities for introducing cultural information, as does the use of specific visual aids (Kreidler, 1971) and the general use of the bulletin board (Rees, 1970).

However, learning to know a culture is a lifetime work; many native speakers come upon aspects of their own culture from time to time of which they are completely unaware and which they may very well misinterpret. It behooves the non-native speaker to go slowly in trying to assimilate cultural information. Students should not expect to learn everything about the culture immediately, but bits and pieces of cultural information digested simultaneously with language will allow students to achieve a greater degree of communicative competence. They will better understand the social use of language.

Nonverbal Communication

Nonverbal communication is an important part of cultural behavior. A higher percentage of meaning is communicated through facial expression and body language (gestures and body motion) than one would think. Such nonverbal communication is language specific and should be learned as a corollary of the linguistic aspects of language. It cannot be learned all at once, but should be absorbed a little at a time, often by careful observation of one's peers.

Watching films and television is helpful in learning gestures and other types of body language. Role playing in the classroom should include appropriate nonverbal signals (gestures and body stance, for example). H. Taylor (1976) points out that just being a " 'doer' of American body language" does not enable one to teach it; he suggests that teachers should become more aware of the role of nonverbal communication in teaching English to speakers of other languages.

Textbook Evaluation

There are checklists available to help teachers evaluate textbooks they may wish to consider for adoption (Stevens, 1971; Cowles, 1976; Rivers, 1968). Joiner (1974) offers a special checklist for analyzing the cultural content of textbooks. Such checklists provide a handy reference for teachers who wish to ensure adequate coverage of various important aspects of learning a second language. Below is an outline suggestive of things to be considered in selecting a textbook for classroom use. It is not meant to be inclusive; individual teachers will think of additional items pertinent to their own particular situation.

Textbook Evaluation Checklist

1. Goals of the course in which the text will be used (Will this text help accomplish these goals?)
2. Background of students (Does this text fit the students' background?)

    a. age

    b. native language and culture (homogeneous or hetero-geneous class?)

    c. educational background

    d. motivation for learning the language

3. Learning theory and theory of grammar on which text is based (Will this cause a problem for the teacher?)

4. Skills emphasized (Is there a balanced approach toward the skills? Does the text emphasize skills which the curriculum is particularly interested in emphasizing?)

    a. listening

    b. speaking

    c. reading

    d. writing

5. Quantity of practice material (Is there a sufficient amount for the size class in which the text will be used?)

6. Quality of content (Does it reflect what is now known about language and language learning?)

    a. naturalness of language

    b. clarity of directions (for students and teacher)

    c. validity (Do the materials accomplish what they purport to?)

    d. variety and flexibility

    e. proficiency level (Does the text conform to the level it purports to serve?)

    f. datedness

7. Sequencing (Is there some general organizational plan?)

    a. by structures

    b. by skills

    c. by situations

    d. some combination of the above

8. Vocabulary (Does the text pay sufficient attention to this aspect of language learning?)

    a. relevance

    b. density

9. Use of special notation (Will this be easily understood by teachers and students?)

    a. phonetic symbols

    b. stress and intonation markings

    c. grammatical diagramming

10. Variety of English (Will this cause a problem?)

    a. British

    b. American

    c. particular American dialect

11. Cultural content (Is there evidence of some kind of cultural bias?)
    a. social
    b. sexual
    c. national
12. Format (Is the text attractive, usable, and durable?)
    a. clarity of type
    b. density of material on page
    c. size of book
    d. binding of book
    e. illustrations
    f. quality of editing
    g. index and chapter headings
13. Accompanying materials (Are there useful supplementary materials available?)
    a. teacher's manual
    b. workbook
    c. tapes
    d. flash cards
    e. posters

Classroom Management

Classroom teaching combines substance and technique. It requires a knowledge of content (substance) and the management of materials and procedures (technique) in such a way that the best possible learning situation is created. We have discussed both substance and technique throughout this book, but it seems appropriate now to focus attention directly on what comprises classroom teaching. We will do this by posing questions that will reveal some of the important factors implicit in classroom teaching. These questions are only suggestive of many more that could be posed. (See also Rivers, 1968:372–81; Finocchiaro, 1969:239–81; and Bumpass, 1963:186–87.) Each teacher can think of other questions that could be added to this inventory. Individual teachers will give more importance to some questions than to others, for teaching, after all, is a very personal, creative activity. Questions will be raised in relation to the three aspects of classroom teaching: the class, the teacher, and the lesson.

The Class

The class is made up of a group of students of a particular age, number, level of proficiency, and specific interests. All of these factors will have an effect on how the class is taught, which textbooks are used, what kinds of activities are appropriate, and how much material can be covered in a class period.

The physical aspects of the classroom are not at all unimportant. Are the desks movable or fixed? If movable, can they be arranged as desired each day or is there some restriction on how they can be placed? Is the room itself attractive or ugly? If the room is particularly ugly, are there ways in which it can be made more attractive? (Pictures, posters, or plants can sometimes improve the appearance of a room.) In addition to blackboard space — which should be considerable — is there a place for the display of visual material, such as a bulletin board? Is the room well ventilated? (Nothing is worse than a stuffy classroom!) Is it noisy? (If there is a pattern to the noise, classroom activities can sometimes be scheduled around the noise.) Is it too hot or too cold? Is there space for the teacher and students to move around? Few classrooms are physically perfect, but the teacher should try to minimize whatever defects exist in order to provide physical surroundings that are as attractive and comfortable as possible.

In addition to the physical characteristics of the room, there is the matter of classroom atmosphere — the mood set by the teacher. Is the atmosphere light and informal? Is the teacher's attitude helpful and positive? Does the teacher have control of the class without being stern and autocratic? Are tensions that sometimes arise between teacher and student or between students handled well? Does the teacher treat all students alike? Is there a balance between voluntary and obligatory responses so that each student has some responsibility to participate?

The Teacher

In regard to the second aspect of classroom teaching, the single most important factor is whether you, the classroom teacher, have made adequate preparation before you enter the classroom. Do you have a clear understanding of why you are teaching what is in the lesson? And do you see the relationship of what is being taught on a daily basis to the overall curriculum? Have you prepared the lesson so as to include a variety of activities during a class period? Do you have right at hand any special materials to be used during the class period? (Nothing is worse than to get to class and discover that some special material on which your lesson depends is somewhere else!) Do you know the names of the students in your class? (Do the students know each other's names?) Do you have an idea of the attendance record of the students? (Even though such a record may not be required, it may indicate that the student is having a problem which could interfere with learning.) Do you make yourself available to students who want to talk to you outside of class?

Participation in professional activities is a means of keeping up-to-date in your chosen field.[4] Do you subscribe or have access to the professional publications that will provide information about research in language learning and language teaching (which may confirm or disconfirm some of your most cherished beliefs about teaching), and about techniques that may liven your classroom.[5] Do you experiment and try to find out what works and does not work in your classroom? (See Brown, 1977, for suggestions about the ''teacher as researcher.'') Do you share your successes and failures in teaching with others who may profit from your experience? Do you participate in in-service training activities in your field when they are available? Do you ever take the initiative in requesting or in planning a workshop or meeting for teachers in your field?

The Lesson

The success of a given lesson is essentially dependent upon presentation and materials. The materials usually include a textbook and/or materials specially selected or devised by the teacher. If a textbook is used, do you rely on it too heavily? Have you adapted it as much as possible to your own students?

(For example, do you substitute vocabulary items that may be more appropriate for your students than those in the text?) Do you make sufficient use of the blackboard? (There are some who say that the blackboard is still the best visual aid a teacher can have!) Do you provide supplementary materials or activities to reinforce learning visually and to make the lesson more interesting and realistic? (Pictures, tapes, videotapes, and field trips belong in this category.) If you distribute materials that you have duplicated for class use, are they readable?

In bringing variety to the lesson, have you used the following types of presentation? (The choice, of course, will depend upon the specific objective of the total curriculum.)

Oral drills: individual or choral; dialogues
Listening activities
Dictation exercises
Speaking activities
Reading activities
Writing activities
Testing exercises
Oral reports
Dramatization or role playing
Free conversation
Games
Songs

In organizing the lesson have you reviewed old material? Have you introduced new material clearly? Have you provided adequate directions and examples for each exercise? Have you allowed sufficient practice so that most students feel they have learned the new item(s)? (You will have to decide what percentage of students will satisfy your feeling for 'most' in these circumstances.) Do the students seem to understand the relevance of what they are learning? Is the sequencing you are following a useful one? (Have you been hindered by the students' not having been introduced to an item that you feel is necessary at this point? Perhaps this is an indication of a need for a change in sequence.) Do you provide some way for students to realize how much they have learned (other than test scores)? ('Before' and 'after' tapes are useful for demonstrating improvement in the use of language. Students are taped on their first rendition of a dialogue or reading of a passage, then again after several practice periods.) Do you talk too much in class? (Teachers should concentrate on providing as much time as possible for students to use the language, as often as possible in a communicative way.) Do you allow students to comment (anonymously) on what they like or do not like about your class? Finally, do you continually ask yourself, "Are the students learning to communicate in the language?" If the answer is "yes," you are achieving your purpose, and there is no greater satisfaction to a teacher.

Analysis of a Lesson

In this section a detailed analysis is presented of the first lesson in Book One of the newly revised (third edition) of *English for Today* (McGraw-Hill, forthcoming), edited by William Slager. This lesson was selected for analysis for several reasons, not the least of which is the fact that I serve on the Editorial Advisory Committee for this series. A second, and far more important reason, however, is the fact that this textbook series is a joint venture of the National Council of Teachers of English and a commercial publisher to produce a series that reflects as nearly as possible the latest information about the English language and language pedagogy.

Since the lesson was not yet printed when this book went to press, it appears here without illustrations, which will greatly enhance its appearance. The text of the lesson is reprinted here in its entirety (in the left column), with notes to the teacher (in brackets) which will appear in the Teacher's Edition alongside the text material rather than in the midst of the text as they are shown here.

My comments on specific sections of the lesson appear in the right column. It is hoped that this analysis will be useful as an illustration of the way in which teachers may want to look at the materials they are using to see how they conform to the principles we have been discussing in this book. It also may provide ideas for ways in which materials may be adapted for more appropriate use in the classroom.

Lesson One: Getting Acquainted

The title indicates a specific communicative context, giving students the feeling they are learning English that will be useful outside the classroom.

GRAMMAR

am
I, *your*
Contraction: *I* + *am* > *I'm*

The grammar box indicates new items being introduced. Both students and teacher know exactly what is being presented. This provides Stevick's (1971) quality of 'transparency'. Also, the contracted form used in speech is clearly shown.

LISTENING

[Introduce yourself to the class.]
    Teacher

        Hello.
        I'm Mr./Mrs./Miss _____.
        I'm your teacher.
Hello
I
am
your
teacher

This listening activity is an integral part of each lesson, enabling students to become accustomed to paying close attention to the teacher's model. This first monologue (the predecessor of dialogues to come) provides a useful means of introducing the teacher but, more important, the initial setting for listening practice.

The vocabulary items in the left margin throughout the lesson are a helpful reminder of the new lexical items as they appear.

PRONUNCIATION

[Model the pronunciation of *I* /ay/, *am* /æm/, and *I'm* /aym/. Explain that contractions are necessary in natural conversational English.]
    Repeat:

Pronunciation also becomes an integral part of the lesson. Here is the immediate disclosure of the normalcy of contractions in speech and their relation to the full forms.

Permission to reprint Lesson One from the forthcoming third edition of *English for Today*, Book One, was granted by the publishers, McGraw-Hill Publishing Company and the National Council of Teachers of English.

1. I
2. am
3. I am
4. I'm

DIALOGUE

[Here, as in all future lessons, you should, whenever possible, introduce structure and vocabulary by referring the students to objects in the classroom.

Have the students introduce themselves to one another. Explain that the introduction with *hi* is informal.]

    S₁: Hi, I'm _____.

    S₂: I'm _____.

The directions to the teacher emphasize the importance of making the classroom activities as relevant to the students' own experience as possible.

Distinguishing between informal and formal kinds of language calls attention to the importance of the appropriate (as well as the grammatical) use of language.

Although S₁ and S₂ can be two different students in these dialogues, sometimes they can designate larger groups if the class is very large, e.g., rows of students or half the class.

GRAMMAR

> This is Marie.
> Is this Marie? Yes. No.

The grammar box indicates that a simple *yes* or *no* provides a sufficient answer to a yes/no question at this point.

LISTENING

[Walk along the front row. As you stand close to each student, say "This is _____." Then pick out students at random and ask, "Is this _____?" Have them answer with *yes* or *no*.

Now point to the chart or to illustrations as you say: "This is Marie; This is Ken;" etc. Next point to the figures at random as you ask questions with "Is this _____?" Call attention to the way your voice rises by raising your hand at the end of the question.]

The listening exercise requires *truthful* answers; language is being practiced in a meaningful way.

The use of the hand to indicate the rise in pitch on these questions is a helpful visual aid.

PRACTICE

Answer with *yes* or *no*.

Teacher: Student(s):

1. Is this Marie?   Yes (or) No.
2. Is this David?   _____
3. Is this Mark?   _____
4. Is this Kathy?   _____
5. Is this Joyce?   _____
6. Is this Ken?   _____

[Before students practice the following formal introduction, model the pronunciation of *Mr.* /místər/, *Mrs.* /mísəz/, and *Miss* /mis/. Then have students come before the class and model the dialogue.]

DIALOGUE

S₁: Mr./Mrs./Miss _____, this is Mr./Mrs./Miss _____.
S₂: How do you do?
S₃: How do you do?

GRAMMAR

| WH questions with *who* |
| Who's this?   (Ken) |
| Contraction: *who* + *is* > *who's* |

[Introduce *who* by using students in the class. As you stand close to each student, ask "Who's this?" and ask another student to supply the name.]

PRONUNCIATION

Repeat:

1. who
2. is
3. who is
4. who's

PRACTICE

Teacher (indicating a student):
  Who's this?
Another student: (name)   _____

This practice, which is based on charts or illustrations that provide information, again offers an opportunity for meaningful responses.

The use of a formal introduction (as well as the preceding informal introduction) indicates the appropriate social use of language.

Items that may be difficult to pronounce are practiced beforehand so that the dialogue will be produced more fluently.

The role-playing activity provides a more 'realistic' setting for language practice.

The grammar box highlights the grammatical item that is coming next in the lesson. The contracted form indicates the way in which it is spelled as well as emphasizing this important characteristic of spoken English.

Introducing grammatical items by involving the students themselves make the activities more meaningful to the students.

This exercise emphasizes the distinction between contracted and uncontracted forms.

[Now point to illustrations in random order and ask "Who's this?" Call attention to the way your voice falls at the end of these WH questions by lowering your hand:

Who's THIS?

Have the class imitate you.]

Gestures indicating the fall of the voice on these questions are useful visual aids.

GRAMMAR

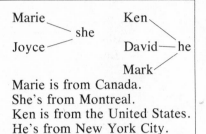

Marie is from Canada.
She's from Montreal.
Ken is from the United States.
He's from New York City.
Contractions: *she* + *is* > *she's*
            he + *is* > *he's*

The grammar box uses illustrations that are as close to an actual sequence in language as possible: *Marie is from Canada; she's from Montreal.* (Another more commonly used means of illustrating the same point is to repeat the sentence: *Marie is from Canada; she's from Canada.* However, this is not a natural sequence.)

[Point to cue cards or illustrations in the book. Say *he* or *she* as you point. Go around the room and point to students as you say *he* for males and *she* for females. If your students are all males or all females, use stick figures or pictures in the book.]
[Model the pronunciation of the individual words and of the contractions:

   she /šiy/ + *is* /iz/ > *she's* /šiyz/
   he /hiy/ + *is* /iz/ > *he's* /hiyz/]

The simplest possible explanation of lexical meaning is pointed out. The comment regarding the composition of classes emphasizes the fact that the teacher should consider his/her own students at all times when preparing the lesson.

Giving practice on the contracted forms alleviates the difficulty of producing them in the practice below.

PRONUNCIATION

Repeat:

1. she	1. he
2. is	2. is
3. she is	3. he is
4. she's	4. he's

PRACTICE

[Before you ask the students to repeat, model the pronunciation of the last names, the countries, and the cities: for example, *Martin*, *Canada*, *Montreal*.]

Giving practice on the individual vocabulary items will facilitate fluency in the following exercise.

Repeat:

[Pictures will be in the book or on posters.]

This is Marie Martin.
She's from Canada.
She's from Montreal.

This is David Campos.
He's from Mexico.
He's from Mexico City.

This is Ken Baker.
He's from the United States.
He's from New York City.

This is Kathy Baker.
She's from the United States.
She's from New York City.

This is Joyce Scott.
She's from the United States.
She's from Indiana.

[Explain that Indiana is one of the states in the United States.]

Learning the language can also include learning about the country in which the language is spoken.

This is Mark Scott.
He's from the United States.
He's from Indiana.

LISTENING

[Find out whether your students can hear the difference between *he* and *she* in questions. Pronounce the questions rapidly. The /h/ in *he* /hiy/ is often omitted when the word is unstressed: *Is he* /iy/ *from Mexico?*]

Follow the model. Respond with *he* or *she*.

Teacher: Student(s):
1. Is he from Mexico?   he

Discrimination practice is helpful in alerting the student to minute differences in sounds. In English this is especially important since many of these discriminatory problems may also involve differences between the spoken and written forms (e.g., *he* pronounced without /h/). The admonition to pronounce sentences rapidly is also important, since slowing down the rate of speech is

2. Is she from Mexico?   she
3. Is she from Canada?   she
4. Is she from the
   United States   _____
5. Is he from the
   United States?   _____
6. Is he from Mexico?   _____
7. Is she from Mexico?   _____
8. Is he from Canada?   _____

not going to help the student when he is faced with having to make this distinction outside the classroom.

PRACTICE

[Use cue cards or illustrations.] Answer with *yes* or *no* as appropriate.

The use of charts or illustrations means that students can make meaningful responses. In other words, the answers must be truthful.

Teacher: Student(s):
1. Is Marie from
   Mexico?   No.
2. Is she from the
   United States?   _____
3. Is she from
   Canada?   _____
4. Is Joyce from
   Canada?   _____
5. Is she from the
   United States?   _____
6. Is she from New
   York City?   _____
7. Is she from
   Indiana?   _____
8. Is Ken from
   Mexico?   _____
9. Is he from
   Canada?   _____
10. Is he from the
    United States?   _____
11. Is he from Indiana? _____
12. Is he from New
    York City?   _____
13. Is David from
    Canada?   _____
14. Is he from the
    United States?   _____
15. Is he from Mexico? _____

Follow the model.

    Model: Marie . . . Canada
           Marie   is   from
           Canada.

1. Marie . . . Canada
   Marie is from Canada.
2. Ken . . . the United States
   Ken is from _____.
3. Joyce . . . the United States
   Joyce is _____.
4. David . . . Mexico
   David _____.
5. Kathy . . . the United States
   Kathy _____.
6. Mark . . . the United States
   _____.

This kind of guided or controlled practice in producing statements provides the specific vocabulary needed but also forces students to recall the grammatical structure rather than providing for simple repetition.

Follow the model.

    Model: Marie . . . Montreal
           She's from Montreal.

1. Marie . . . Montreal
   She's _____ Montreal.
2. Ken . . . New York City
   He's _____ New York City.
3. Joyce . . . Indiana
   She _____.
4. David . . . Mexico City

   _____.
5. Kathy . . . New York City

   _____.
6. Mark . . . Indiana

   _____.

[The following drill combines the two previous ones and requires the students to remember these cues and form two consecutive sentences. It should be a challenge for the more advanced students. However, it is optional: your students can progress in the lesson if you choose to omit the drill.]

    Model: Marie . . . Canada
          . . . Montreal

         Marie   is   from
         Canada.
         She's from Montreal.

1. Marie . . . Canada . . .
    Montreal

    _____.

    _____.

2. Ken . . . the United States
    . . . New York City

    _____.

    _____.

3. Joyce . . . the United States
    . . . Indiana

    _____.

    _____.

4. David . . . Mexico . . .
    Mexico City

    _____.

    _____.

5. Kathy . . . the United States
    . . . New York City

    _____.

    _____.

6. Mark . . . the United States
    . . . Indiana

    _____.

    _____.

READING

Marie Martin is from Canada.
She's from Montreal.

Ken Baker is from the United
States.
He's from New York City.

David Campos is from Mexico.
He's from Mexico City.

Joyce Scott is from the United
States.
She's from Indiana.

Supply the name of the country:

1. Marie is from _____.
2. Ken is from _____.
3. David is from _____.
4. Joyce is from _____.

This exercise in reading follows
the pedagogically sound belief that
it is best in the early stages of reading to practice reading what has
been learned orally.

This cloze exercise provides an
opportunity for students to substitute items on a meaningful basis.

Supply *He's* or *She's*.
1. David: _____ from Mexico City.
2. Marie: _____ from Montreal.
3. Joyce: _____ from Indiana.
4. Ken: _____ from New York City.

[Be sure that all students have the opportunity to ask questions as well as to answer them.]

Follow the model.

David . . . Canada
S_1: Is David from Canada?
S_2: No.

Marie . . . Canada
S_1: Is Marie from Canada?
S_2: Yes.

1. David . . . Canada
S_1: Is _____?
S_2: No.

2. Marie . . . Canada
S_1: Is _____?
S_2: _____.

3. Ken . . . the United States
S_1: _____?
S_2: _____.

4. David . . . the United States
S_1: _____?
S_2: _____.

5. David . . . Mexico
S_1: _____?
S_2: _____.

6. Joyce . . . Canada
S_1: _____?
S_2: _____.

The use of S_1, S_2, etc. indicates that as many students as possible be given an opportunity to participate. In large classes, the S_1 role could be half the class, or the class could be divided by rows, with S_1 being one row and S_2 another.

Note that all the responses are based on the reading and are meaningful.

OPTIONAL EXERCISE

[A *no* answer in the following drill requires the students to supply the correct information:

These optional exercises are provided for students who have grasped the preceding exercises well. Not all students will be able

S₁: Is David from Canada?
    (wrong country)
S₂: No, he's from Mexico. (The
    correct country is supplied.)

to handle them, but those who can
should be encouraged to do so.

A *yes* answer requires the students to supply additional information.

S₁: Is Marie from Canada?
    (right country)
S₂: Yes, she's from Montreal.
    (additional information —
    the right city)

This makes heavy demands on the students' memory. A chart on the board may be helpful — for example:

```
              ╱(country) Canada
    Marie
              ╲(city) Montreal]
```

Follow the model:

S₁: Is David from Canada?
S₂: No, he's from Mexico.
S₁: Is Marie from Canada?
S₂: Yes, she's from Montreal.
S₁: Is Ken from Canada?
S₂: ____, _____.
S₁: Is Marie from Canada?
S₂: ____, _____.
S₁: Is Ken from the United
    States?
S₂: ____, _____.
S₁: Is David from the United
    States?
S₂: ____, _____.

GRAMMAR

	WH questions with *what*: What's your name?
what her his name first last	Possessive pronouns: *her*, *his*, *your*: What's her name? Marie Martin. What's her first name? Marie. What's her last name? Martin. What's his name? David Campos. What's your name?

[Make sure your students know that in English the last name is the family name. You can use names of famous people that your students already know. Or you can draw stick figures of members of a family on the board and show that they all have the same last or family name.]

Teacher: What's your first name?
Student: _____.
Teacher: What's your last name?
Student: _____.

[Introduce *his* and *her* by pointing to a student's book. Point to the book of a male student and say "his book." Point to the book of a female student and say "her book." If your students are all males or all females you will need to use pictures or the illustrations in the book. Model both the question and the reply so that the students will understand that they can supply a single-word answer.]

Model:

Teacher: What's his first name?
Ken.

Teacher: What's his first name?
S_1: _____

Teacher: What's his last name?
S_2: _____

Teacher: What's her first name?
S_3: _____

The note regarding first and last names illustrates the importance of cultural differences and the ways in which lexical items involving such differences may be explained.

Teacher: What's her last
      name?
S₄: —————————

LISTENING

[Make sure students can hear the difference between *his*, *her*, and *your*. The /h/ in *his* and *her* is often dropped when these words are unstressed.]
Respond with *his*, *her*, or *your*:

Teacher: Student(s):
1. What's her name?   her
2. What's his name?   ————
3. What's her name?   ————
4. What's your name?   ————
5. What's his name?   ————
6. What's your name?   ————

Emphasis upon listening discrimination exercises like this alert the student to the need for listening carefully to these unstressed words. It also helps to explain why English sounds different from the way it is written.

PRONUNCIATION

Repeat:
1. what   1. who
2. is   2. is
3. what is   3. who is
4. what's   4. who's

Again, the pronunciation exercise on contracted forms and their relationship to full forms makes this English pronunciation process clear.

PRACTICE

[Point to a picture of Marie as you model the drill.]
Teacher: What's her first
      name?
      Marie.
      What's her last
      name?
      Martin.

PRACTICE

Ask about Marie:
S₁: What's her first name?
S₂: Marie.
S₁: What's her last name?
S₂: ————.
Ask about Ken:
S₃: What's ————?

The practice is based on information available to all students so that the responses are meaningful.

S_4: _____.
S_3: What's _____?
S_4: _____.
Ask about Joyce:
S_5: What's _____?
S_6: _____.
S_5: What's _____?
S_6: _____.
Ask about David:
S_7: What's _____?
S_8: _____.
S_7: What's _____?
S_8: _____.

GRAMMAR

	WH questions with *where*: Where's he from? Where's she from?
are you where	*you are* Where are you from? Contraction: *where* + *is* > *where's*

[Introduce *you are*. Point to yourself and say, "I am _____." Point to a student and say, "You are _____."

PRACTICE

[In the contrastive situation below, be sure to stress *you*: Where are YOU from?

Have the students practice first with the name of their city and then with the name of their country. Teach them to pronounce the name of their city and country in English. If your students are all from the same city and country, you should make this practice very brief.]

Teacher: I'm from _____.
         Where are you from?
Student: I'm from _____.

Attention to the stress on *you* in the sequence "I'm from _____. Where are you from?" will help both teacher and student to use natural sounding language.

COMMUNICATION

[This is the first of the many communication drills you will find in this text. If you have a very large class, you might find it necessary to limit the activity to no more than 10 minutes at a time.]

[Make sure the students use the following intonation:

What's your NAME?

Where are you FROM?]

Here students are being asked to respond to questions that may well occur outside the classroom.

Ask your classmates:
1. What's your name?
2. Where are you from?

PRONUNCIATION

Repeat:

1. where	1. what
2. is	2. is
3. where is	3. what is
4. where's	4. what's

Practice on the contractions *where's* and *what's* is particularly important since the /r/ sound is difficult for many speakers of other languages.

Ask about Marie:
[Allow either full answers (*Her name is Marie*) or single words (*Marie*).]

S_1: What's her name?
S_2: _____.
S_1: Where's she from?
S_2: _____.

Ask about Ken:
S_3: What's _____?
S_4: _____.
S_3: Where's _____?
S_4: _____.

Ask about Joyce:
S_5: What's _____?
S_6: _____.
S_5: Where's _____?
S_6: _____.

Ask about David:
S_7: What's _____?

S$_8$: _____.
S$_7$: Where's _____?
S$_8$:_____.

PRACTICE WITH NUMBERS:

[Use flash cards or refer to numbers on the board.]

Repeat the name of the number.

1 one	7 seven
2 two	8 eight
3 three	9 nine
4 four	10 ten
5 five	11 eleven
6 six	12 twelve

[Count from one to twelve. Ask the students to listen carefully several times. Then ask them to try it themselves.]

Count from one to twelve.

Telephone Numbers:

[Explain that telephone numbers in the Untied States contain seven numbers. The first three are pronounced one at a time. Then, after a short pause, the next four are pronounced one at a time.

Supply other numbers if more practice is needed, and write the numbers on the board so that students don't have to memorize them.

The number *0* is referred to as the letter *O* or as "zero."]

Repeat:

1. 359-1704 _____
2. 822-6135 _____
3. 487-6018 _____
4. 338-6719 _____
5. 490-0536 _____
6. 509-6712 _____

Even though Arabic numerals may be familiar to students, they have to learn the English words that are used to refer to them.

Cultural information such as this regarding the pattern of telephone numbers helps students learn the appropriate use of language.

DIALOGUE

[Supply the meaning of "I have the wrong number." There is no need at this point to analyze the sentence.]

S₁: Hello?
S₂: Hello. Is this 233-1456?
S₁: No. This is 233-1457.
S₂: Sorry. I have the wrong number.

S₁: Hello?
S₂: Hello. Is (Ken) there?
S₁: (Ken)? (Ken) who?
S₂: Is this 322-4758?
S₁: No. This is 422-4758.
S₂: Sorry. I have the wrong number.

Supplying the meaning of a particular phrase, such as "I have the wrong number," allows for a much more normal use of language than if such phrases are avoided. Although lessons should not be overloaded with such items, they are useful in appropriate contexts.

GRAMMAR SUMMARY

Sentences (statements, *yes/no* and WH questions) with *am*, *is*, *are*
Pronouns
I
you, your
he, his
she, her
Structure words: *from*, *what*, *where*, *who*

The grammar summary allows both teacher and students to be aware of the items that are presented in the lesson.

WRITING

[Even if your students use the same alphabet in their own language, you should give practice in naming the letters in English.]

The Alphabet

Print

Early emphasis upon writing provides a balanced approach toward teaching the language.

Here, as with the numerals, students will need to learn the names of the letters even though they may be familiar with the alphabet.

Capital	*Small*	*Capital*	*Small*
A	a	B	b
C	c	D	d
E	e	F	f
G	g	H	h

I	i	J	j
K	k	L	l
M	m	N	n
O	o	P	p
Q	q	R	r
S	s	T	t
U	u	V	v
W	w	X	x
Y	y	Z	z

PRACTICE

Repeat the name of each letter above.

Learn the alphabet song.

[You may find that singing the alphabet song will not be an appropriate activity for older students.

Explain the importance of being able to spell one's name letter by letter. For example, point out that it is often difficult to understand someone over the telephone. Therefore, it's particularly important for your students to practice spelling out loud.]

Say your name. Then spell it.

　S_1: My name is (Ken Baker).

　　(K-E-N B-A-K-E-R).

Cursive

Writing Practice:

1. Copy:

1. *g*___   5. *t*___

2. *j*___   6. *y*___

3. *f*___   7. *m*___

4. *h*___   8. *z*___

2. Copy:

1. *F*___   5. *O*___

2. *G*___   6. *R*___

3. *J*___   7. *T*___

4. *L*___   8. *W*___

3. Write the numbers your teacher dictates.

[Use only numbers one through twelve in the exercise below.]

Follow the model.

Teacher:	Student(s):
one	*1*
seven	*7*
three	*3*

4. Write the small letters your teacher dictates. Follow the model.

Teacher:	Student(s):
a	*a*
d	*d*
f	*f*

If a person is unfamiliar with the Roman alphabet, specific practice in forming the letters is needed. Also, users of the Roman alphabet often differ in the way they form the letters.

Simple dictation exercises like these provide excellent listening practice. They can also be used as testing exercises to ascertain which students may need remedial help with identifying numbers or letters.

SUPPLEMENTARY ACTIVITIES

1. Ask about telephone numbers.

[If most of the class members do not have home telephone numbers, this exercise should be skipped or you could substitute the following: "What's the telephone number of your doctor? Your school? The police?" etc.]

S$_1$: What's your telephone number?

S$_2$: ———.

2. Ask about people's names.

[Have students bring magazines and newspapers with pictures of famous people (for example, movie stars or historical figures) to class. Make sure the students answer with the name only.]

S$_1$: Who's this?

S$_2$: ———.

3. Practice spelling.

[This is called a "spelling bee." The leader says the words introduced in this lesson; the other students spell them. If a student misspells a word, that student is out of the game and takes a seat. The winner is the last student standing.]

These supplementary activities appear throughout the book and offer the opportunity for less structured practice than is usually attempted in the classroom. They extend the content of the lessons to activities that will directly apply to communication outside the class and that will be particularly enjoyable to students.

Notice that in the first and second supplementary exercises the responses are simple (only numbers or a name). This is a perfectly natural use of language that avoids the necessity of pronouncing the difficult consonant cluster in *its* . . . or choosing between *this is* . . . or *that is* . . . in this first lesson.

The spelling bee is not only useful, it is part of English-speaking culture, a direct result of the complexity of the spelling-sound relationships in English.

right	Leader: Spell the word *hello*.
you + are	Student: H-E-L-L-O.
you're	Leader: Right. (or, I'm sorry. You're wrong.)

Exercises

A. Write a dialogue (or select one from a textbook) that illustrates the formulas for introductions. How could this dialogue be changed to fit particular situations?

B. Write an example of each of the following types of structural drills illustrated in Chapter 1: imitation, substitution, transformation, and response. If your students are all of the same language background, also write a translation exercise.

C. Write a dictation exercise that will provide practice on the comprehension of reduced forms (e.g., contractions and unstressed pronouns).

D. List the kinds of grammatical constructions that would probably be needed in order to use English in the following communicative situations.

requesting information	wishing
expressing likes and dislikes	affirming
describing things	closing conversations
advising	expressing possibility
expressing ability	expressing conditions

E. Select a given grammatical construction and devise a series of mechanical, meaningful, and communicative exercises such as those illustrated on pages 207–10. Or write a manipulation-communication exercise patterned after that on pages 210, 211.

F. Develop a minimal pair exercise using words and sentences to practice the comprehension and production of any of the following sounds (or any other pair of sounds your students may be having difficulty with): /iy/ and /i/; /š/ and /č/; /v/ and /w/; /l/ and /r/; /ə/ and /a/; /f/ and /p/.

G. Observe your own 'classroom talk'. Make a note of anything you say that might be somewhat unnatural or that reflects your attempt to 'help' students better understand what you are saying.

H. If you teach young children, prepare a story to present to your class (*not* "The Three Bears"), using pictures, puppets, or other visual aids.

I. Make a list of the telephone numbers in your community that provide recorded messages useful for students to call for listening practice. Devise specific questions that they could obtain answers to by calling one or another of these numbers.

J. Record two dialogues — one formal, the other informal. Note the items that characterize the style of each. Play them for students as a means of helping them identify these clues.

K. Devise a dialogue that will provide practice on some linguistic item on which students make frequent errors. This could be used as a 'before' and 'after' sample of their speech if recorded early in the term and then again later after they have had practice on the particular item.

L. Make up an exercise like Exercises D and E on page 200 for guessing the meaning of words from context.

M. Select a short reading (or write one) and make up comprehension questions of the five types described by Norris and listed in this chapter.

N. Prepare a guided writing exercise similar to the examples in this chapter.

O. Select a title for a composition that you think will elicit a particular grammatical construction. Provide two or three sentences of the type you would like to find in such a composition.

P. Select a reading passage and note the devices used to relate sentences to each other (the use of pronouns and words like *however*, *in addition*, etc.).

Q. Re-read an American short story and note any cultural content that might be difficult for a non-native English speaker to understand. How would you attempt to make the reading of the story easier?

R. Analyze the use of nonverbal communication on a television program. List the gestures, body motion, use of space, and facial expressions that occur in a fifteen-minute segment.

S. Analyze the management of your classroom (or that of a

classroom you are able to observe). What questions would you add to those posed in this chapter regarding the class, the teacher, and the lesson?

Notes

1. Allen, Allen, and Shute (1966) is an excellent resource for spelling-sound correspondence in English.

2. Motivation is a very strong factor in reading. I recall that the very first thing my son learned to 'read' was the Coca Cola sign which appeared outside every *cafetin* across the island of Puerto Rico. He knew what interested him, and he looked for it everywhere!

3. In writing this section, I have profited greatly from discussions with Dennis Godfrey.

4. TESOL, an association of Teachers of English to Speakers of Other Languages, is the largest organization devoted entirely to English as a Second Language, English as a Second Dialect, and Bilingual Education. ATESL, Association of Teachers of English as a Second Language, is a section of the National Association for Foreign Student Affairs, and its membership includes those who are primarily interested in teaching English to speakers of other languages in colleges and universities. Within other organizations such as the National Association of Bilingual Education, National Council of Teachers of English, National Association of Continuing Basic Education there are also groups with special interest in teaching English to speakers of other languages.

5. Professional publications containing articles of interest and use to teachers of English to speakers of other languages are listed in the bibliography. In the United States, TESOL issues a newsletter and plans annual conventions, in addition to publishing *TESOL Quarterly*. It also regularly publishes a directory of teacher preparation programs in ESL and bilingual education (Blatchford, 1977). There are also state and regional affiliates of TESOL that publish newsletters and hold workshops and conferences. Overseas teachers have access to materials published by the United States Information Services, which include *English Teaching Forum*, a journal for teachers. These materials are available through U.S. embassies and consulate offices.

8

Testing

As in any discipline, evaluation plays an important part in teaching and learning English as a second or foreign language. Teachers and students alike are eager to know how well they are each achieving their goals. It must be remembered that there is a very fine line to be drawn between teaching and testing; as a matter of fact, they often overlap. Testing can be a very effective means of teaching, and teachers and students alike know that tests often provide a very strong motivation for learning. Furthermore, teachers are constantly engaged in an informal evaluation of their students' performance. In this chapter, however, we will be primarily concerned with testing in formal situations.

Types of Tests

Evaluative instruments — tests — are of several kinds and can be classified in various ways. One way to categorize them is in terms of who produces them. If they are commercially published and available for widespread use, they are referred to as *standardized* tests. If they are created by individual teachers for their own use, they are *classroom* or *teacher-made* tests.

Harris (1969:13) has set forth the following criteria for good tests of all kinds.

> All good tests possess three qualities: *validity*, *reliability*, and *practicality*. That is to say, any test that we use must be

appropriate in terms of our objectives, *dependable* in the evidence it provides, and *applicable* to our particular situation.

Valid tests are those that do the job for which they were designed. A test has little validity if it measures something other than what it is supposed to measure. For example, a test that purportedly measures control of English grammar but that contains such difficult vocabulary that it is actually measuring knowledge of lexicon is not a valid test of grammar.

Reliability refers to consistency in measuring whatever is being evaluated. In other words, reliable tests are dependable tests. If you give the same test twice to the same group with a minimum time lapse between, you will get the same results. Reliability is also directly related to adequacy of the sample used in measuring. Thus, in a classroom situation the average of scores on several short quizzes or compositions over a period of time will provide more reliable information than the score on one long examination.

Harris's third quality, practicality, is especially important from the teacher's point of view. Facility in administration (no need for special pencils or equipment, for example) and ease of scoring are factors to consider in a testing program.

Standardized tests usually meet all three of Harris's criteria. They have usually demonstrated a high degree of validity and reliability, and are easy to administer and score. Normative information (often in terms of age and grade level) is generally available for scores on standardized tests. Such information allows users to compare scores that their own students receive on the tests with the scores of similar populations across the country (or around the world, in the case of internationally administered tests). However, populations used for norming must be considered carefully when applying norms to other groups. For example, grade norms obtained for one population cannot be universally applied, since this may work to the disadvantage of certain schools and certain types of students (minority children, for example). Brière and Brown (1971) provide a helpful discussion of norming procedures, and they emphasize the importance of knowing the characteristics of the group on which norms are based.

Classroom tests form an important part of any instructional program; and, depending upon their quality, they can be effective measures of language ability. They can often assess skills that standardized tests, constructed to be as easy as possible to administer, do not attempt to evaluate: i.e., actual productive use of the language. In addition, teacher-made tests can be specifically tailored to the particular instructional situation.

Purposes for Which Tests Are Used

A second method of classifying tests is by the purpose for which they are used. A *general proficiency* test is one that is designed to measure total competence in a subject. It includes items that range from easy to very difficult in order to discriminate clearly between levels of proficiency. A language proficiency test will usually measure a wide range of skills (listening comprehension, reading comprehension, writing ability) as well as subject matter (grammar, vocabulary, pronunciation).

An *achievement* test, on the other hand, is utilized to discover how much has been learned of what has been taught. If on completion of a specified amount of subject matter the teacher wishes to know how well students have assimilated the particular material that has been taught, an achievement test is in order. Such a test will include only that which has been taught and for which the students are held responsible. Many teacher-made tests are achievement tests.

Sometimes it is useful to discover whether or not students possess a talent for language learning. In such cases an *aptitude* (or *prognostic*) test is used. One widely known language aptitude test, the Carroll-Sapon Modern Language Aptitude Test (1959), includes exercises in number learning, phonetic script, spelling clues, functions of words in sentences, and memorization of paired associate words. Another, the Pimsleur Language Aptitude Battery (1966), assesses vocabulary knowledge in English, skill in language analysis (using a hypothetical language), discrimination of sounds (using sentences in Ewe, a language spoken in Ghana), and sound-symbol association. Both of these aptitude tests stress the role of memory, sound-symbol association, and sensitivity to grammatical structure, competence in which is thought to reflect aptitude for language learning.

By far the most frequently used tests are those of achievement and general proficiency, the former usually for evaluating recently acquired knowledge and the latter for assessing overall, long-term acquisition of knowledge. Both proficiency and achievement tests may be used as *diagnostic* tests to discover particular points of difficulty students may be having. They may also be used as *placement* tests to ascertain at what level students should enter a language program. Of course, specific tests may be developed for diagnosis or placement. Ilson (1962) recommends the dicto-comp for diagnostic and placement purposes.

Testing students' grasp of a second culture can be done, but it is not easily accomplished. Lado (1961), Seelye (1966), Upshur (1966), and Yousef (1968) suggest ways in which cross-cultural knowledge can be assessed. Below is an item used by Yousef (1968:230) to test the knowledge of American culture acquired by Middle-Eastern employees of an American business organization.

> The two friends John Smith (an American) and Ahmed Ali (a Saudi Arab) have belonged to the same club for a period of time. Lately, Ali was out of town on a work assignment.
> He is now back for a few days. Yesterday afternoon, Ali went to the club to see his old friends and spend some time with them. His friends were sitting and chatting in the lounge. As soon as John saw Ali he waved his hand and asked Ali to come and join them. According to American culture, John's attitude was
>
> a. rude   b. indifferent
> c. incomprehensible   d. friendly

Yousef makes the following comments on the responses to this item.

The answers spread over the three wrong choices. Only fif-
teen students of the one hundred and twenty thought John's
attitude was friendly, because according to Middle-Eastern
culture, John should have gotten up, hugged, shaken the hand
of his friend, expressed pleasure at seeing him, and asked how
he was. The majority of the students saw the situation only in
terms of their native culture.

A word of caution is in order concerning the use of
standardized tests for purposes other than that for which they
are designed. For example, standardized reading tests designed
for middle-class Anglos are not valid measures when administered to Navaho children on a reservation or to Chicano children
in an urban ghetto. Another misuse of standardized general
proficiency tests has been by researchers attempting to measure
the effectiveness of various teaching methods. Only specially
designed achievement tests would be valid in this case. In other
words, great care must be taken to ensure that tests are not
misused or test results misinterpreted.

Discrete-Point and Integrative Tests

Another way in which tests can be distinguished is in terms of
what Carroll (1961) calls the "discrete structure-point" or "integrative" approach. Tests that evaluate control of specific linguistic items are *discrete-point* tests; those that require an integrated
use of language are *integrative* tests. Carroll says that the former
can best be used to measure knowledge of such things as items of
structure (morphology and syntax), items of the lexicon (vocabulary and "idiomatic phrases"), and auditory discrimination (contrasts in sounds, stress, and intonation). He says that the latter
kind of test (integrative) is what is required for evaluating listening comprehension, speaking, reading comprehension, and written composition.

Because of the seeming ability of integrative tests to measure
overall language proficiency (Darnell, 1970; Oller, 1973b), much
emphasis is now placed on developing and utilizing such tests.
This tendency is also a result of a changing attitude in language

teaching methodology from the strict audio-lingual to a more communicative approach.

Oller (1971) is a strong proponent of the use of *dictation* as an integrative test because he has found that it is a reliable device for evaluating general language proficiency. Oller and Conrad (1971) believe that the *cloze* test is also a reliable measure of proficiency. They provide the following explanatory comments about its origin (183).

> The word "cloze" was invented by W. L. Taylor (1953) to refer to a type of test originally designed to measure the readability of passages of prose. The test was constructed by deleting words from a selection and requiring the examinee to fill in the blanks. The average score for a large group of subjects was taken as an index of the level of difficulty of the passage. The term 'cloze' was used with the notion of Gestalt "closure" in mind, referring to the natural human psychological tendency to fill in gaps in patterns. The restoration of words deleted from a selection of prose in order for the passage to make sense is a special use of this ability to comprehend broken patterns.

Cloze tasks demand of examinees that they bring to bear on the particular passage before them all the knowledge they possess of the language. Oller and Conrad point out a major advantage of the cloze test (187).

> The most important argument in its favor is that it requires the student to perform a task which is not unlike what native, speakers do in sending and receiving messages. In listening, we anticipate what the speaker will say next and frequently (either overtly or covertly) supply missing words or phrases. In speaking, we sometimes find ourselves groping for a word halfway into a sentence.

In addition, the cloze test fulfills Harris's criterion of practicality, as Oller and Conrad also point out (187).

> A second important advantage of the cloze test is its ease of construction and scoring. All that a person preparing the test need do is (1) select a passage of prose of suitable difficulty — definable in terms of a population and its language objectives

— of approximately 250 to 500 words in length. (2) Delete every *n*th word (where *n* usually is a number between 5 and 10). This mechanical method of selecting blanks to be filled in by the student can, in the long run, be expected to reflect the frequency of occurrence of grammatical and lexical forms in the languages tested.

Below are excerpts from a cloze test of reading in which every sixth word has been deleted. A key to the exact words to be replaced is supplied at the end of the passage. An alternative to exact-word scoring permits acceptable substitutes for these items, usually those that native speakers may supply when asked to perform the task. Such acceptable substitutes are also provided for the cloze sample below.

Thomas Alva Edison[1]

In the history of applied ——(1)——, Thomas Alva Edison stands alone. ——(2)—— a thousand patents are credited ——(3)—— him. A Congressional committee once ——(4)—— the value of his inventions ——(5)—— $15,599,000. He was a man ——(6)—— tremendous energy and phenomenal intelligence.

——(7)—— was born in Milan, Ohio, ——(8)—— February 11, 1874. He started ——(9)—— work when he was twelve ——(10)—— old. He began working as ——(11)—— train boy in order to ——(12)—— support himself. Three years later, ——(13)—— began publishing a small newspaper ——(14)—— the railroad employees.

. . . Edison avoided ——(48)—— in social activities because he ——(49)—— that they were a waste ——(50)—— time. He never remembered to ——(51)—— his appointments, much to the ——(52)—— of his wife and ——(53)——. Edison continued to live in ——(54)—— manner until his death in 1931. ——(55)—— life was an illustration of ——(56)—— own formula for success: "Two ——(57)—— inspiration and ninety-eight percent perspiration."

Key
(Acceptable alternatives in parentheses)

1. science
2. Over (Approximately)
3. to
4. placed (estimated)
5. at
6. of
7. Edison
8. on
9. to
10. years
11. a
12. help

13. he	52. annoyance (chagrin)
14. for	53. friends (acquaintances)
48. participating	54. this
49. felt (thought, believed)	55. His
50. of	56. his
51. keep	57. percent

"Exact-word" and "acceptable substitute" cloze tests correlate very highly with each other (Oller, 1972); a relatively long test of one type will measure students' abilities about as well as the other. Each has advantages. The exact-word type is easier to score when large numbers of students are being tested, but the acceptable substitute type may be more pedagogically useful to teachers in assessing the control that individuals have over the language.

A type of modified cloze test that Harris (1976) calls "rational deletion" involves the omission of particular linguistic items selected by the teacher for this purpose. Oller and Inal (1971) describe such a test of prepositions. It could be equally useful with other structural items such as articles or pronouns.

Another type of cloze test is the multiple-choice (M-C) cloze test which provides several items from which students make a selection. Jonz (1976) found that an M-C cloze test, which took about twenty minutes to administer and less than a minute each to score, was as reliable in ninety percent of the cases as a three-hour placement test that took thirty minutes each to score.

Test Scoring

Objective tests are those in which individual items have only one correct answer. Therefore, they are easy to score, and scorer reliability is high; i.e., several raters will score the test in the same way. *Subjective* tests, on the other hand, contain items that may be scored differently by different raters. They are more difficult to use, but in some instances — for example, in testing the ability to write a composition — subjective scoring is unavoidable. It need not, however, be unreliable if raters are given specific training in such scoring (Harris, 1969:70).

Students from other countries often have had little or no exposure to objective tests and initially, at least, find them confusing. Care must be taken to provide sufficient practice in taking objective tests before subjecting students to a battery of tests that are unlike those with which they have been familiar.

Types of Test Items

There are several excellent reference books that illustrate in detail various types of items which can be used to evaluate control of both the linguistic aspects of language (grammar, pronunciation, vocabulary) and the language skills (listening and reading comprehension, speaking and writing ability). The reader is referred especially to Dacanay (1963), Harris (1969), Heaton (1975), Lado (1961), and Valette (1977).

Most testing experts mention the following types of testing techniques: completion, multiple choice, composition, and oral production. Examples of each of these frequently used types of testing exercises follow.

COMPLETION

Fill the blank with an appropriate preposition.

Mary lives _____ 2607 River Road.

MULTIPLE CHOICE

Select the item that is closest in meaning to the underlined part of the sentence.

They postponed their trip until next year.

        a. put on
        b. put off
        c. put out
        d. put through

COMPOSITION

(This item is taken from Harris [1969:78], who emphasizes the importance of providing unambiguous directions for writing a composition.)

Describe an interesting member of your family: one of your parents or grandparents, a brother or sister, cousin, aunt, or uncle. Be specific in describing the special characteristics that you think make him or her an interesting person. You may wish to give examples of things this person has said or done which illustrate these characteristics.

ORAL PRODUCTION

Structured speech sample: The examinee is asked to read aloud several sentences, each containing one or two pronunciation problems.

With pictures as stimulus: The examinee is given a series of pictures to look at for a brief period and then asked to describe what is happening in the pictures.

Unstructured interview: The examiner (or preferably examiners) conducts an informal interview with the examinee on a topic that the person interviewed has not been informed of beforehand.

Although multiple-choice items are very commonly used in objective tests, they require considerable time to prepare. Most classroom teachers find that other types of items may be written more easily and still be objective. For example, the completion type is objective in that only one correct answer is possible. Another equally objective item could be produced by restating the original multiple-choice item given above (containing the underlined word *postponed*) thus: "Explain the underlined portion of the sentence in your own words." Harris (personal communication) suggests the following to teachers who want to use multiple-choice items on tests for large groups of incoming students in the fall but find them too time-consuming to construct: "Give free-response items to this year's classes and use the most frequent 'wrong answers' to create multiple-choice items for next fall's entering class."

Standardized tests of general proficiency in English now quite often utilize short conversations or two-line dialogues as context for multiple-choice questions. These tend to provide a setting for the language item being tested and give the feeling of a more realistic language situation. Below are two examples of this kind of item.

"Do you mind closing the window?"
"_____. It's too cool with it open."
  a. Yes, I don't.
  b. No, I don't.
  c. Yes, I do.
  d. No, I mind.

"How old is Susan?"
"She's younger _____ her sister."
  a. of
  b. than
  c. that
  d. for

Testing Exercises

Teacher-made exercises can comprise a test. For example, after dealing with the distinction between the past and the present perfect tenses in English, it might be desirable to test whether or not students have learned the difference in form between these tenses and, what is probably more important as well as more difficult, are able to use the two forms in appropriate situations.

An exercise that tests control of form alone might be something like (A), whereas (B) tests both form and appropriate use.

A. Fill in the correct past form of the verb in parentheses.
  1. Bill (live) _____ in New York from 1970 to 1974.
  2. Before that, he (move) _____ from place to place.
  3. He never (stay) _____ in one city very long.

B. Use the appropriate form of the verb in parentheses (past or present perfect).
  Allen (live) _____ in St. Louis since 1970. Before that he (move) _____ from place to place. At that time he (want)

_____ to travel, so he never (stay) _____ in one city more than a year. A few years ago he (change) _____ his mind. As a matter of fact, he (own) _____ a house in St. Louis for the past two years.

Single exercises like these can be a test of sorts, but it must be remembered that only a large number of such discrete-point exercises will provide reliable information about an individual's control of the language.

Test making is not an easy task. Many traps lie in wait for the unwary, as any experienced teacher knows; and students have a way of springing these traps with relish. Test items should be carefully worked out by the teacher before using them. Better still, if the test is one that will be utilized many times, pretesting the items will assure the teacher of a more reliable test. An item that everyone answers correctly is too easy and should be discarded. If a particular item is missed by almost everyone, it may mean that the item deals with information that has not been well taught and needs further attention (if it is an achievement test item), the item is too difficult for everyone (if it is a proficiency test item), or the item is poorly written — perhaps ambiguous. A poorly constructed item should be discarded during the pretesting stage; if a defective item appears when pretesting has not been possible, it should not be counted in the scoring.

Improving Classroom Tests and Their Use

Some ideas for improving the construction of classroom tests have already been suggested: items should be checked carefully before actual use and discarded if found to be too easy or too difficult; unambiguous instructions should always be provided; practice in taking objective tests should be given to those not familiar with this technique. In addition, in sequencing test items it is best to begin with those that are easy and work toward the more difficult so that examinees do not become discouraged early in the examination.

If pictures are used as stimuli in tests of oral production, they should be culture-free; that is, as far as possible they should be capable of being interpreted in the same way by a member of any culture.

For ease in scoring multiple-choice tests the use of separate answer sheets is suggested, since they can be corrected rapidly with a stencil overlay and the test booklet can be used again.

Finally, the use of classroom tests can be improved by paying careful attention to the purpose for which they were designed and the ways in which the results are interpreted. Tests are not infallible measures; they should be regarded as a relative rather than an absolute assessment of ability.

Available Tests of English for Speakers of Other Languages

English language tests for non-native speakers of the language are different from those for native speakers. Many items on such tests would seem simplistic to the native speaker. Conversely, English tests for native speakers usually emphasize matters of style and usage, which, although important at a very advanced level, will not provide the necessary discrimination of the language proficiency of non-native speakers who have not attained the highest levels of competency.

Testing is an essential component of any ESL/EFL instructional program. It provides the means of assessing students' overall proficiency in the language, of identifying specific problems students are having in learning the language, of placing students at an appropriate instructional level, and of indicating areas in which teaching may not have been very effective. There are many tests of English for speakers of other languages which have been developed for commercial use. A short list of bibliographies of tests of English for speakers of other languages and a selected list of standardized ESL/EFL tests will be found in the bibliography for this chapter.

Exercises

A. Make up a one-paragraph cloze exercise to test control of the use of pronoun forms in English.

B. Make up a ten-item exercise to test control of the use of regular and irregular noun plurals. Try to contextualize the ten items (i.e., do not use unrelated sentences). If you find it impossible to use one context for all the sentences, group them in sets of three or four sentences.

C. Consider what you have taught recently or have observed in a language classroom and devise a set of testing exercises which could comprise part of an achievement test of that material. If you are unable to observe a language class, select three or four items that you may pretend to have taught and write an exercise to test control of those items.

D. Which of the following would you consider to be a better test item? Why?

1. What do you need?   a. tea
                                   b. furniture
      I need a _____.   c. chair
                                     d. pens

2. What do you need?   a. typewriters
                                    b. pen
      I need a _____.   c. stamps
                                     d. pencils

E. Analyze the responses on a recent achievement test you have administered and see if there is any pattern to the errors. If a certain item was missed by several students, try to account for this in one of the following ways: Was it too difficult or was it confusing because of the way in which it was presented?

F. Make up a paragraph for dictation that will test students' ability to hear unstressed prepositions.

G. To test ability to use stress and intonation appropriate to context, ask students to produce the part of the following items that does not appear in parentheses. (The parenthetical material is the information that gives the contextual clues.)

1. (I studied all afternoon yesterday and became very tired.)
   What did you do then?
   (I went to the movies to relax.)
2. (I didn't study yesterday afternoon because I didn't feel like it.)
   What did you do then?
   (I went to visit a friend of mine instead.)
3. (We've been spending a lot of money recently on new furniture and a new car.)
   I heard that you had new furniture, but I didn't know you had a new car.
4. I want to go, (but I can't.)
5. I want to go, (but she doesn't.)
6. The chairman can't come, (but he sent the report).
7. The chairman can't come, (but the vice chairman is here.)

H. Select a paragraph and devise a multiple-choice cloze test of the passage. Decide which words you want to delete (every 5th, 6th, 7th, etc.), then select at least three items to use as choices for the deletions. (An easy way to obtain choices is to administer the passage as a regular cloze test and use incorrect choices, which students supply, as distractors (incorrect alternatives) for the multiple-choice cloze items.

Note

1. Adapted from *English Conversation Practices* by Maxine Guin Phinney, et al. (Ann Arbor: University of Michigan Press, 1968), p. 114.

BIBLIOGRAPHY

Bibliography

	Abbreviations — Periodicals
ELT	English Language Teaching
FLA	Foreign Language Annals
IRAL	International Review of
	Applied Linguistics
LL	Language Learning
MLJ	Modern Language Journal
TQ	TESOL Quarterly

Part 1. The English Language

Chap. 1. The Grammatical System

General References

Alexander, L. G., W. Stannard Allen, R. A. Close, and R. J. O'Neill. 1975. English Grammatical Structure: A General Syllabus for Teachers. London: Longman.

Close, R. A. 1975. A Reference Grammar for Students of English. London: Longman.

Curme, George O. 1947. English Grammar. New York: Barnes and Noble.

Dacanay, Fe R. 1963. Techniques and Procedures in Second Language Teaching. Chapters I and II. Dobbs Ferry, N.Y.: Oceana Publications.

Finocchiaro, Mary. 1969. Teaching English as a Second Language. Rev. ed. A Course of Study for Beginning Language Learners, pp. 65–82. New York: Harper and Row.

Francis, W. Nelson. 1958. The Structure of American English. New York: Ronald Press.

Frank, Marcella. 1972. Modern English: A Practical Reference Guide. Englewood Cliffs, N.J.: Prentice-Hall.

Fries, Charles C. 1945. Teaching and Learning English as a Foreign Language. Chapter III. Ann Arbor: University of Michigan Press.

Huddleston, Rodney D. 1971. The Sentence in Written English: A Syntactic Study Based on an Analysis of Scientific Texts. Cambridge: Cambridge University Press.

———. 1976. An Introduction to English Transformational Syntax. London: Longman.

Jespersen, Otto. 1964. Essentials of English Grammar. University, Alabama: University of Alabama Press.

Leech, Geoffrey N. 1971. Meaning and the English Verb. London: Longman.

——, and Jan Svartvik. 1975. A Communicative Grammar of English. London: Longman.

Quirk, Randolph, Sidney Greenbaum, Geoffrey Leech, and Jan Svartvik. 1972. A Grammar of Contemporary English. New York: Seminar Press.

——, and Sidney Greenbaum. 1973. A Concise Grammar of Contemporary English. New York: Harcourt Brace Jovanovich.

Traugott, Elizabeth C. 1972. The History of English Syntax. New York: Holt, Rinehart and Winston.

Whitman, Randal L. 1975. English and English Linguistics. New York: Holt, Rinehart and Winston.

Resource Articles

Bolinger, Dwight. 1968. Entailment and the meaning of structures. Glossa 2:119–27.

Cook, V. J. 1968. Some types of oral structure drills. LL 18:155–64.

Hok, Ruth. 1964. Oral exercises: their type and form. MLJ 48:222–26.

Kaszmarski, Stanislaw P. 1965. Language drills and exercises: a tentative classification. IRAL 3:195–204.

Ney, James W. 1967. Oral drills: methodology. Selected Conference Papers of the Association of Teachers of English as a Second Language, 57–63. Washington, D.C.: National Association for Foreign Student Affairs.

Paulston, Christina B. 1970. Structural pattern drills: a classification. FLA 4:187–93.

——. 1971. The sequencing of structural pattern drills. TQ 5:197–208.

Teaching Texts (secondary students and adults)

Bruder, Mary Newton. 1973. MMC: Developing Communicative Competence in English as a Second Language. Pittsburgh: University of Pittsburgh, University Center for International Studies.

Danielson, Dorothy, and Rebecca Hayden. 1973. Using English: Your Second Language. Englewood Cliffs, N.J.: Prentice-Hall.

Frank, Marcella. 1972. Modern English: Exercises for Non-Native Speakers. Part I: Parts of Speech. Englewood Cliffs, N.J.: Prentice-Hall.

——. 1972. Modern English: Exercises for Non-Native Speakers. Part II. Sentences and Complex Structures. Englewood Cliffs, N.J.: Prentice-Hall.

Krohn, Robert. 1971. English Sentence Structure. Ann Arbor: University of Michigan Press.

Praninskas, Jean. 1975. Rapid Review of English Grammar. 2nd ed. Englewood Cliffs, N.J.: Prentice-Hall.

Rutherford, William. 1975. Modern English. 2nd ed. 2 vols. New York: Harcourt Brace Jovanovich.

Teaching Texts (elementary students)

English around the World. 1970, 1975. Levels 1–5. Glenview, Ill.: Scott, Foresman.

English for a Changing World. 1976. Books 1–2. Glenview, Ill.: Scott, Foresman.

English for Today. 1972. 2nd ed. Books 1–6. New York: McGraw-Hill.

Lado English Series. 1970. Books 1–6. New York: Regents.

Look, Listen and Learn. 1971, 1972. Books 1–4. London: Longman.

New Horizons in English. 1974. Books 1–6. Reading, Mass.: Addison-Wesley.

Chap. 2. The Sound System

General References

Ladefoged, Peter. 1975. A Course in Phonetics. New York: Harcourt Brace Jovanovich.

Lewis, J. Windsor. 1972. A Concise Pronouncing Dictionary of British and American English. London: Oxford University Press.

Resource Articles

Allen, Harold B. 1973. Language variants and TESOL. TQ 7:13–23.

Bowen, J. Donald. 1973. Contextualizing pronunciation practice in the ESOL classroom. TQ 6:83–94.

Dickerson, Wayne B. 1976. Phonological variability in pronunciation instruction: a principled approach. TQ 10:177–91.

Robinett, Betty Wallace. 1964. Teaching English consonant clusters. Studies in Language and Linguistics in Honor of Charles C. Fries, 335–42. Ann Arbor: University of Michigan Press.

———. 1965. Simple classroom techniques for teaching pronunciation. On Teaching English to Speakers of Other Languages, ed. by V. F. Allen, 135–38. Champaign, Ill.: NCTE.

Teaching Texts

Allen, Robert L., Virginia French Allen, and Margaret Shute. 1966. English Sounds and Their Spellings. New York: Thomas Y. Crowell.

Bens, Allis. 1977. Active English: Pronunciation and Speech. Englewood Cliffs, N.J.: Prentice-Hall.

Bowen, J. Donald. 1975. Patterns of English Pronunciation. Rowley, Mass.: Newbury House.

Davidson, Walter. 1973. Sound to Speech: A Pronunciation Manual for English as a Foreign Language. Pittsburgh: University Center for International Studies, University of Pittsburgh.

Grate, Harriette Gordon. 1974. English Pronunciation for Japanese Students. New York: Regents.

Marelli, Leonard R. 1971. Pronunciation and Dictation. New York: American Language Institute.

Morley, Joan. 1978. Improving Spoken English: An Intensive Personalized Program in Perception, Pronunciation, Practice in Context. 2 vols. Ann Arbor: University of Michigan Press.

Nilsen, Don L., and Alleen P. Nilsen. 1971. Pronunciation Contrasts in English. New York: Regents.

Prator, Clifford H., and Betty Wallace Robinett. 1972. Manual of American English Pronunciation. 3rd ed. New York: Holt, Rinehart and Winston.

Chap. 3. The Vocabulary System

General References

American Heritage Dictionary of the English Language. 1969. New York: Houghton Mifflin.

A Dictionary of American Idioms. 1975. Rev. ed. Woodbury, N.Y.: Barron's Educational Series.

Oxford Advanced Learner's Dictionary of Current English. 1974. 3rd ed. London: Oxford University Press.

Praninskas, Jean. 1972. American University Word List. London: Longman.

Webster's Third New International Dictionary. 1966. Springfield, Mass.: G. and C. Merriam Company.

Resource Articles

Croft, Kenneth. 1967. Some co-occurrences in American clichés. TQ 1:47-49.

Norris, William E. 1970. Advanced reading: goals, techniques, and procedures. TQ 4:17–35.

Richards, Jack C. 1976. The role of vocabulary teaching. TQ 10:77–89.
Twaddell, W. Freeman. 1973. Vocabulary expansion in the ESOL classroom. TQ 7:61–78.

Teaching Texts

Barnard, Helen. 1971. Advanced English Vocabulary. Workbooks 1–3. Rowley, Mass.: Newbury House.
Croft, Kenneth. 1960. Reading and Word Study. Englewood Cliffs, N.J.: Prentice-Hall.
Dixson, Robert J. 1971. Essential Idioms in English. Rev. ed. New York: Regents.
Franklin, Harry B., Herbert G. Meikle, and Jeris E. Strain. 1968. Vocabulary in Context. Ann Arbor: University of Michigan Press.
Hill, L. A. 1965. A Picture Vocabulary. 2 vols. London: Oxford University Press.
Kurilecz, Margaret. 1969. Man and His World. New York: Thomas Y. Crowell.
McCallum, George P. 1970. Idiom Drills. New York: Thomas Y. Crowell.
———. 1978. More Idiom Drills. New York: Thomas Y. Crowell.
Osman, Neile. 1965. Word Formation and Dictionary Use: A Work-Book for Advanced Learners of English. London: Oxford University Press.
Pittman, G. A. 1965. Activating Advanced English Vocabulary. London: Longman.
Reeves, George. 1975. Idioms in Action. Rowley, Mass.: Newbury House.
Saitz, Robert L., and Donna Carr. 1972. Selected Readings in English: for Students of English as a Second Language. Cambridge, Mass.: Winthrop Publishers.

Part 2. Teaching English to Speakers of Other Languages

Chap. 4. Language and Culture

Allen, Walter Powell. 1956. Selecting Reading Materials for Foreign Students: A Technique for Selecting Reading Materials Which Provide Cultural Background for Learning English. Rockville, Md.: Washington Educational Research Associates, Inc.
Benedict, Ruth. 1934. Patterns of Culture. New York: Houghton Mifflin.
Birdwhistell, Ray L. 1970. Kinesics and Context: Essays on Body Motion Communication. Philadelphia: University of Pennsylvania Press.
Brislin, Richard W. 1974. Seating as a measure of behavior: you are where you sit. Topics in Culture Learning 2:103–16. East-West Center, Honolulu, Hawaii.
Brooks, Nelson. 1964. Language and Language Learning. 2nd ed. New York: Harcourt Brace & World.
Burling, Robbins. 1970. Man's Many Voices. New York: Holt, Rinehart and Winston.
Carroll, John B. (ed.). 1956. Language, Thought, and Reality: Selected Writings of Benjamin Lee Whorf. Cambridge, Mass.: MIT Press.
Clark, Virginia P., Paul A. Eschholz, and Alfred A. Rosa. 1977. Language: Introductory Readings. 2nd ed. New York: St. Martin's Press.
Clarke, Mark A. 1976. Second language acquisition as a clash of consciousness. LL 26:377–90.
Ervin-Tripp, Susan. 1964. An analysis of the interaction of language, topic, and listener. American Anthropologist 66:6 (Part 2), 86–102.
Farb, Peter. 1974. Word Play: What Happens When People Talk. New York: Alfred A. Knopf.
Fast, Julius. 1970. Body Language. New York: N. Evans and Company.
Fries, Charles C. 1945. Teaching and Learning English as a Foreign Language. Chap. V. Ann Arbor: University of Michigan Press.
Geary, James A. 1943. The Proto-Algonquian form for 'I-thee'. Language 19:147–51.
Green, Kathleen. 1975. Values clarification theory in ESL and bilingual education. TQ 9:155–64.
Grimshaw, Allen D. 1973. Rules, social interaction, and language behavior. TQ 7:99–115.

Gumperz, John J. 1964. Linguistic and social interaction in two communities. American Anthropologist 66:6 (Part 2), 137–53.

———, and Dell Hymes (eds.). 1964. The Ethnography of Communication. American Anthropologist, Special Publication, 66:6 (Part 2).

———. 1972. Directions in Sociolinguistics: The Ethnography of Communication. New York: Holt, Rinehart and Winston.

Hall, Edward T. 1959. The Silent Language. New York: Doubleday & Company.

———. 1966. The Hidden Dimension. New York: Doubleday & Company.

Hannerz, Ulf. 1973. The second language: an anthropological view. TQ 7:235–48.

Hoebel, E. Adamson. 1958. Man in the Primitive World. 2nd ed. New York: McGraw-Hill.

Hoijer, Harry. 1954. The Sapir-Whorf hypothesis. Language and Culture, ed. by Harry Hoijer, 92–105. Proceedings of a Conference on the Interrelations of Language and Other Aspects of Culture. American Anthropologist 56:6 (Part 2).

Hymes, Dell. 1962. The ethnography of speaking. Anthropology and Human Behavior, ed. by T. Gladwin and W. Sturtevant, 15–53. Washington, D.C.: Anthropological Association of Washington.

———. 1972. Models of interaction of language and social life. Directions in Sociolinguistics, ed. by John J. Gumperz and Dell Hymes, 35–71. New York: Holt, Rinehart and Winston.

———. 1974. Foundations of Sociolinguistics: An Ethnographic Approach. Philadelphia: University of Pennsylvania Press.

Joos, Martin. 1961. The Five Clocks. New York: Harcourt Brace & World.

Jourard, S. M. 1966. An exploratory study of body-accessibility. British Journal of Social and Clinical Psychology 5:221–31.

Keating, Caroline. 1976. Nonverbal aspects of communication. Topics in Culture Learning 4:12–13. East-West Center, Honolulu, Hawaii.

Kluckhohn, Clyde. 1961. Notes on some anthropological aspects of communication. American Anthropologist 63:895–910.

Lakoff, Robin. 1973. Language and women's place. Language in Society 2:45–80.

Matluck, Joseph H., and Betty J. Mace-Matluck. 1975. Language and culture in the multi-ethnic community: spoken-language assessment. MLJ 59:250–55.

Murdock, George P., et al. 1961. Outline of Cultural Materials. New Haven: Yale University Press.

Nostrand, Howard Lee. 1966. Understanding Complex Cultures: A Language Teacher's Handbook. New York: Blaisdell.

Ota, Akira. 1971. Comparison of English and Japanese with special reference to tense and aspect. Working Papers in Linguistics, ed. by Randal L. Whitman and Kenneth L. Jackson, 3:121–64.

Paulston, Christina Bratt. 1974. Linguistic and communicative competence. TQ 8:347–62.

Pearson, Bruce L. 1977. Introduction to Linguistic Concepts. New York: Alfred A. Knopf.

Pike, Eunice V. 1956. Not Alone. Chicago: Moody Press.

Sapir, Edward. 1921. Language. New York: Harcourt, Brace and Company.

———. 1929. The status of linguistics as a science. Language 5:205–14.

Seelye, H. Ned. 1974. Teaching Culture: Strategies for Foreign Language Educators. Skokie, Ill.: National Textbook Company.

Trudgill, Peter. 1974. Sociolinguistics: An Introduction. New York: Penguin Books.

Watson, Karen Ann. 1974. Understanding human interaction: the study of everyday life and ordinary talk. Topics in Culture Learning 2:57–66. East-West Center, Honolulu, Hawaii.

Whorf, Benjamin Lee. 1940. Science and linguistics. Technology Review (MIT) 42:229–31, 247–48.

Wolfart, H. Christoph. 1973. Plains Cree: a grammatical study. Transactions of the American Philosophical Society 63, Part 5.

Chap. 5. Current Trends and Issues in Language Teaching

Bolinger, Dwight. 1968. The theorist and the language teacher. FLA 2:30–41.
——. 1972. The influence of linguistics: plus and minus. TQ 6:107–20.
Brooks, Nelson. 1975. The meaning of audiolingual. MLJ 59:5–6, 234–39.
Carroll, John B. 1971. Current issues in psycholinguistics and second language teaching. TQ 5:101–14.
Chastain, Kenneth. 1976. Developing Second-Language Skills: Theory to Practice. 2nd ed. Chicago: Rand McNally.
Chomsky, Noam. 1957. Syntactic Structures. The Hague: Mouton.
——. 1965. Aspects of the Theory of Syntax. Cambridge, Mass.: MIT Press.
Close, R. A. 1977. Banners and bandwagons. ELT 31:175–83.
Cohen, Andrew D. 1975. Error correction and the training of language teachers. MLJ 59:414–22.
Common errors in Ceylon Schools Research Group. 1972. ELT 27:73–76.
Corder, S. Pit. 1967. The significance of learner's errors. IRAL 5:161–70.
——. 1975a. The language of second-language learners. MLJ 59:409–13.
——. 1975b. Error analysis, interlanguage and second language acquisition. Language Teaching & Linguistics: Abstracts 8:201–18.
Cowan, J. Ronayne. 1975. Reading, perceptual strategies, and contrastive analysis. TESL Studies 1:24–37.
Curran, Charles M. 1972. Counseling-Learning: A Whole-Person Model for Education. New York: Grune and Stratton.
Cuyer, Andre. 1972. The Saint-Cloud method: what it has achieved. ELT 27:19–24.
Dickerson, Lonna J. 1975. The learner's interlanguage as a system of variable rules. TQ 9:401–7.
Dulay, Heidi, and Marina K. Burt. 1972. Goofing: an indicator of children's second language learning strategies. LL 22:235–52.
Ferguson, Charles A. 1968. Contrastive analysis and language development. Report of the Nineteenth Annual Round Table Meeting of Linguistics and Language Studies, ed. by James E. Alatis, 101–12. Washington, D.C.: Georgetown University Press.
Fries, Charles C. 1945. Teaching and Learning English as a Foreign Language. Ann Arbor: University of Michigan Press.
Gattegno, Caleb. 1972. Teaching Foreign Languages in Schools: The Silent Way. New York: Educational Solutions.
Hammerly, Hector. 1971. Recent methods and trends in second language teaching. MLJ 55:499–505.
——. 1975. The deduction/induction controversy. MLJ 59:15–18.
Hanzeli, Victor E. 1975. Learner's language: implications of recent research for foreign language instruction. MLJ 59:426–32.
Jakobovits, Leon A. 1974. Transactional engineering analysis and foreign language teaching: a reply to Ney. MLJ 58:201–3.
——, and Barbara Gordon. 1974. The Context of Foreign Language Teaching. Rowley, Mass.: Newbury House.
Jarvis, G. A., 1972. Teaching education goals: they're tearing up the street where I was born. FLA 6:198–205.
Jespersen, Otto. 1904. How to Teach a Foreign Language. London: George Allen & Unwin.
Lado, Robert. 1957. Linguistics across Cultures. Ann Arbor: University of Michigan Press.
Lambert, Wallace E. 1963. Psychological approaches to the study of language. MLJ 47:51–62, 114–21.
——. 1969. Psychological aspects of motivation in language learning. Linguistic-Cultural Differences and American Education (Special Anthology Issue of Florida FL Reporter), ed. by Alfred C. Aarons, Barbara Y. Gordon, and William A. Stewart, 95–98.

Marckwardt, Albert H. 1965. Old paths and new directions. On Teaching English to Speakers of Other Languages, ed. by Virginia F. Allen, 3–8. Champaign, Ill.: National Council of Teachers of English.

Matthews-Bresky, R. J. H. 1972. Translation as a testing device. ELT 27:58–65.

Ney, James W. 1974. Contradictions in theoretical approaches to the teaching of foreign languages. MLJ 58:197–200.

Palmer, Harold E. 1917. The Scientific Study & Teaching of Languages. London: George C. Harrap & Company.

Parkinson, Frank C. 1972. Transformational grammar and the practical teacher. ELT 27:2–8.

Paulston, Christina B., and Mary N. Bruder. 1975. From Substitution to Substance: A Handbook of Structural Pattern Drills. Rowley, Mass.: Newbury House.

———. 1976. Teaching English as a Second Language: Techniques and Procedures. Cambridge, Mass.: Winthrop.

Piaget, Jean. 1959. The Language and Thought of the Child. 3rd ed. London: Routledge & Kegan Paul.

Postovsky, Valerian A. 1975. On paradoxes in foreign language teaching. MLJ 59:18–21.

Prator, Clifford H. 1965. Development of a manipulation-communication scale. NAFSA Studies and Papers, English Language Series 10:385–91. Washington, D.C.: National Association for Foreign Student Affairs.

Richards, Jack C. 1971. A non-contrastive approach to error analysis. ELT 25:204–19.

——— (ed.). 1974. Error Analysis: Perspectives on Second Language Acquisition. London: Longman.

———. 1976. The role of vocabulary teaching. TQ 10:77–89.

Rigg, Pat. 1976. Choosing and using dialogues. TQ 10:291–98.

Ritchie, William C. 1968. On the explanation of phonic interference. LL 18:183–97.

Rivers, Wilga M. 1964. The Psychologist and the Foreign-Language Teacher. Chicago: University of Chicago Press.

Robinett, Betty Wallace. 1977. Characteristics of an effective second language teacher. Viewpoints on English as a Second Language, ed. by Marina K. Burt, Heidi Dulay, and Mary Finocchiaro, 35–44. New York: Regents.

Rubin, Joan. 1975. What the "good language learner" can teach us. TQ 9:41–51.

Schachter, Jacquelyn. 1974. An error in error analysis. LL 24:205–14.

Selinker, Larry. 1972. Interlanguage. IRAL 10:219–31. Reprinted in Richards (1974), 31–54.

Southern, K. R. 1972. The long and the short of it? ELT 27:35–37.

Stevick, Earl W. 1974a. The meaning of drills and exercises. LL 24:1–22.

———. 1974b. Language instruction must do an about-face. MLJ 58:379–84.

———. 1975. One simple visual aid: a psychodynamic view. LL 25:63–72.

———. 1976. Memory, Meaning, and Method. Rowley, Mass.: Newbury House.

Stratton, Florence. 1977. Putting the communicative syllabus in its place. TQ 11:131–41.

Taylor, C. V. 1972. Why throw out translation? ELT 27:56–58.

Valdman, Albert. 1975. Error analysis and grading in the preparation of teaching materials. MLJ 59:422–26.

Wagner-Gough, Judy, and Evelyn Hatch. 1975. The importance of in-put data in second language acquisition studies. LL 25:297–308.

Wardhaugh, Ronald. 1968. Linguistics, psychology, and pedagogy: trinity or unity? TQ 2:80–87.

———. 1970. The contrastive analysis hypothesis. TQ 4:123–30.

Wilkins, D. A. 1972. Linguistics in Language Teaching. Cambridge, Mass.: MIT Press.

———. 1976. Notional Syllabuses. London: Oxford University Press.

Chap. 6. Acquiring Second Language Skills

Allen, G. D. 1975. Speech rhythm: its relation to performance universals and articulatory timing. Journal of Phonetics 3:75–86.

Allen, Robert L., Virginia F. Allen, and Margaret Shute. 1966. English Sounds and Their Spellings. New York: Thomas Y. Crowell.

Allen, Virginia French. 1966. Listening and reading. Selected Conference Papers of the Association of Teachers of English as a Second Language, 66–72. Washington, D.C.: National Association for Foreign Student Affairs.

———. 1973. Trends in the teaching of reading. TESL Reporter 6 (4):1, 2, 15–19.

Birdwhistell, Ray L. 1970. Kinesics and Context: Essays on Body Motion Communication. Philadelphia: University of Pennsylvania Press.

Brière, Eugène J. 1966. An investigation of phonological interference. Language 42:768–96.

Brown, H. Douglas (ed.). 1976. Papers in Second Language Acquisition. Special Issue, Number 4, LL.

Carroll, John B. 1966. Research in foreign language teaching: the last five years. Language Teaching: Broader Contexts, Northeast Conference on the Teaching of Foreign Languages, ed. by R. G. Mead, Jr., 12–42. New York: MLA Materials Center.

———. 1971. Current issues in psycholinguistics and second language teaching. TQ 5:101–14.

———, P. Davies, and B. Richman. 1971. The American Heritage Word Frequency Book. New York: Houghton Mifflin.

Cook, V. J. 1978. Second-language learning: a psycholinguistic perspective. Language Teaching & Linguistics Abstracts 11:73–89.

Cowan, J. Ronayne. 1974. Lexical and syntactic research for the design of EFL reading materials. TQ 8:389–99.

Eskey, David. 1973. A model program for teaching advanced reading to students of English as a foreign language. LL 23:169–84.

Ewer, J. R., and G. Hughes-Davies. 1971. Further notes on developing an English programme for students of science and technology. (1) ELT 26:65–70. (2) ELT 26:269–73.

Fries, Charles C. 1962. Linguistics and Reading. New York: Holt, Rinehart and Winston.

———, and Agnes C. Fries. 1961. Foundations for English Teaching. Tokyo: Kenkyusha.

Gaies, Stephen J. 1976. The syntax of ESL teachers' classroom language: a preliminary report. Paper presented at the Second Conference on Second Language Learning and Teaching, State University of New York College at Oswego, Oswego, N.Y.

Gatbonton, E. C., and G. R. Tucker. 1971. Cultural orientation and the teaching of foreign literature. TQ 5:137–43.

Hatch, Evelyn. 1973. Research on reading a second language. Workpapers in Teaching English as a Second Language 7:1–10. University of California, Los Angeles.

Henzl, Vera M. 1973. Linguistic register of foreign language instruction. LL 23:207–21.

Huddleston, Rodney D. 1971. The Sentence in Written English: A Syntactic Study Based on an Analysis of Scientific Texts. Cambridge: Cambridge University Press.

Jakobson, R., C. G. Fant, and M. Halle. 1969. Preliminaries to Speech Analysis. Cambridge, Mass.: MIT Press.

Kaplan, Robert. 1966. Cultural thought patterns in intercultural education. LL 16:1–20.

Key, Mary Ritchie. 1975. Paralanguage and Kinesics (Nonverbal Communication). Metuchen, N.J.: The Scarecrow Press.

Lackstrom, J. E., L. Selinker, and L. P. Trimble. 1970. Grammar and technical English. English as a Second Language: Current Issues, ed. by R. C. Lugton, 101–34. Philadelphia: Center for Curriculum Develpoment.

Morley, Joan. 1975. Round robin on the teaching of pronunciation. TQ 9:83–86.

Morris, Joyce. 1968. Barriers to successful reading for second-language students at the secondary level. TQ 2:158–63.

Newmark, L., J. Mintz, and J. L. Hinsley. 1964. Using American English. New York: Harper and Row.

Norris, William E. 1970. Teaching second language reading at the advanced level: goals, techniques, and procedures. TQ 4:17–35.

Oller, John W., Jr. 1972. Assessing competence in ESL: reading. TQ 4:313–23.

———, and J. R. Tullius. 1973. Reading skills of non-native speakers of English. IRAL 11:69–80.

Povey, John F. 1967. Literature in TESOL programs: the language and the culture. TQ 1:40–46.

Prator, Clifford H., and Betty Wallace Robinett. 1972. Manual of American English Pronunciation. 3rd ed. New York: Holt, Rinehart and Winston.

Richards, Jack C. (ed.). 1976. Teaching English for Science and Technology. Anthology Series No. 2. SEAMO Regional English Language Centre.

Rivers, Wilga M. 1976. The natural and the normal in language learning. Papers in Second Language Acquisition, ed. by H. Douglas Brown, 1–8. Special Issue, Number 4, LL.

Scherer, G. A. C., and M. Wertheimer. 1964. A Psycholinguistic Experiment in Foreign Language Teaching. New York: McGraw-Hill.

Seliger, Herbert W. 1972. Language practice at the intermediate level and the concept of presupposition. MLJ 56:436–40.

Selinker, Larry, R. M. Todd Trimble, and Louis Trimble. 1976. Pre-suppositional rhetorical information and EST discourse. TQ 10:281–90.

Shillan, David. 1967. An articulatory unit for speech and text. ELT 21:150–55.

Steyaert, Marcia. 1978. A comparison of the speech of ESL teachers to native speakers and non-native learners of English. Minnesota Working Papers in Linguistics and Philosophy of Language, Number 5.

Taylor, Harvey M. 1976. Training teachers for the role of nonverbal communication in the classroom. Papers in ESL: Selected Conference Papers (1974 and 1975), 45–51. Washington, D.C.: National Association for Foreign Student Affairs.

Thorndike, E. L., and I. Lorge. 1944. The Teacher's Word Book of 30,000 Words. New York: Teachers College, Columbia University.

Twaddell, W. Freeman. 1973. Uses of reading. MLJ 57:393–96.

Wallace, Betty J. 1949. The importance of classroom atmosphere. LL 2:73–75.

Wardhaugh, Ronald. 1969. Reading: A Linguistic Perspective. New York: Harcourt Brace and World.

West, Michael. 1953. A General Service List of English Words. New York: Longmans Green.

Widdowson, H. G. 1972. The teaching of English as communication. ELT 27:15–19.

Wilkins, D. A. 1974. Second-Language Learning and Teaching. London: Edward Arnold.

Willis, Hulon. 1967. Structural Grammar and Composition. New York: Holt, Rinehart and Winston.

Yorio, Carlos. 1976. Discussion of "Explaining Sequence and Variation in Second Language Acquisition." Papers in Second Language Acquisition, ed. by H. Douglas Brown, 59–63. Special Issue, Number 4, LL.

Chap. 7. Teaching the Communication Skills

Allen, Harold B., and Russell N. Campbell (eds.). 1972. Teaching English as a Second Language: A Book of Readings. 2nd ed. New York: McGraw-Hill.

Allen, Robert L., Virginia French Allen, and Margaret Shute. 1966. English Sounds and Their Spellings. New York: Thomas Y. Crowell.

Allen, Virginia F. 1953. People in Livingston: A Reader for Adults Learning English. New York: Thomas Y. Crowell.

———. 1957. People in Fact and Fiction: Selections Adapted for Students of English as a Foreign Language. New York: Thomas Y. Crowell.

————. 1958. The preparation of dialogue and narrative materials for students of English as a foreign language. LL, Special Issue, 97–101.

Arapoff, Nancy. 1970. Writing through Understanding. New York: Holt, Rinehart and Winston.

Bander, Robert G. 1978. American English Rhetoric: A Two-Track Writing Program for Intermediate and Advanced Students of English as a Second Language. 2nd ed. New York: Holt, Rinehart and Winston.

Barnard, Helen. 1971. Advanced English Vocabulary. Workbooks 1–3. Rowley Mass.: Newbury House.

Baskoff, Florence. 1971. Guided Composition. Philadelphia: Center for Curriculum Development.

Baudoin, Margaret, Ellen S. Bober, Mark A. Clarke, Barbara K. Dobson, and Sandra Silberstein. 1977. Reader's Choice: A Reading Skills Textbook for Students of English as a Second Language. Ann Arbor: University of Michigan Press.

Bird, Deirdre. 1975. Listening comprehension for ESL using tapes. Unpublished paper, Program in English as a Second Language, University of Minnesota.

Black, Colin. 1970. A Handbook of Free Conversation. London: Oxford University Press.

Blatchford, Charles H. 1973. Newspapers: vehicles for teaching ESOL with a cultural focus. TQ 7:145–51.

————, (ed.). 1977. Directory of Teacher Preparation Programs in TESOL and Bilingual Education. Washington, D.C.: Teachers of English to Speakers of Other Languages.

Bolinger, Dwight. 1968. The theorist and the language teacher. FLA 2:30–41.

Bontner, Maxine T., and John E. Gates. 1975. A Dictionary of American Idioms. Woodbury, New York: Barron's Educational Series.

Brière, Eugène J. 1966. Quantity before quality in second language composition. LL 16:141–51.

Brooks, Nelson. 1964. Language and Language Learning: Theory and Practice. 2nd ed. New York: Harcourt Brace & World.

Brown, H. Douglas. 1977. The English teacher as researcher. ELT 31:274–79.

Brown, T. Grant. 1969. In defense of pattern practice. LL 19:191–203.

Bruder, Mary Newton. 1973. MMC: Developing Communicative Competence in English as a Second Language. Pittsburgh: University Center for International Studies, University of Pittsburgh.

Bumpass, Faye L. 1963. Teaching Young Students English as a Foreign Language. New York: American Book Company.

Chastain, Kenneth. 1976. Developing Second-Language Skills: Theory to Practice. 2nd ed. Chicago: Rand McNally.

Combe-Martin, M. H. 1970. Listening and Comprehending. London: Macmillan and Company.

Cook, V. J. 1968. Some types of oral structure drills. LL 18:155–64.

Cowles, Hovey M. 1976. Textual materials checklist. FLA 9:300–303.

Croft, Kenneth. 1960. Reading and Word Study. Englewood Cliffs, N.J.: Prentice-Hall.

————. 1972. Readings on English as a Second Language. Cambridge, Mass.: Winthrop Publishers.

Dacanay, Fe R. 1963. Techniques and Procedures in Second Language Teaching. Dobbs Ferry, N.Y.: Oceana Publications.

Danielson, Dorothy. 1965. Teaching composition at the intermediate level. On Teaching English to Speakers of Other Languages, ed. by V. F. Allen, 143–45. Champaign, Ill.: National Council of Teachers of English.

————, and Rebecca Hayden. 1973. Using English: Your Second Language. Englewood Cliffs, N.J.: Prentice-Hall.

Dixson, Robert J. 1971. Essential Idioms in English. Rev. ed. New York: Regents.

Dobbyn, Michael. 1977. Prepared dictation and the under-employed language laboratory. ELT 32:55–60.

Dobson, Julia M. 1974. Effective Techniques for English Conversation Groups. Rowley, Mass.: Newbury House.

Dorry, Gertrude Nye. 1966. Games for Second Language Learning. New York: McGraw-Hill.

Doty, Gladys, and Janet Ross. 1973. Language and Life in the U.S.A. 3rd ed. Volume II: Reading English. New York: Harper and Row.

Dubin, Fraida, and Elite Olshtain. 1977. Facilitating Language Learning: A Guidebook for the ESL/EFL Teacher. New York: McGraw-Hill.

English for Today. (forthcoming) 3rd ed. New York: McGraw-Hill.

Erazmus, Edward T. 1960. Second language composition teaching at the intermediate level. LL 10:25–33.

Farid, Anne. 1976. Communication in the classroom: student-improvised dialogues. TQ 10:299–304.

Finocchiaro, Mary. 1964. Teaching Children Foreign Languages. New York: McGraw-Hill.

———. 1969. Teaching English as a Second Language. Rev. ed. New York: Harper and Row.

Fowles, J. 1970. Ho ho ho: cartoons in the language class. TQ 4:155–59.

Franklin, Harry B., Herbert G. Meikle, and Jeris E. Strain. 1968. Vocabulary in Context. Ann Arbor: University of Michigan Press.

Fries, Charles C. 1963. Linguistics and Reading. New York: Holt, Rinehart and Winston.

———, and Agnes C. Fries. 1961. Foundations for English Teaching. Tokyo: Kenkyusha.

Godfrey, Dennis. 1977. Listening instruction and practice for advanced second language students. LL 27:109–22.

Gougher, Ronald L. (ed.). 1972. Individualization of Instruction in Foreign Languages: A Practical Guide. Philadelphia: Center for Curriculum Development.

Greathouse, Jean, and Nancy Wilcox Peterson. 1978. A model for listening comprehension units using the content of other disciplines. Papers in ESL: Selected Conference Papers (1976 and 1977). Washington, D.C.: National Association for Foreign Student Affairs.

Gurrey, P. 1955. Teaching English as a Foreign Language. London: Longmans Green.

Hall, Eugene J. 1970. Orientation in American English. Washington, D.C.: Institute of Modern Languages.

Harding, Deborah, Gilles Delisle, and Blanca Escorcia. 1969. A Microwave Course in English as a Second Language. La Jolla, California: Lingoco Corporation.

Harris, David P. 1966. Reading Improvement Exercises for Students of English as a Second Language. Englewood Cliffs, N.J.: Prentice-Hall.

Haskell, John F. 1977. How to select suitable reading materials. Interview 3 (1):1–2. New York: Collier Macmillan International.

Hauptman, Philip, and Jack Upshur. 1975. Fun with English. New York: Collier Macmillan International.

Hirasawa, Louise, and Linda Markstein. 1974. Developing Reading Skills: Advanced. Rowley, Mass.: Newbury House.

Hok, Ruth. 1964. Oral exercises: their type and form. MLJ 48:222–26.

Horn, Vivian. 1977. Composition Steps. Rowley, Mass.: Newbury House.

Ilson, Robert. 1962. The dicto-comp: a specialized technique for controlling speech and writing in language learning. LL 12:299–301.

Johnson, Francis C. 1971. English as a Second Language: An Individualized Approach. Melbourne: Jacaranda Press.

Joiner, Elizabeth G. 1974. Evaluating the cultural content of foreign-language texts. MLJ 58:242–44.

Judson, Horace. 1972. The Techniques of Reading. 3rd ed. New York: Harcourt Brace Jovanovich.

Kaplan, Robert B. 1966. Cultural thought patterns in intercultural education. LL 16:1–20.

Kaszmarski, Stanislaw P. 1965. Language drills and exercises: a tentative classification. IRAL 3:195–204.

Knapp, Donald. 1965. A focused, efficient method to relate composition correction to teaching aims. On Teaching English to Speakers of Other Languages, ed. by V. F. Allen, 149–53. Champaign, Ill.: National Council of Teachers of English.

Kreidler, Carol J. 1971. Effective use of visual aids in the ESOL classroom. TQ 5:19–37.

Kurilecz, Margaret. 1969. Man and His World. New York: Thomas Y. Crowell.

Lawrence, Mary S. 1972. Writing as a Thinking Process. Ann Arbor: University of Michigan Press.

———. 1975. Reading, Thinking, Writing. Ann Arbor: University of Michigan Press.

Lee, W. R. 1965. Language Teaching Games and Contests. London: Oxford University Press.

Markstein, Linda, and Louise Hirasawa. 1977. Expanding Reading Skills: Advanced. Rowley, Mass.: Newbury House.

McCallum, George P. 1970. Idiom Drills. New York: Thomas Y. Crowell.

———. 1978. More Idiom Drills. New York: Thomas Y. Crowell.

Molina, Herbert. 1971. Language games and the Mexican-American child learning English. TQ 5:145–48.

Morley, Joan. 1972. Improving Aural Comprehension. Ann Arbor: University of Michigan Press.

———. 1973. Films for EFL Practice: Listening, Speaking, Vocabulary Building. Ann Arbor: Follett's Bookstore.

———. 1976. Listening Dictation: Understanding English Sentence Structure. Ann Arbor: University of Michigan Press.

———. 1978. Improving Spoken English: An Intensive Personalized Program in Perception, Pronunciation, Practice in Context. 2 vols. Ann Arbor: University of Michigan Press.

———, and Mary S. Lawrence. 1971. The use of films in teaching English as a second language. LL 21:117–35.

Ney, James W. 1967. Oral drills: methodology. Selected Conference Papers of the Association of Teachers of English as a Second Language. Washington, D.C.: National Association for Foreign Student Affairs.

———. 1968. The oral approach: a re-appraisal. LL 18:3–13.

Nida, Eugene. 1953. Selective listening. LL 4:92–101.

Norris, William E. 1970. Advanced reading: goals, techniques, and procedures. TQ 4:17–35.

O'Neil, Robert, and Roger Scott. 1974. Viewpoints: Interviews for Listening Comprehension. London: Longman.

Paulston, Christina Bratt. 1970. Structural pattern drills: a classification. FLA 4:187–93.

———. 1971. The sequencing of structural pattern drills. TQ 5:197–208.

———. 1972. Teaching writing in the ESOL classroom: techniques of controlled composition. TQ 6:33–59.

———, and Mary Newton Bruder. 1975. From Substitution to Substance: A Handbook of Structural Pattern Drills. Rowley, Mass.: Newbury House.

———, and Mary Newton Bruder. 1976. Teaching English as a Second Language: Techniques and Procedures. Cambridge, Mass.: Winthrop Publishers.

———, and Gerald Drykstra. 1973. Controlled Composition in English as a Second Language. New York: Regents.

Pimsleur, Paul, and Donald Berger. 1974. Encounters. New York: Harcourt Brace Jovanovich.

Plaister, Ted. 1976. Developing Listening Comprehension for ESL Students. Englewood Cliffs, N.J.: Prentice-Hall.

Porter, Patricia A., and Allen Sharp. 1977. Active English. 3 books. Englewood Cliffs, N.J.: Prentice-Hall.

Praninskas, Jean. 1965. Controlled composition. On Teaching English to Speakers of

Other Languages, ed. by V. F. Allen, 146–48. Champaign, Ill.: National Council of Teachers of English.

———. 1975. Rapid Review of English Grammar. 2nd ed. Englewood Cliffs, N.J.: Prentice-Hall.

Prator, Clifford H. 1965. Development of a manipulation-communication scale. Selected Conference Papers of the Association of Teachers of English as a Second Language, 57–62. Washington, D.C.: National Association for Foreign Student Affairs. Reprinted in Croft (1972), 402–8.

Rees, A. L. W. 1970. The display board in language teaching. TQ 4:161–64.

Reeves, George. 1975. Idioms in Action. Rowley, Mass.: Newbury House.

Richards, Jack, and Michael Poloquin. 1972. English Through Songs: A Songbook for ESL. Rowley, Mass.: Newbury House.

Rigg, Pat. 1976. Choosing and using dialogs. TQ 10:291–98.

Rivers, Wilga M. 1966. Listening comprehension. MLJ 50:196–202. Reprinted in Croft (1972), 87–99.

———. 1968. Teaching Foreign-Language Skills. Chicago: University of Chicago Press.

———. 1972. Speaking in Many Tongues: Essays in Foreign-Language Teaching. Rowley, Mass.: Newbury House.

———, and Mary S. Temperley. 1978. A Practical Guide to the Teaching of English as a Second or Foreign Language. New York: Oxford University Press.

Robinett, Betty Wallace. 1972. On the horns of a dilemma: correcting compositions. Studies in Honor of Albert H. Marckwardt, ed. by J. E. Alatis, 143–50. Washington, D.C.: Teachers of English to Speakers of Other Languages.

Robinson, Lois. 1975. Guided Writing and Free Writing. 2nd ed. New York: Harper and Row.

Rojas, Pauline M. 1968. Writing to learn. TQ 2:127–29.

Ross, Janet, and Gladys Doty. 1975. Writing English: A Composition Text in English as a Foreign Language. 2nd ed. New York: Harper and Row.

Rutherford, William E. 1975. Modern English. 2 vols. 2nd ed. New York: Harcourt Brace Jovanovich.

Saitz, Robert L., and Donna Carr. 1972. Selected Readings in English: for Students of English as a Second Language. Cambridge, Mass.: Winthrop Publishers.

Saporta, Sol. 1966. Applied linguistics and generative grammar. Trends in Language Teaching, ed. by A. Valdman, 81–91. New York: McGraw-Hill.

Sawyer, J., and S. Silver. 1961. Dictation in language learning. LL 11:33–42.

Schutz, Noel W., Jr., and Bruce L. Derwing. 1978. A theoretical defense of the pattern drill. Papers in ESL: Selected Conference Papers (1976 and 1977). Washington, D.C.: National Association for Foreign Student Affairs.

Seliger, Herbert W. 1972. Language practice at the intermediate level and the concept of presupposition. MLJ 56:436–40.

Sittler, Richard. 1964. Teaching aural comprehension. The ABC English as a Second Language Bulletin. New York: American Book Company.

Slager, William. 1966. Classroom techniques for controlling composition. Selected Conference Papers of the Association of Teachers of English as a Second Language, 77–85. Reprinted in Croft (1972), 232–44.

———. 1973. Creating contexts for language practice. TQ 7:35–50.

Smith, Frank. 1971. Understanding Reading: A Psycholinguistic Study of Reading and Learning to Read. New York: Holt, Rinehart and Winston.

SRA International Reading Laboratory. 1969. Willowdale, Ontario: Science Research Associates.

Starting English Early. 1967. 30-minute color film. Academic Communication Facility, University of California, Los Angeles.

Stern, Rhoda H. 1976. Sexism in foreign language textbooks. FLA 9:294–99.

Stevens, Edith B. 1971. Textbook evaluation form: beginning foreign language texts. Accent on ACTFL 2:8–9.

Stevick, Earl W. 1971. Adapting and Writing Language Lessons. Washington, D.C.: Foreign Service Institute.

Sutaria, Minda C. n.d. Basic Readers for English Teaching. Quezon City, Philippines: Phoenix Publishing House.

Sutherland, Kenton. 1967. Dictation in the language classroom. TQ 1:24–29. Reprinted in Croft (1972), 224–31.

Taylor, Barry P. 1978. Teaching composition skills to low-level ESL students: cause-effect and comparison-contrast. Papers in ESL: Selected Conference Papers (1976 and 1977). Washington, D.C.: National Association for Foreign Students Affairs.

Taylor, Harvey M. 1976. Training teachers for the role of nonverbal communication in the classroom. Papers in ESL: Selected Conference Papers (1974 and 1975), 45–51. Washington, D.C.: National Association for Foreign Student Affairs.

Thonis, Eleanor W. 1970. Teaching Reading to Non-English Speakers. New York: Collier Macmillan Company.

Valdman, Albert (ed.). 1966. Trends in Language Teaching. New York: McGraw-Hill.

Via, Richard A. 1972. TESL and creative drama. TESL Reporter 5:1–3.

————. 1976. English in Three Acts. Honolulu: University of Hawaii Press.

Wishon, George E., and Julia M. Burks. 1968. Let's Write English. Books 1 and 2. New York: American Book Company.

Wissot, Jay. 1970. The English-as-a-second-language trip: its structure and value. TQ 4:165–68.

Yorkey, Richard C. 1970. Study Skills for Students of English as a Second Language. New York: McGraw-Hill.

Bibliographies and Instructional Materials Lists

Escobar, Joanne E., and John Dougherty. 1976. An Annotated Bibliography of Adult ESL Instructional Materials. Illinois ESL/ABE Service Center, 500 S. Dwyer Avenue, Arlington Heights, Illinois 60005.

Croft, Kenneth. 1974. A Composite Bibliography for ESOL Teacher Training. Washington, D.C.: Teachers of English to Speakers of Other Languages.

Fox, Robert P. 1975. A Selected List of Instructional Materials for English as a Second Language: College Level. Washington, D.C.: Center for Applied Linguistics.

Marckwardt, Maybelle D. 1975. A Selected List of Instructional Materials for English as a Second Language: Elementary Level. Washington, D.C.: Center for Applied Linguistics.

————. 1975. A Selected List of Instructional Materials for English as a Second Language: Secondary Level. Washington, D.C.: Center for Applied Linguistics.

Ohannessian, Sirarpi. 1964. Reference List of Materials for English as a Second Language. Part 1: Texts, Readers, Dictionaries, Tests. Washington, D.C.: Center for Applied Linguistics.

————. 1966. Reference List of Materials for English as a Second Language. Part 2: Background Materials, Methodology. Washington, D.C.: Center for Applied Linguistics.

Pedtke, Dorothy A., Bernarda Erwin, and Anna Marie Malkoc. 1969. Reference List of Materials for English as a Second Language, Supplement 1964–68. Washington, D.C.: Center for Applied Linguistics.

Record Albums for Teaching English As a Second Language

Goodbye Rainbow. 1974. London: Longman.

Hard to Learn That English as a Second Language Blues. 1975. New York: Collier Macmillan International.

Mister Monday and Other Songs for the Teaching of English. 1971. London: Longman.

Sunday Afternoon. 1973. London: Longman.

Periodicals

TESOL Quarterly (Publication of the association of Teachers of English to Speakers of Other Languages)
455 Nevils Building
Georgetown University
Washington, D.C. 20057

English Language Teaching (Published in association with the British Council)
Oxford University Press
200 Madison Avenue Press Road
New York, New York 10016 Neasden, London NW10 England

Language Learning (A journal of applied linguistics)
2001 North University Building
University of Michigan
Ann Arbor, Michigan 48109

Foreign Language Annals (Publication of the American Council on the Teaching of Foreign Languages)
2 Park Avenue
New York, New York 10016

Modern Language Journal (Publication of the National Association of Modern Language Teachers)
Richard S. Thill
Department of Foreign Languages
University of Nebraska
Omaha, Nebraska 68101

Professional Organizations

TESOL (Teachers of English to Speakers of Other Languages)
455 Nevils Building
Georgetown University
Washington, D.C. 20057

ATESL of NAFSA (Association of Teachers of English as a Second Language of the National Association for Foreign Student Affairs)
1860 19th Street N.W.
Washington, D.C. 20009

ACTFL (American Council on the Teaching of Foreign Languages)
62 Fifth Avenue
New York, New York 10011

AEA (Adult Education Association)
810 18th Street N.W.
Washington, D.C. 20006

NAPCAE (National Association of Public Continuing and Adult Education)
1201 16th Street N.W.
Washington, D.C. 20036

NCTE (National Council of Teachers of English)
1111 Kenyon Road
Urbana, Illinois 61801

Chap. 8. Testing

Allen, J. P. B., and Alan Davies (eds.). 1977. Testing and Experimental Methods. London: Oxford University Press.

Beardsmore, H. Baetens, and A. Renkin. 1971. A test of spoken English. IRAL 9:1–11.

Brière, Eugène J., and Richard H. Brown. 1971. Norming tests of ESL among Amerindian children. TQ 5:327–33.

Carroll, John B. 1961. Fundamental considerations in testing English language proficiency of foreign students. Testing the English Language Proficiency of Foreign Students. Washington, D.C.: Center for Applied Linguistics.

Carroll-Sapon Modern Language Aptitude Test. 1959. New York: The Psychological Corporation.

Clark, John L. D. 1972. Foreign Language Testing: Theory and Practice. Philadelphia: The Center for Curriculum Development.

Dacanay, Fe R. 1963. Techniques and Procedures in Second Language Teaching. Chapter VII: Testing the English language, 450–521. Dobbs Ferry, N.Y.: Oceana Publications.

Darnell, D. K. 1970. Clozentropy: the procedure for testing English language proficiency of foreign students. Speech Monographs 37:36–46.

Davies, Alan (ed.). 1968. Language Testing Symposium: A Psycholinguistic Approach. London: Oxford University Press.

———. 1978. Language testing. Language Teaching and Linguistics: Abstract 11:145–59.

Harris, David P. 1969. Testing English as a Second Language. New York: McGraw-Hill.

———. 1976. Testing reading comprehension in ESL: background and state of the art. Papers in ESL: Selected Conference Papers (1974 and 1975), 25–30. Washington, D.C.: National Association for Foreign Student Affairs.

Heaton, J. B. 1975. Writing English Language Tests: A Practical Guide for Teachers of English as a Second or Foreign Language. London: Longman.

Ilson, Robert. 1962. The dicto-comp: a specialized technique for controlling speech and writing in language. LL 12:299–301.

Jones, Randall, and Bernard Spolsky (eds.). 1975. Testing Language Proficiency. Washington, D.C.: Center for Applied Linguistics.

Jonz, Jon. 1976. Improving on the basic egg: the M-C cloze. LL 26:255–65.

Lado, Robert. 1961. Language Testing: The Construction and Use of Foreign Language Tests. London: Longmans Green.

O'Brien, Maureen C. (ed.). 1974. Testing in Second Language Teaching: New Dimensions. Dublin: University of Dublin Press.

Oller, John W., Jr. 1971. Dictation as a device for testing foreign-language proficiency. ELT 25:254–59.

———. Scoring methods and difficulty levels for cloze tests of proficiency in English as a second language. MLJ 56:151–58.

———. 1973a. Cloze tests of second language proficiency and what they measure. LL 23:105–18.

———. 1973b. Discrete-point tests versus tests of integrative skills. Focus on the Learner, ed. by J. W. Oller, Jr. and Jack C. Richards, 184–98. Rowley, Mass.: Newbury House.

———. 1975. Research with Cloze Procedure in Measuring the Proficiency of Non-Native Speakers of English: An Annotated Bibliography. Washington, D.C.: ERIC Clearinghouse on Languages and Linguistics, Center for Applied Linguistics.

———, and Christine A. Conrad. 1971. The cloze technique and ESL proficiency. LL 21:183–95.

———, and Nevin Inal. 1971. A cloze test of prepositions. TQ 5:315–25.

Palmer, Adrian. 1972. Testing communication. IRAL 10:35–45.

Palmer, Leslie, and Bernard Spolsky (eds.). 1975. Papers on Language Testing 1967–74. Washington, D.C.: Teachers of English to Speakers of Other Languages.

Perren, George. 1967. Testing ability in English as a second language: 1 Problems. ELT 21:99–106. 2 Techniques. ELT 21:197–202. 3 Spoken language. ELT 22:22–29.

Pimsleur Language Aptitude Battery. 1966. New York: Harcourt Brace and World.

Rand, Earl. 1963. A short test of oral English proficiency. LL 13:203–10.

Seelye, H. Ned. 1966. Field notes on cross-cultural testing. LL 16:77–85.

Taylor, E. L. 1953. Cloze procedure: a new tool for measuring readibility. Journalism Quarterly 30:415–33.

Upshur, John A. 1966. Cross-cultural testing: what to test. LL 16:183–96.

———. 1971. Objective evaluation of oral proficiency in the ESOL classroom. TQ 5:47–59.

———, and Julia Fata (eds.). 1968. Problems in Foreign Language Testing. Special Issue, Number 3, LL.

Valette, Rebecca M. 1977. Modern Language Testing: A Handbook. 2nd ed. New York: Harcourt Brace and World.

Yousef, Fathi S. 1968. Cross-cultural testing: an aspect of resistance reaction. LL 18:227–34.

Bibliographies

Garcia-Zamor, Marie, and David Birdsong. 1977. Testing in English as a Second Language: A Selected Annotated Bibliography. Washington, D.C.: ERIC Clearinghouse on Languages and Linguistics, Center for Applied Linguistics.

Indochinese Refugee Education Guides. Testing English Language Proficiency. Washington, D.C.: National Indochinese Clearinghouse, Center for Applied Linguistics.

Representative Tests of English as a Second Language

This list was compiled from information in the following two publications: *Indochinese Refugee Education Guides — General Information Series: Testing English Language Proficiency* (Washington, D.C.: Center for Applied Linguistics, n.d.) and *Guidelines: English Language Proficiency* (Washington, D.C.: National Association for Foreign Student Affairs, 1977).

Comprehensive English Language Test (CELT)

Developed by: David P. Harris and Leslie A. Palmer
Available from: McGraw-Hill Book Company
                1221 Avenue of the Americas
                New York, New York 10020

A battery of three tests (listening comprehension, structure, vocabulary) to measure general English proficiency. Intended for use at the intermediate and advanced levels.

Grade range: high school-adult
Testing time: 45 minutes for each test

English Placement Test

Developed by: Mary Spaan and Laura Strowe
Available from: English Language Institute
                University of Michigan
                Ann Arbor, Michigan 48109

A 100-item test of listening comprehension, grammar, vocabulary, and reading yielding one score. Intended for quick placement of students at all levels of proficiency in intensive English language programs.

Grade range: high school-adult
Testing time: 75 minutes

Ilyin Oral Interview

Developed by: Donna Ilyin
Available from: Newbury House Publishers
68 Middle Raod
Rowley, Massachusetts 01969

Designed to test students' ability to use English orally in response to hearing it, in a controlled situation. Consists of 50 items scored for accuracy of information and structure, including word order, verb structure, and other structures.

Grade range: 7-adult
Testing time: 5-30 minutes

English Language Structure Tests

Developed by: Donna Ilyin and J. Best
Available from: Newbury House Publishers
68 Middle Road
Rowley, Massachusetts 01969

Six tests of English structure that can be correlated with the Ilyin Oral Interview test for placement of students. Two forms each of beginning, intermediate, and advanced levels.

Grade range: 7-adult
Testing time: 30 minutes each form

Michigan Test of Aural Comprehension

Developed by: John A. Upshur, Mary Spaan, and
Randolph Thrasher
Available from: English Language Institute
University of Michigan
Ann Arbor, Michigan 48109

A 90-item test of listening comprehension to accompany the Michigan Test of English Language Proficiency. Intended for use at the intermediate and advanced levels. Three forms available.

Grade range: high school-adult
Testing time: 25 minutes for each form

Michigan Test of English Language Proficiency (MTELP)

Developed by: John A. Upshur, et al.
Available from: English Language Institute
University of Michigan
Ann Arbor, Michigan 48109

A 100-item test of general English proficiency (grammar, vocabulary, reading comprehension) yielding one score. Intended for use with university-level adults to determine language readiness for academic programs. Several forms available.

Grade range: adult (academically oriented)
Testing time: 75 minutes for each form

Test of English As a Foreign Language (TOEFL)

Available from: Educational Testing Service
Princeton, New Jersey 08540

A three-part English proficiency test (listening comprehension, reading comprehension and vocabulary, structure and written expression) used extensively for admission and placement of foreign students in institutions of higher learning. Under an "institutional testing plan" arrangements can be made for local administration of the test. Many forms used.

Grade range: adults (academically oriented)
Testing time: 2½-3 hours

Bilingual Syntax Measure

Developed by: Marina K. Burt, Heidi Dulay, and
E. Hernandez

Available from: Harcourt Brace Jovanovich
757 Third Avenue
New York, New York 10017

Designed to measure a child's structural proficiency in English. It can also be used for diagnosis and placement. Child response booklets are available in English and Spanish.

Grade range: pre K-3
Testing time: not specified

INDEX

Index